REFLECTIONS OF A PILOT, PART 2

Danger in the Desert

by

Leonard Porter, Jr.

RoseDog Books

PITTSBURGH, PENNSYLVANIA 15222

The contents of this work including, but not limited to, the accuracy of events, people, and places depicted; opinions expressed; permission to use previously published materials included; and any advice given or actions advocated are solely the responsibility of the author, who assumes all liability for said work and indemnifies the publisher against any claims stemming from publication of the work.

ISBN: 978-1-4349-8124-0
eISBN: 978-1-4349-4367-5
Printed in the United States of America

First Printing

For more information or to order additional books, please contact:
RoseDog Books
701 Smithfield Street
Pittsburgh, Pennsylvania 15222
U.S.A.
1-800-834-1803
www.rosedogbookstore.com

Many if not all names mentioned in this book have been changed where necessary to protect their privacy. This is especially true for the Arabs as I did not always know their names.

I wish to dedicate this book to my wife, Martha along with my son and his family. Martha learned early on there would be hardships in pursuing a flying career with me, but chose to share this lifestyle. Without her support and dedicated help, my continued success would be in doubt. We made many moves due to the demands of the service and requirements of civilian employment. She handled each move with strength, determination and efficiency. Many times I was not available to lend a helping hand, but that did not faze her. She got the job done. We were separated many times throughout the years and she handled it as routine.

She was indeed a very strong asset, socially as well as everyday life. My sincere thanks to you, Martha.

David also proved to be a "Trooper." From a very early age he was subjected to being uprooted and moved many times. He handled all these moves with strength of character beyond his years. He left close friends behind many times and faced the unknown in new schools, classmates and neighbors. He was not pleased of course, but accepted the inevitable with stoicism.

David's wife Rita has proven to be a jewel in our new family tree. Their children, Stacy and David, Jr. (Our Grandchildren) are our pride and joy. We are truly blessed.

All have been very supportive of me as I struggled through the years with completion of this chronicle.

With love and affection,

Leonard (Husband, Father, & Grandfather)

Career Two 2, Danger in the Desert

GUIDE:

FLYING IN SAUDI ARABIA AND MIDDLE EAST, 1964-1981

My retirement from the Air Force was effective in October 1964 in San Diego, California. We were there to visit Marti's parents while waiting for a word from United Airlines about possible employment as a Training Captain in Denver, Colorado. Both of us were raised and educated in Kansas City, Missouri. We even went to the same school, Northeast Senior High School. While enjoying the climate and beauty of San Diego, I thought I might send a résumé to our "Home town" airline. Within a very short time, I received a phone call from TWA in Kansas City asking me if I would come there for an interview. The person on the line explained there would be a ticket waiting for me at their ticket office on Lindbergh Field, San Diego. Very soon I was on my way to Kansas City.

First, after arrival, I reported to 10 Richards Road, their Personnel Office, where I signed in and was directed to call the manager of Flight Training, located at 13th and Baltimore in Downtown Kansas City. My call there got me an appointment with the manager and after arrival, an interview with two of the training captains separately, followed by a battery of written tests. They also gave me a ride in one of their aircraft simulators to check my piloting skills. The above was followed by a final interview by the manager of Flight Training.

Trans World Airlines, Kansas City, Missouri, then offered me employment as a "Contract Captain" in December of 1964. My starting assignment would be in Saudi Arabia. My contact in TWA to learn all the details of traveling to Saudi Arabia was Joe Laterza. He was a really nice person and well versed in his job. Joe had all the answers and would make our arrangements for travel. The way he handled everything helped increase my appreciation of the manner TWA personnel had done things so far. He would remain a friend long after my employment had terminated in retirement.

TWA had a management contract with Saudi Arabia to furnish supervision, maintenance and operational training for that country's national airline. This included assigning pilots to provide instruction in operational flying. At first, all of the foreign pilots were contract captains, like me, except none were permanent as I was. However, I was to learn later most of them had quite different backgrounds from mine. TWA Line Captains became part of the mix much later.

The national airline was small and flew mostly Piston aircraft on all its routes. They had recently bought three Boeing 720B's from TWA. These were slightly smaller versions of the vaunted Boeing 707's. In addition, they operated twelve DC-3's, ten Convair 340's and five DC-6's. The DC-3's were twin engine aircraft with twenty-two seats in all but the King's aircraft. The Convairs were also twin engine, but much more modern with "tricycle" landing gear as opposed to the "tail dragger" construction of the older aircraft. This airplane carried forty four seats, except for the King's plane, which had thirty nine. The DC-6's were modern four engine, 87 seat passenger aircraft. I had accumulated several thousand hours in that type aircraft in the military. But "seniority" being the operational theme, I would start on the DC-3, a WW2 vintage airplane with a heroic reputation as a C-47 in the military. If you read my first book, you might remember I unofficially checked myself out in that type aircraft while in combat in 1944. Then later, while assigned to various bases in the United States, including Alaska and Thule, Greenland, I flew it many thousands of hours. Now, of course, I would be checked out in the civilian manner.

One of the DC-3's was the first aircraft owned by Saudi Arabia. It was a gift from President Roosevelt to King Saud in 1945. The tail number was SAR-1. It was still configured for the King, with a private room up front on the right side. It had a huge king-sized leather chair and a table for his use. Later when they got their first Convair 340 (SAR-1), it too was configured for the King and was his personal airplane until the DC-6's arrived. Of course, one of those was now re-configured with kingly accouterments, including a huge leather chair. All of these aircraft, including one of the new 720B's, once designated the King's, were never changed. They were to fly on regular routes with ordinary passengers but would remain configured for the King. Some of the ranking princes also got into the act and two or three DC-3's and four Convairs ended up with a SAR tail number. The SAR stood for Saudi Arabia Royal. All of the other aircraft had tail numbers beginning with HZ, such as HZAAB.

When I first arrived, the name for the airline was SAUDAIR and, of course, this was painted in large letters on the sides and tail of all Kingdom aircraft. Later the name was changed to SAUDIA. The story was that some wag had loosely interpreted SAUDAIR as meaning, "The King's Penis." I can't vouch for that, but the name was changed.

I am a little ahead of myself; however, I thought a little background might help in view of some of the material that will follow.

Right after the New Year in1965, I received written orders to start my travel to Saudi Arabia along with TWA tickets. The travel orders and tickets were initiated by Joe Laterza in Personnel. I would leave my wife and son behind in San Diego as quarters would not be immediately available. Actually, I believe the real reason was, would I stay once I got a look at the country, people and conditions. Also would the Saudis accept me? There were people that had been sent over there and once they got a look at the place, returned on the first available transportation. Some couldn't stand the climate it was hot. Others were just plain homesick. There were those that had trouble with the cultural differences. There were quite a few. Then some realized the difficulty they would face with the language. In any event an early return of a new employee represented quite a loss. The "contract," or minimum time, one was expected to stay there was eighteen months. These eighteen months also coincided with United States requirements for income tax relief. (Or credit)

I departed San Diego at 8:18 AM on the morning of 6 January 1965 and, after a routine flight, arrived in Kansas City about noon. Kansas City had been my home and my parents still lived in nearby Independence. My niece, Serena Olah, also lived in Independence, so I called her to see if she could pick me up. She drove by and picked up my mom, and then drove downtown to pick me up. I spent that evening and night at home visiting, and then Serena drove me back to the hotel in downtown Kansas City about noon. Many thanks, Serena, you were always a big help. About 1445, a bus arrived to take several of us to the International Airport located about seventeen miles north of Kansas City. We were briefed on the flight and after about a two-hour wait, we were loaded aboard Saudi Arabian Boeing 720B, HZACA for a short flight to New York. This aircraft had just been given an overhaul by TWA and represented a convenient vehicle to transport several new employees and some old employees returning from vacation. We stayed in New York that night and at 0530 on the eighth of January, we departed for Gander, Newfoundland for a fuel stop. Weather at Gander on arrival was not too good. They were experiencing blowing snow and the visibility was poor. Captain Sam Bigler made one go-around and on the next approach was able to sneak it in ok. That was the good news. The bad news was, the field was now below minimums in blowing snow and we had a wait on the ground for about nine hours. There was a snack bar and some seating space, but no place to really rest. It was a long day. I did use the time to become more acquainted

4

with the other passengers, though. I met another pilot going over to Saudi for the first time. So we had much in common from that standpoint. His background was much different from mine as he was not an ex military pilot, but rather a "journeyman" pilot who had been in the employ of many small airlines. I later learned that was true of many of the other pilots that were employed to help operate the airline. His name is Bob Wells and we were to be friends for quite some time. Finally departed that evening and arrived Paris about 0330Z.Note: The z stands for, Greenwich mean time, from which all time zones are computed. Zero is represented by a time line drawn north south through England. It was raining there and Captain "Jake Nahar" made the approach and landing. "Jake's" name was actually Nahar Nasser. He was a Saudi National and was one of the first Saudis to become a captain. He was also the King's pilot along with Sam Bigler. Never learned why he was called "Jake." Sam Bigler was the number one contract captain and the "Manager" of the Boeing aircraft fleet. For some reason, we were kept isolated in the Orly Terminal (Paris Airport). Also we had to wait until 0600Z time before being allowed to depart due to some kind of curfew. Noise abatement, I think.

I got my first view of Saudi Arabia on the morning of January 9, 1965 (Friday) from the air as we approached from the north along the western edge of that land. The Red Sea was on our right as we approached Jeddah which was our destination. Jeddah is a port city midway down the Red Sea from Suez and is a very old city. The spelling is not firm, as one might see it spelled many different ways. Some maps and/or books show it as Jiddah, Djiddah, Djeddah, Jeddah, Jidda, etc. Many spellings of other Arabic words are shown phonetically and the spelling becomes secondary. The word, Jeddah in Arabic, has variously been interpreted as meaning "road" or "grandmother," depending upon pronunciation. Some maintain the city was named for Eve (of Adam and Eve) and there is a walled area there that is reputed to contain Eve's tomb. More about that later.

Jeddah was to be my home for the next eighteen months, although I didn't know it at the time.

We taxied up to the terminal about 1030 local time and exited the aircraft into a very warm humid atmosphere. We lined up and walked into Customs where we were required to hand over our passports and to show current shot records. We were not to see our passports again until departing the Kingdom. A little scary when you think of it. You had to pick out your own bags and then get one of the Customs officials to clear them for you. They looked in some and not others. If ok, they marked them with chalk and you stacked the bags nearby. The Customs officials were dressed in their normal Arabic fashion. They wore a long white "gown," with long sleeves and usually a "Mandarin" collar, topped off with a "Ghutra" (cloth) on their heads held in place by an "Agal," two joined circles of fine black wool rope about a half inch in diameter. Under the ghutra, is worn a "Kufiyyah" a small tight-fitting crocheted skullcap. The "gown" referred to is called a "thobe" or "Galibeia" in Arabic.

The interior of the building was very large, not air-conditioned, and strange to most of us with a lot of commotion going on. Those of us that were new arrivals had no clue what was going on and no apparent way to find out. Some of the returning employees tried to be helpful, but even they were harried by the turmoil. Those who might have helped were not allowed in the Customs area. Although the temperature was only in the upper eighties, the humidity and stress was making it very uncomfortable. None of the Customs officials seemed to be able to speak English, except for a few brief commands. We later found out most of them could indeed speak English but preferred not to for some reason. I suspected intimidation purposes.

Waiting noisily at the entrance to Customs was a group of Yemeni natives waiting to grab our luggage and whisk it out to waiting trucks. Of course we didn't know of this impending development and when we observed our bags being hustled out of the area by little men in strange garbs, our anxiety level increased immediately. Our shouts of stop, wait, come back here fell on deaf ears it seemed. We had to shove our way through the mass of humanity, trying our best to keep our eyes on which of the little strangers (thieves?) had which of our bags and where were they taking them. I elbowed my way through the shouting jostling mass in time to see my bags thrown up into a truck. Now I was besieged by thrusting little hands, exhorting me to, "Atini floose, Baksheesh, Baksheesh." They wanted to be paid for carrying my bags. How did I know? Lucky for me one of the airline employees, who was there to help, paid the gratuity. (Baksheesh) Later I was to learn this was the common word to say, "Pay me," or, "Gift." Most of the Americans interpreted the word as "bribe." By this time I was dripping wet with perspiration and really thirsty. Some of us were loaded on small buses and driven about a mile and offloaded in the heat of the day in front of the Hotel Al Haramain Palace. Of course, this added to our anxieties as we were again separated from our collective baggage. We were guided into the lobby to be assigned rooms. Fortunately, the desk clerk spoke excellent English and the job was soon accomplished. We had already been advised not to drink the local water and I was really thirsty. I asked for something bottled to drink and was soon introduced to Evian Water. I opened and drank a whole liter. The desk clerk I alluded to above was Sudanese and his name was Omar. He was soft spoken with a very likeable personality, although not at all outgoing. He offered nothing, but would readily answer your questions with apparent honesty. He seemed to be definitely in charge. He was intelligent and really had a grasp on local procedures and the operation of the hotel. I learned to rely on him heavily. He was much more then just a clerk! I later asked him where he learned to speak such good English. He said he went to a Christian school near his home in Sudan.

About this time there was a commotion outside, so I took a look. Somebody was having an altercation with a cab driver. It was Bob Wells. He hadn't been as lucky as we. His "Basket Boys" had taken his bags to a waiting taxi and, not knowing the procedure, he got in. The driver took him to the right place, but now* wanted five Riyals (about $1.25) for the ride. Of course, Bob did not have any local money and couldn't understand the driver anyway. Soon someone bailed him out and he too, was duly signed up. The "someone" was part of the team that was on hand at the airport to greet us, but had been sidetracked by the local customs people. They caught up with us at the hotel and proceeded to help in every way they could. They gave us a briefing pamphlet and an envelope with some local money to tide us over until we could get settled. The local money was courtesy of one of the airline's employees, a Mr. Tino Bonnofonti. He was a mechanic and had a money changing business on the side. He proved to be a convenience for those employees who did not want to go to town to cash a check, especially a personal check. Yes, he charged a small percentage for any transaction, but no more than those in town.

The Al Haramain Palace Hotel was a five-story building, actually six stories, counting the "ground" floor. It was new and about the best they had to offer, but certainly not "first class" by our standards. Omar is on the right and the electrician is center standing in the photo. (See Photo section) Omar is wearing the typical* Saudi dress sans the Ghutra and Agal. The ground floor had a large dining room, a very nice lounge area, and office space. The rooms were spacious and air conditioned. The air conditioners were all window units and did cool the room, albeit quite noisy. The electric power was two twenty volts, European style and not very reliable. We soon learned that when the power failed, one would lose air conditioning. The power for the building was set up in a complicated grid and* when a section failed, the building maintenance "expert" could and did switch from one section to another. If your section failed, one should quickly complain loudly and often. Sometimes this might cause the "expert" to switch your power back on at the expense of other rooms. You were not immune from another "switch" later on, so it was prudent to stay alert. The "expert" referred to was a Palestinian who had training in building maintenance and electrical systems. He could also

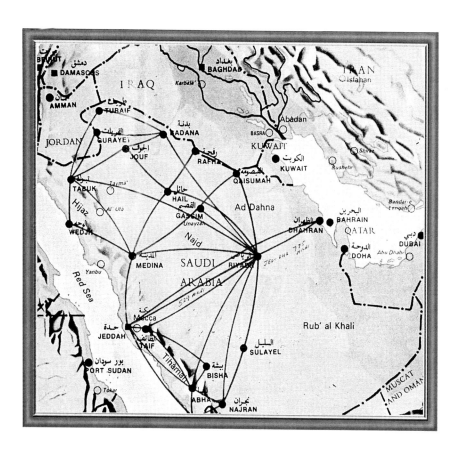

Al Haramain Hotel, David with Volkswagon, 1966

speak English which was a big help to us. We learned later he had rewired the entire building and it no longer complied with the electrical diagrams. Only he knew which circuit breakers controlled which areas of the system. A unique approach to job security.

We were advised on the sanitary conditions (lack of) on the local economy and encouraged not to drink the tap water anywhere. Do not eat salads or any other uncooked food in any of the local eateries including the hotel restaurant. Each of us was invited to have dinner with one of the employee's families that evening. Captain Carter Jones invited me and Captain Jim Money for dinner at his house. Allow me to digress for a moment or two.

I learned that Captain Money was referred to as, Captain "Floose" by Americans and Saudis alike. Money in Arabic was pronounced "Floose," therefore; he was Captain "Floose" to all! Anyway, Captain Jones came by the hotel and took us to his home for a very nice steak dinner.

Prior to dinner, we were introduced to "sadeki." This was a homemade alcohol produced using a formula provided by Aramco, the big American oil conglomerate in Saudi Arabia. They had many employees in Dhahran on the east coast where the oil fields were. They became aware their employees were using unsafe methods to produce alcohol in this "very dry" country. That is, alcohol was forbidden. So to prevent sickness, blindness and/or possibly death, one of the chemists came up with a simple formula that did not use grains or fruit. Just sugar, yeast and a catalyst, let it ferment, and then cook it. Keep all equipment clean and be careful with the whole process. Most cooked and ran it twice to increase the alcohol content and to help purify. Some of the purists cooked it a third time. This aided greatly in removing the "yeasty" taste and smell. The end product tested out to about 180 or 190 proof. This would then be "cut" to a more useable 80 or 90 proof. Some of this product was quite palatable and certainly produced the desired effect. By the way, the word, "Sadeki" means "Friend" in Arabic. Go figure!

Let's get back to the steaks. They were not local. There just was no such thing. Some of the steaks available were shipped in from Australia frozen. Some, very few, were ordered from the States and flown back by one of the crews returning from the TWA overhaul base in Kansas City. More were ordered from a wholesaler in Beirut and flown in by one of the crews. Some of the pilots would make up a list and collect the money from those ordering and take it to Beirut. Awkward, but it worked. That is, most of the time! There were times when an aircraft would go out of commission and the delay would prove to be too long to save the meat. Just don't attempt to bring in any pork products because pork was definitely on their "Hit List," FORBIDDEN. A pork dinner could prove to be quite costly.

We really enjoyed the meal and appreciated the thoughtfulness of those who took strangers into their homes to make them welcome. This was not a company sponsored thing but rather a very thoughtful gesture on the part of all the families involved in this "Welcome to Jeddah" event. That effort not only got us out of a very lonely hotel room in a strange part of the world, but gave us chance to learn a lot from those who had been there for sometime. Not only did I learn a lot from Carter, but his wife Shirley gave me many helpful tips on how to prepare for the eventual arrival of Marti. Both proceeded to give us many insights about the local structure, the people, Arabs and Westerners and how to respond to them. Also some of the dos and don'ts. Regarding the westerners, we were advised all of the embassies were located here in Jeddah. None were allowed in Riyadh, the capital of Saudi Arabia. Later, we were to enjoy entertainment by and with the staff of several of these embassies. Carter drove us back to the hotel about 2100 and we expressed our heartfelt thanks for the evening and their largesse.

I went to bed very soon after arrival and slept about an hour, then tossed and turned the rest of the night. The strange surroundings contributed to my restlessness as did the time change. Another factor was a very noisy diesel generator, seemingly just outside my window. One would think

Son David in Saudi
Daily Dress, with Cape

Al Amoudi on right, safe with money in back.

the window air conditioner would block the sound of that generator, but of course it did not. My room was small and dreary in addition to the generator noise. The following morning, I asked Omar to find a better room for me and why. He agreed he would make arrangements as soon as possible.

Bob Wells and I walked to the Airline Operation Building (about a mile) the next morning. It was just a short half block to a main road direct to the airport. This main road was referred to as "Airport Road" and we would call it that thereafter, although it was designated, "Baghdadiah Street" on the Town Plan. Taking Airport Road the opposite direction would lead one to the big circle where an old fort was located on the left; the Finance building on your right then continuing on* around would lead to the entry to Abdul Azzis Street, which was the main street. Just prior to reaching the old fort on the left was a large walled in lot with gates on the north and south sides. Legend had it that was the burial place of Eve of Adam and Eve. Adam was supposedly buried elsewhere, possibly in Iraq. Legend also indicated both were very tall, perhaps as much as twenty feet. Peering through the gate, I could see a long mound inside the wall that was very likely a bit longer than twenty feet. In the picture of the entrance to Eve's Tomb, there is a pole visible with a cross near the top. A bit ironic, particularly in this case.

The actual Operations building was just across the road from the airport. It was a partially walled-in two-story former home of a Saudi and did not convert very well to offices. The "grounds" were devoid of any cover such as grass or shrubbery and there was no pavement. The entry and parking area was "au na'turel." We had noticed on our walk to the airport that the street was not paved, and would later learn there was only one short paved road so far. The natural ground was desert-like, but not porous. That became quite obvious when we walked onto the grounds of the Operations building. There were several indentations filled with water. We learned the last rain had been several days earlier and the water would simply have to evaporate. Winter months brought rain showers from time to time and, since there was very little slope to aid in runoff, standing water could and did create some hazards.

We had hoped to learn something about our assignments. It was not to be. Captain MacDougal was the DC-3 Supervisor and it became readily apparent, everything was more or less disorganized. Actually, that observation at this time was a bit premature. This was Saturday and almost no one was there. Saturday is the Muslim Sabbath and is observed as such by all. Friday is treated and observed as (our) Saturday. We leisurely returned to the hotel by a different route to get a feel for the area. We saw many strange sights and many different people. It was an interesting walk, but it seems most of those people were not capable of making themselves understood. We spoke slowly and distinctly too. I did notice a used car lot on the north side of the road. I think this road was a continuance of Airport Road which seems to make a loop up to the airport and then back towards the town area. I made a mental note to return there after we had a little more information.

It did not surprise us that we had difficulty making ourselves understood. After all, we were now in a very foreign country which was only just now starting to enter the 1900's. We both understood very soon that we were the foreigners and should comport ourselves accordingly. This was a country that did not allow tourism and still does not to this day. The city of Jeddah had only one paved street when we arrived in January of 1965. The entire "souq" (shopping area) was unpaved. The streets were graded, compacted desert. The merchants "watered down" the areas in front of their shops to control the dust.

I woke up in the morning and realized it was Sunday and was probably a normal work day so possibly we might learn a little more. Admittedly, I was entertaining the thought that I already did not care very much for the surroundings, after the frustration of yesterday and having to spend another night listening to that infernal generator. Another little word with Omar was on my agenda. He was very apologetic and promised to work on changing my room very soon.

Bob and I again walked up to Operations. The weather was certainly pleasant enough. Today was about like yesterday, so far in the mid seventies. Yesterday ended about seventy-nine and the night was cool. No air conditioner needed at night, so of course outside noises were more intrusive. Anyway it was a nice walk.

Captain MacDougal, the DC-3 supervisor was on a trip, so was not available. No one in the office seemed to know if there was a set procedure to check new people out and get them started. We pressed a little and met Captain Leroy Johnson who at the time was a DC-3 instructor. (Note: I learned many years later, Leroy was from Clinton, Missouri and his wife was still there. I was to later meet many fine people living in Clinton and enjoyed golfing, fishing and hunting with them. Small world.)

The actual scheduling was not Leroy's responsibility; however he was very helpful giving us a probable schedule. Very likely we would fly a few local hours with an instructor, including some night flying with some landings, and get a check ride by the supervisor. We would then be scheduled for some trips to various destinations in the Kingdom for familiarization with routes and airports. Between trips, we would be attending ground school in the Convair 340 twin engine aircraft. Sometime in February, the FAA Inspector domiciled in Beirut would come to Jeddah to administer check rides for type ratings in the appropriate aircraft. He came very close to being correct on all counts. We (Bob Wells) and I flew our first local in a DC-3 with Leroy Johnson as the instructor, on January 12th. It was enjoyable to be back in the seat of an airplane, even though somewhat awkward at first as it had been several years since my last flight in a C-47 (DC-3). I soon caught on, though, and made several takeoffs and landings before turning it over to Bob.

We had been given a manual on operation of the DC-3 and had reviewed it prior to this flight and would spend the remainder of the duty day studying same.

When I returned to the hotel, Omar greeted me with a big grin to inform me my new room would be available to move in bukra (tomorrow). I would have to listen to that bloody generator one more night! I did not mention that to him of course. He was trying to please.

Bob and I decided to try the restaurant in the hotel this evening. The restaurant was on the ground floor and was quite spacious with nice furniture and arrangement. We ordered as best we could to insure a fully cooked meal and NO salad. I requested an unopened bottle of Evian water for our drink. All the waiters were Sudanese. I don't know where they got their training, but they were the best waiters I had ever encountered. They all dressed in white galibeas and wore a wrapped white turban on their heads, Sudanese style. They were very attentive without being intrusive and served with great style. We ate there often when the menu seemed in concert with my limited tastes. Food would turn out to be quite a problem for me.

Wednesday, the 13th of January, I moved into my new room. Room number 308 was very nice and quite large. I would guess it to be about fourteen by sixteen feet with a small entry hall and a separate bath room. The furniture was adequate and very plain. There was a separate air conditioner in place through a hole cut in the outside wall for that purpose. Also there was a ceiling fan. There were double doors leading out to a small balcony and a window along side. The ceiling height was at least ten feet. All in all a very nice room.

The person in charge of the inner workings of the hotel was a tall slender Sudanese named Sulieman. He was a quiet serious young man always dressed in the Arab white thobe with appropriate head gear. Sulieman spoke very good English, was intelligent and had very firm control of all of the workers in the hotel. We sought him when we had any problem and he would see it done, or quietly explain why the delay, or an alternative. A good man.

Thursday 14th of January, flew two hours and twenty five minutes in a DC-3 aircraft with Leroy Johnson. I made several takeoffs and landings along with some air work, including practice instrument flying. Bit of a crosswind for the takeoffs and landings, but good to help get reacquainted with the DC-3.

The weather so far had been wonderful. The temperature would rise during the day to the high seventies and cool at night to sweater conditions. We would later learn how fortunate we were to arrive in the "winter."

Bob and I used the next few days getting acquainted. We learned to use the taxis, how much to pay, (anywhere in town for two riyals, about fifty cents U.S.) and how to direct the driver. All the taxis were large cars, mostly Chevrolets, and driven by many different nationalities, including Yemenis, Sudanese, Pakistanis, etc. There were no street numbers for places one would want to go, so it became a direction thing. Straight ahead (al atuwl), right (al yameen), left (as shmal), stop, (owguf). All the drivers had a tendency to drive much too fast (especially for their skill and experience level), and we frequently had to admonish with "shway shway," (slowly, carefully) or, "slow down, dammit," spoken with a shout. Also, we learned some of those drivers did not understand Arabic any better than we did. Then we reverted to hand signals. There was no shortage of taxis, so we were safe getting out of the car almost anywhere even if we were wrong. Most of the locals relied on many other forms of travel in their daily lives. They traveled by foot, bicycle, and motorbike or on the "ghersh" buses. These were small Volkswagen ten or twelve passenger buses that moved almost constantly on given routes. Their name derives from the cost, i.e., four ghersh. This would amount to about four cents U.S.

All Saudi drivers had one thing in common besides speed and that was constant use of the horn, and the taxi drivers compounded that tendency by installing super loud horns. I mean many, many decibels! That was very annoying, of course, and later we observed police roadblocks to check for type of horn installed. They would raise the hood, toot the horn, and if it was one of the loud ones, would remove the offending noise maker with bolt cutters. The driver of the taxi would then be sent to have a proper horn installed.

I almost forgot to mention the car radio. The radio was always on playing Arab type music at a high volume. It was very difficult to get the driver to lower the volume or turn it off

The drivers liked to decorate the inside of the automobile. The seats might be covered with a thick material woven in bright purples and indigos. The dashboard is usually fringed by some furry material in several colors, many in pastels. The steering wheel is taped in many colors and the gear lever is garnished with some kind of dangle. The rear window may be almost concealed by multicolored, tasseled curtains. Plump pillows encased in silver spangles may rest on the ledge behind the seat back.

All that was probably a lot more than you needed to know about the local transportation, but I think it does add to the feel of the environment. None of the taxis were air-conditioned and became very uncomfortable in the heat of summer.

The "Market Place" or "Suq, Suuq, Ssuuq, Sook," whatever the spelling, was in a relatively small area right in the "downtown" of Jeddah. King Abdul Aziz Street was the main street. People usually turned into the souk off the main street onto Gaabel Street; however, directions were usually given by, "Turn into the street with the orange juice stand." There was an orange juice sidewalk café style store on the left just past the barber shop on the corner. There was seating inside and out, similar to a Paris sidewalk café. Most all directions to a given place usually started out with, "You know where the orange juice stand is?" "Ok, from there you go——

On the right, across from the orange juice stand, was a baby clothes shop, then a children's shop, a boutique, a film store, then Al Amoudi's money changer shop, or "booth." The money changers sat on a platform about waist high. Behind them was a huge open safe which displayed tens of thousands of dollars in currency and coin of many, if not all, countries of the world. Perhaps hundreds of thousands of dollars were represented here. One of the bills displayed on

Entrance to Souk, Jeddah, 1965

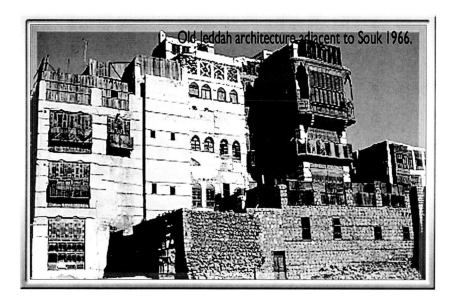

Old Jeddah architecture adjacent to Souk 1966.

Covered Souk, Jedda, SA, 1966

Lawrence of Arabia met Sherif of Mecca in 1917 here.

the top right of the contents was a United States thousand dollar bill. (See photos)*

In addition, there were rows and rows of gold coins minted by and for many different countries. Even gold bullion, from tiny gold bars to very large ones, was stacked behind the changer. All were marked with content and weight. You ask for it, they would probably find it for you. There were a couple more money changers further along on this street.

I favored Al Amoudi's as a money changer after my very first experience in cashing a check. I was running short of local currency after a few days and asked friends where one should go to cash a personal check. Just go to the souk, I was instructed, and ask one of the money changers to cash it for you. With some feeling of possibly having my leg pulled, I approached the money changer across from the orange juice stand and asked if they would cash a check for me. Al Amoudi (it was he in person) answered, "Sure, Captain, how much do you want?" I was so surprised; I almost forgot how to respond. Number one, his English was very good. Number two, how did he know I was a captain? Number three, was he really going to accept my personal check without any other identification in this far off land? The answer to number three was, yes he did. Number two was answered for me after I had been there for a while. Their intelligence system was excellent. They knew when new people arrived and what company they were with and what their jobs were. They were also pretty sure you were not going anywhere without them knowing about it. The local government had your passport and kept it until you were authorized to depart and a visa had been issued. Very interesting! Yes, all money changers charged a small percentage of every transaction. Some could be better by decimals and it might be worthwhile to shop around, but experience proved Al Amoudi was overall the best.

On the left side of this street, after passing the orange juice stand, were several shoe stores. After the shoe stores, we come to a pedestrian cross street. Although cars were not supposed to use this street, donkey carts, bicycles, and motor bikes did, along with throngs of people. Occasionally a small truck or complete jerk in a car would bull their way through, horn tooting, and complicate the movement of all.

The "souk" was separated in sections by the type of merchandise being sold. Carpets generally in one section, pots and pans, materials, paper, gold, silver, hardware, shoes, etc, each in their own area. Even "charcoal," "animal" and "hubbly bubbly" (for water pipes or "Hookahs."). Not a bad idea! It sure made it simple to comparison shop. In the evenings, it was a very interesting place to be. Shoppers filled the streets, many different types of people. Many Saudis, men and women, each in their own manner of dress. Many other nationalities were present as well, each in their own costume, dress, or clothing. During this period of unrest with the Yemeni fighting the Egyptians, who were attempting to invade their country, there were many Yemeni soldiers to be seen. Saudi Arabia was backing the Yemeni, furnishing them with money and very likely, munitions as well. Anyway, they really added to the ambience of the souk. Their uniforms consisted of garments very much like dresses which ended at the knees or thereabouts. The color of the garment was khaki and I think buttoned up the front. They wore a large pocketed belt which held the ever present Arab curved scabbard with dagger in the center of their abdomen. Many also carried a rifle with bandoleer of cartridges slung over the shoulder. Most favored shoulder length hair and, along with the rest of their costume, were a formidable appearing group.

The noise really added to the overall interest of the place. There was a constant babble of voices, music coming from various shops, occasional automobile horns, and shouts from Yemeni with donkey carts trying to get through the mass of people. Sometimes a car would attempt to go through or a lunatic on a motorcycle would challenge the mass. I failed to mention that none of the "streets" in the souk were paved and the merchants had a practice of "watering" down the dust from time to time. This provided one with another hazard to watch out for, as the water tended to puddle here and there. Also a little "donkey doo" would show up from time to time, creating a bit of a "mine field."

Bob and I went to the souk Thursday evening, January 14, 1965 and tried to traverse the whole of it. We were "lost" several times due to cut backs and "blind" alleys and the fact that the "streets" were not exactly straight. Yes, we did ask questions and sometimes understood the directions given. We were having so much fun exploring this exotic, exciting place, being lost seemed to be just part of it. The sights, sounds and smells were something to behold and to experience! The sounds of many voices sometimes speaking different languages or dialects and shouts of laughter blended well with the tinkling of bells and Arab music blaring from several nearby radios. All of this was punctuated occasionally with the cacophonous blaring of an automobile horn or the braying of a donkey pulling a cart through the mass of constantly moving humanity.

Tables out in the open, piled high with dates, figs, and other fruits and vegetables we were unable to identify, provided an aroma that was heady and pleasant. That is, for the most part. Flies were thick at times, hovering over and alighting on the displayed fruit. The attendant would sometimes attempt to ward them off with a lion's tail "shoo-fly" wand or fly swatter. Just as often though, he would use a "flit" gun to spray the fruit or vegetables with a 'bug killer" of some kind. Enough to make one wary of eating any of the fruit or vegetables without washing them. The most exotic aromas were produced by the merchants who sold spices. They displayed their wares in open containers and sold them by weight. I did not know there were so many different spices in the world.

Perhaps right next to the merchant who sold spices would be one who specialized in frankincense and myrrh, both aromatic resinous substances used in perfumery and incense along with other types of incense. The hardened resins were in various size pieces and shades of amber and were priced accordingly. Naturally the merchant would keep some of this material burning to produce the aromatic smoke. Close by, one could find basins of henna. Many of the older men would die their beards with henna to signify having been on the Hajj (Pilgrimage) to Mecca. Also there were those who dyed parts of their donkeys and those with camels used it freely to make unusual designs on them. I saw one donkey that was completely covered with a henna dyed design along with having parts of his hide shaved to enhance the effect. Much later we saw camels that had been "beautified" in much the same manner.

The "souk" would prove to be a large part of our entertainment in the months to come. The women loved the place. The souk areas were an almost constant hubbub of activity. Not only just the movement, jostling and sounds, but an awful lot of bargaining was in progress. It apparently was not considered couth or proper to accept the first price offered. One had to learn to "counter offer." That practice soon evolved into a great game. I learned to enjoy the back and forth struggle. I even brought that method back to the states with me. The automobile dealers in the United States did not appreciate my newly acquired skills when I returned home.

The next day, Friday was different as the Arabs viewed this day as their Saturday and the following day (Saturday) as their holy day.

I read a lot, wrote to Marti and David and generally "goofed" off. Went for a long walk to get acquainted with the local area. Most of the stores were closed Friday afternoon and all day Saturday for the weekend. I passed many locals on the streets and all seemed friendly, most certainly non-threatening. I vowed to learn some Arabic as soon as possible. At least enough to greet people with a "good morning," etc. This "free time" was very rewarding and gave me a chance to evaluate my circumstances. Sure was glad the weather was so pleasant this time of year.

Flew local with Leroy Johnson again today. Later in the month I flew again with Leroy and also had rides with Captain "Goody" Goodman, a great guy and the proverbial itinerant pilot. Later I was "lucky" enough to receive instruction from Captain MacDougal, the self styled "World's greatest pilot." (Sic). This may or may not have been of great benefit to me.

Sunday the 17ᵗʰ of January 1965, I checked in to the United States Embassy and asked for the Air Attaché Office. There I met a Mrs. Freeman who was not only friendly, but very knowledgeable in many ways. She offered many helpful ideas and got approval for me to use their mail until I could get U.S. Military approval (MAAG) to use the APO address.

Next I looked for and found the location of the MAAG House. This building housed the members of the United States Military Assistance Group, their headquarters and the mess hall (dining facility). The members of this group were specialists in various aspects of the military and were in Saudi Arabia in an advisory capacity for their counterparts in the Saudi Air Force. I talked to a Major McKaig in Administration and received the necessary permission to use their APO (Army Post Office) address for my mail. The MAAG had a small Post Exchange (PX) in the building stocked with shaving materials, candy, cigarettes, film and many other small necessaries. Major McKaig denied me permission to purchase items there. After some discussion, he agreed to check with Dhahran MAAG headquarters. Retired Air Force officers, which of course apply to me, are authorized use of Military Exchanges. Admittedly this privilege is with the concurrence of the Commanding Officer of the organization.

Within days, permission was granted by the Commanding General of MAAG located in Dhahran, Saudi Arabia. Major McKaig now added another proviso. All such purchases must be reported to Saudi customs and it was up to me to talk to customs officials and provide him, McKaig, with the procedure. This was not being done in Riyadh nor in Dhahran and for a very good reason. The Arabs themselves provide the reason why not. They maintain it is very bad to allow the camel's nose to intrude under the tent edge. To do so is to allow the camel access and he will soon occupy the tent.

Luckily, cooler heads prevailed after becoming aware of McKaig's intentions and soon I could purchase from the PX.

Lt. Colonel Keefe, the local MAAG Commanding Officer, returned from a short leave and offered me the opportunity to join them for meals in their mess hall along with other amenities. This was the beginning of a long and very beneficial relationship for me and my family after they joined me. Now might be a good time to mention, the MAAG showed movies on their roof almost every night and of course we were invited. There were no theatres in Saudi Arabia for the public, as movies were not allowed. The embassy also had a theatre in their main building and later we would have access to that as well. Things were looking up!

FIRST TRIP

Within a day or two I was scheduled for my first trip, not as the captain, but for familiarization with the routes to be flown and "navigation" of same. Captain Akram, a Saudi National was to be administered a "route check" by Captain Leroy Johnson. This "route check" was always given to any captain who had not flown that particular trip in a given time span. The route was scheduled to depart Jeddah for Wedj (north on the red sea coast), land, offload passengers, load any passengers or cargo and proceed to Tabuk, which is slightly inland and further north. Again land, offload/on load and proceed to Badana. Badana is basically an Aramco station on the oil pipeline that runs from Dhahran on the east coast all the way across the northern portion of Saudi Arabia to seaports in Lebanon. From Badana we were to proceed west to another pipeline station at Turaif which is located very near the borders with Jordan and Iraq. Here we were to spend the night and return the next day via a reverse route. Note: There were other "stations" along this thousand mile long pipeline and I will become very familiar with them in the months to come. The inhabitants were employees of Aramco and their responsibilities included maintenance, inspections and safety of the pipeline. A note about Akram:

He spoke very good English, had gone to school in the U.S and had lived there for a while. While there he married an American girl and she accompanied him back to Saudi Arabia. He was intelligent, a good pilot and a very nice gentlemen. He was also a big help to me.

Now for the actual flight. We departed Jeddah at 0350 in a DC-3, with Captain Akram in the left seat and me in the right as co-pilot. The aircraft lost hydraulic fluid on climb out and we had to return to Jeddah. Captain Akram handled the emergency very well indeed and made a nice landing without the use of flaps or brakes.

The passengers and cargo were reloaded on another DC-3 and we departed Jeddah at 0520 for another try. The flight proceeded as planned to Wedj where Akram made an excellent landing. The agent at Wedj wanted to put more passengers on than we had seats for, and got a little angry when Akram told him no. When he kept insisting, Akram made him take the passengers off he had already loaded. Later, Akram explained to me this agent had done this before to other captains and had actually gotten away with it. The agent would take "baksheesh" (bribe) from the passengers to ensure their getting on board. He would then intimidate the captain to accept them or wait till the captain went to the cockpit and then slip a couple extra on board. The entire trip was a real eye opener to me.

Soon we were airborne en route to Tabuk, where Akram made another smooth landing on the ten thousand foot runway. No further problems loading, refueling, etc. The flight took off on time, destination Badana. Climb out was accomplished to eight thousand feet where we would cruise.

We were now flying in the clear but, within thirty minutes, were between layers of clouds. Soon those layers merged and we were on instruments. Radio contact with Badana revealed they had rain and low ceilings. We knew there could be no approach under those conditions as they did not have any type of radio aid system. After an hour and twenty seven minutes of flight, with about an hour and a half to go, we started our return to Tabuk.

Near Tabuk is where Lawrence of Arabia blew up the railroad during World War I. This was the rail line built by the Turks and it stretched from Medina in Saudi Arabia to Amman, Jordan. If you saw the movie, you saw it happen. The rail has remained unused since that time because of the extensive damage caused by Lawrence and the men he led. Anyway, the Saudis are now starting the process of rebuilding the rails. They also built a very fine ten thousand foot concrete runway at Tabuk. However, there were camels on the runway as we started our approach and we waited until they had been herded off. There is now an Army training center nearby and there is a very large tent city east of town to accommodate the soldiers.

Passengers were off loaded at Tabuk; however, they all opted to return to Jeddah. Later I would learn this was a common occurrence. There were no hotels or motels or any other places one might overnight unless, of course, they had friends or relatives nearby. Also there might not be another flight through that station for several days en route to their desired destination. They just accepted that as the way it is and made little or no protest. Soon we departed for Wedj and thence back to Jeddah arriving at 1635. The day and flight was a long one. The trip turned out to be an eye opener for me in many ways. I now realized many changes were to occur in my planning for all future flights to ensure a safe operation.

It was easy enough to navigate from Jeddah to Wedj as we could almost follow the coast line all the way (2 hours, 20 minutes). However, on a straight line, we would have to be over water just about out of sight of land. From Wedj to Tabuk, not so easy. We had no radio aids. All navigation was dead reckoning aided by "pilotage" which is using a map, spotting "landmarks," visually keeping track in that manner all the way. However, as soon we departed Wedj, there was just desert, sprinkled with bare hills and/or jabals (mountains, small or large). I had no idea which of these should be considered "landmarks." About halfway, we crossed a large lava flow (harrat) which stood out dramatically from the desert color. That, of course, gave us a direction fix, but not a lateral fix. Both Akram and Leroy knew where we were, of course, but let me sweat. They sure got my attention. From that time on, I picked their brains on what to look for and would plot those clues on my map. A clue might be an established camel trail or a wadi. (A wadi is a dry river bed and can be a very good landmark.) Small oases were used, along with different color sand and texture. The color of a mountain (Jabal) might be a good clue. There was a lot of marble in the country and the color of a marble mountain, sometimes stood out clearly for miles. Flying from Jeddah, the check point to make a right turn towards Taif to clear the highest terrain was "The White Mountain." The mountain WAS white and it was indeed marble. Many of the "landmarks" were quite subtle, but readable after one had adjusted to paying close attention.

Lava flows were good, although these were mostly confined to the western portions of the country. The southern mountains had more small villages because of the nature of the land. There was more water near the surface and this was utilized for limited agriculture. The villages grew in those fortunate areas. Some of the mountains were "terraced" and grew many crops. All of these things were duly marked on my maps as I flew each of the various routes, and of course I memorized them. I have remarked many times, I believe I could return to Saudi Arabia and fly every one of those routes by memory. Even "AR RUB AL KHALI" (desert) that covers a large portion of southeastern Arabia has check points, if one knows what to look for. (I could not fly that from memory tho.)

We often flew "off track" to locate and mark on our maps landmarks that might be used if one should get off course due to weather and have to start looking for some recognizable area. Sand storms occurred on occasion, and visibility could be obscured for thousands of feet in the air and the upper air currents could blow one off course very easily. When and if the ground again became visible, there might be some abated panic in the cockpit while we searched for a viable means to establish a position. Most of the time, these sand storms were not "forecast." Our first clue might be looking down and seeing the desert starting to "move." That would mean the wind was picking up on the surface enough to pick up the sand and blow it along. Eventually the blowing sand might begin to rise to higher levels. Other times we might just look ahead and see a huge wall of blowing sand dust blotting out the sky. There was no way to tell how far the visibility would be bad, so the prudent thing was to turn around and go back. Some of these sand storms would reduce visibility from coast to coast, over eight hundred miles. The height of these sand storms could reach altitudes of fifteen to twenty thousand feet.

TWA had been seeking a qualified person to operate Saudi's airline for some time, and was unable to find such a person within their own ranks. They located such a person in Mr. Morton Byers and he had preceded me in Saudi. Mr. Byers had operated many small airlines in the U.S. throughout many years and appeared to be highly qualified. He was to become the General Manager Technical for Saudi Arabian Airlines, reporting to Trans World Airlines. He of course would serve at the pleasure of the Director General of the airline, who was a Saudi.

Bob Wells and I reported to Mr. Byers a few days after our arrival and were given a good briefing on what to expect. I learned that day; Bob Wells had worked in one of those small airlines in the states for Mr. Byers.

Mort Byers was about six feet, seven inches tall and soon was tagged with the sobriquet, "high pockets." Don't know how he felt about that but I never heard of any protests.

Mort Byers invited several of us for cocktails and dinner Thursday evening. Captain Ahearn drove Wells, Johnson, Goodman and I to the affair in his red Cadillac. Ahearn had bought the car used from a Saudi Prince. The car was air-conditioned, had a "Continental" spare on the trunk and very dark glass in all rear windows. The car only had a few miles on it but the low grade gas available there kept it struggling to run. One would have to take the car out on a high speed run often to "burn" the carbon or whatever out. Interesting fact: There were TEN other identical red Cadillacs running around Jeddah, each having been purchased from a local Saudi Prince. The Prince had bought them for his children and ordered them all the same so there would be no prejudice involved. These became available for sale when those were replaced with new.

Byers had a very nice villa in the Aramco compound out on Mecca road. Cocktails were served on the roof, which was pretty much the normal thing for those with villas. All villas seemed to have a flat roof with a waist high wall built up. Probably so families would have a place to sit out in the evenings and not be observed. The dinner was given in honor of the Jack Friers. Frier was a TWA captain and the director of the Flight Training Center in Kansas City. He was in Jeddah for just a short visit. I met a lot of people there and fortunately could remember some of them later. Very interesting.

Martinis were made using "Sadeki" instead of gin and some of the Manhattan's were as well. I tried one of the martinis, but switched when I noticed there was some real Johnny Walker's Scotch available and later saw some Gordon's and Beefeaters Gin. How could that be in a land where alcohol is forbidden? Well, the liquor was smuggled in, of course.

Earlier I had explained about Sadeki and how it evolved. Brand liquor was smuggled in many ways, by truck and camel train over the desert, by boat and sometimes by plane. A few months later, I purchased a case of scotch and it was delivered to me in a bedraggled, dusty, much worn burlap bag. Straight from its burial place out in the desert, I was told. The price of a case of booze was another oddity. Whether you purchased Scotch, Bourbon, Gordon's gin or Beefeater's gin, the price per case was the same. The booze had been smuggled across the desert from Amman, Jordan and buried somewhere near Jeddah until called for. The diplomatic pouch was a bountiful source as well. None of this was really a secret from the Saudis. They apparently simply allowed the westerners their supply of liquor as long as they were discreet and did not furnish any to the local populace. Many of us made our own wine and some became quite adept in the brewing of same. The food was catered as all such events would prove to be and was served buffet style. It was an evening well spent and talking with many different people helped a lot with perspective. Several private companies were represented, several embassies, USGS people and a ranking Saudi or two. I would try to sort it out later.

Will Brown, a flight engineer, had borrowed Fred Wright's Volkswagen while Fred was on vacation. He invited me to go with him to the creek the next day, a Friday. The "creek" is actually an "arm" or inlet from the Red sea, located about twenty-five miles north of Jeddah. Although long sandy beaches extend for miles north and south of Jeddah, access and the danger from sharks makes them unpopular. The most frequented spot is the four mile long creek, between 200 and 800 yards wide. Westerners and Arabs have cabins or villas on both sides of the creek. The villas are all walled and the cabins are collectively walled as they are rather flimsy and don't rate the expense. They have rudimentary water supply and some electricity. Most all accommodations are rented by the year by anyone with the money. Many of these have boat docks built out into the sea, although most are used as a means into or out of the water and/or a place to sun or fish. The cabins are very basic and qualify mostly as a place to change into swimming suits or whatever. The creek is a very popular place on the weekends and is indeed a very beautiful waterway. The water is crystal clear and is teeming with thousands of multicolored tropical fish of many kinds. One has to be careful, of course, as many of those fish are poisonous, and so is the coral. It really is a snorkeler's paradise though, or scuba diving, if that is your sport. I spent quite a bit of time out in the water and sun and later with my family doing the same although Marti was not a big fan. David loved it!

The road to the creek is lightly paved and is fairly straight, but a very dangerous stretch of road nevertheless.

The road itself can be a death-trap. Its straightness encourages high speed. To reach the creek, one leaves town along the Medina road, passing a few lonely cafes with tables and high wicker benches scattered many yards far into the desert. The road points dead ahead to the distant plume of smoke on the horizon that heralds the cement factory. On either side stretches the desert: to the left and out of sight, the sea; to the right, about 40 kilometers away a low range of mountains. Patches of dry scrub grass dance in the heat haze and it is not uncommon to see small herds of camels grazing, their shepherds sitting patiently nearby. Occasionally one sees Bedouin women squatting to cut those patches of grass and bundling them for later use. This road is paved because it is the "highway" to Medina, the second holy city in Saudi Arabia and it leads us to the turnoff for the creek. About sixteen kilometers beyond the cement factory the road passes over a causeway at the landward end of the creek. The turnoff is just beyond the causeway and does not lead one to just a single track or road. You are faced with many choices. One can hope he chooses the right track to best traverse the distance with the least chance of bogging down along the way. Depending on recent weather, some of those trails may still be wet in places (the low spots) and are impassable. In any event, the trick is to stay parallel to the creek and follow the contours of the sand to prevent bogging down.

The locals were not raised with automobiles as most of us were and had very little concept how to drive, nor the skills required. They tended to drive as fast as the car would go and, of course, this resulted in some spectacular accidents from time to time. Sometimes cars overtake three abreast, leaving no place but the desert for oncoming cars. The road was littered with wreckage on either side in a very short time span. In those early days, they apparently saw no need to remove the debris as it was just in the desert and nothing to interfere. Besides, the sight of the mayhem might serve to instill a little caution. Don't think it worked tho. One thing all westerners soon learned was NOT to be on that road at the beginning of the weekend when the Saudis were racing to the creek, AND avoid the road on Saturday evenings when they were returning home.

Bob Wells found a used Volkswagen and plans to purchase it Saturday. I will wait for a new one and plan to go to the dealer in a few days and follow Akram's advice on how to proceed. Several have been to the dealer and he has told them he has no cars. Akram advises go anyway.

Received my Saudi Captain's license for the DC-3 today. The license was issued by Mr. Yousif T. Qutub, Head of Airworthiness for the country. The license still needs the signature of the Director General of Saudi Arabian Airlines. He is presently on vacation. Mr. Qutub says it is ninety percent a license without that signature so go ahead and fly. So okayyyy, will do. I would never do that in the U.S.; however, I am in a different world now.

GASSIM

Scheduling has assigned me to a trip on January 29 to depart Jeddah at 0322Z with following stops: Medina, Hail, Gassim, Zilfi, Riyadh, stay overnight, and return the same route in reverse. Captain Tashkandy (Saudi national) and I will alternate in left seat and command for each leg. He will take off from Jeddah, and I will co-pilot and navigate. The flight was uneventful into and out of each of the villages or towns. We refueled at Gassim and I initiated the takeoff from the left seat, now in command. The weather had deteriorated some and we had a fairly low ceiling with scattered scud below that. Riyadh should have about the same on arrival with a slightly higher ceiling. Riyadh did have a radio aid, so that would help if I should have to make an instrument approach. Gassim is the Airport that serves the towns of Buraydah and Unayzah.

Right after takeoff things went from fair to pretty bad in a hurry! When I called for "gear up," Tashkandy operated the gear handle to "up," but nothing happened. A quick look at the hydraulic pressure revealed why. We had just lost all pressure. Decision time! If I continued the climb, we would quickly be in the clouds and unable to return to Gassim. Should I continue on to Riyadh in the clouds with the gear down causing high* fuel* usage and hope we had enough fuel? And that weather would hold up so we could land? That option seemed to me to be the riskier way to go since I could still see the ground as I had leveled out as soon as the lack of pressure was noted. I called for "gear down," knowing the gear would free fall of its own weight if not already down and possibly "lock down." If it did not, we could "hand crank" it into the locked position. I advised Tashkandy we would return and land at Gassim and for him to call the agent to inform him. We stayed low to remain out of the clouds and circled for a landing. No problem.

There was no maintenance available at this remote village, so we were left with two options. One, advise Jeddah of our problem and wait for them to fly some maintenance people in to fix the aircraft. Two, remain here overnight, waiting for better weather and daylight. Then secure the gear in the down position, add extra fuel, and fly to Riyadh for repairs. We decided to advise Jeddah and fly to Riyadh in the AM.

Sounded simple enough, but there were no facilities for an overnight stay. We had five passengers and there were four in the crew. It was now getting dark as the sun had set and the clouds were still with us.

Tashkandy and the agent for the airline were busily working something out, speaking rapidly in Arabic. How I wished I could understand. Soon they had arrived at a plan, I could tell by their actions, but what? "Tashkandy, what is the plan?" I asked. His reply left a lot of room for further explanation. He was not very fluent in English and had a habit of saying the least he could. I gathered we were to be transported in to the village of Burrayduh for the night. Soon a Land Rover vehicle arrived and the passengers were loaded in the rear.

Tashkandy and I were in the front seat with the driver. The driver wore the usual Arab dress, with khotra and agal (head scarf), and appeared of normal intelligence. That is, until he started to drive across the desert! Then he took on a whole different personality. There was no road, we were traveling across rolling treacherous sand hills, dips and dry wadis at a bone jarring clip. The head lights were alternately shining on sand and the night sky as we negotiated the uneven terrain. When we hit an upslope, the headlights could not illuminate the ground and one had the feeling of about to fly off into an abyss. That tended to give me a real thrill, similar to roller coaster. Only worse. He was busily shifting gears most of the time as we hit areas of soft sand and tended to bog down, whereupon he would increase the engine speed to a roar. The night was truly dark and the truck lights did little to give one a sense of attitude and direction. I was holding on as best I could, trying to keep from breaking something, wind or getting thrown out. I think I may have prayed a little (even to Allah).

I was even starting to question my decision to return and land when seemingly all at once we arrived in the village. The first indication was mud walled buildings suddenly appeared in the light from our headlights. Any lights were dim and came from inside the houses or buildings. The vehicle stopped in front of a walled in enclosure and everybody got out, including me as Tashkandy said, "We are here." After I asked, of course.

I followed him and the others through a doorway in the wall, and entered a courtyard that with the dim light available appeared to be rather large. We trailed across the courtyard and entered a large room which was the ticket office and waiting room. My guess is the room was about fifty feet by fifteen with a very high ceiling, perhaps 16 to 18 feet. The floor was covered with "Persian" rugs and there were chairs and sofas all around. They were all black wood with gold trim and carved backs and arms. The cushions were all light green. We were separated from the agent and passengers, and we four crew members went in a room which had no furniture but did have a very nice Arabic rug on the floor and colorful "pillows" up against the wall.

Capt Porter, Steward Achmed, Local Sheikh @ Guriat, SA, 1965
I was wearing the Sheikh's "Mishla"

Refueling Convair, Gassim, SA, 1966
Captain Porter, Pilot

Capt. Porter
at the "Creek"
Saudi Arabia, 1965

Aligator Gar

Majmah, Saudi Arabia, Airport & Terminal, 1965.   (North from Capital city of Riyadh)

The Arab crew sat on the floor and leaned against the pillows, so I did the same. When I asked Tashkandy, "What are we supposed to do now?" His answer was cryptic as usual, "We will eat soon." Believe me, that did not relieve my mind one bit. I have what has been referred to as a weak stomach. My preference is for plain foods that are tried and true. No experimenting for me. One of the pilots had told me about the Arab food and how it was served. Captain Akkram had verified that for me and had unfortunately informed me the honored guest would be offered the goat's eyeball as a tidbit. Would I be considered the "honored guest?" Man, I hope not!

Soon the agent appeared in the doorway and said, "Come, followed by a few words in Arabic." Like a sheep to slaughter, I followed Tashkandy and the agent through the door and down the hall and into what I will refer to as the "dining" room. There appeared to be a wall to wall rug on the floor, with pillows distributed all around. The center of the room had what appeared to me to be a large platter piled high with food. There were also many smaller dishes containing, cheeses, tuna, meats, round objects, oranges, apples, jams, dates, etc. located conveniently around the center tray. Lots of cooked rice with bits of meat scattered through out and other garnishes unknown. The meat, I learned, was chicken and goat. There were also several dishes of round flat Arabic bread. The Arabs would tear off a piece of this bread and use it to fold over morsels and pop them into their mouths.

The agent and passengers were seated on the floor in a semi-circle around the food with their legs crossed and already starting to eat. We were waved to join. I had a little trouble with that crossed-leg position but managed to get close. I watched them perform the eating ritual as I took my time getting situated. They used their right hand and scooped up a portion of rice and tidbit, rolling the morsel into a ball and popped it into their mouth. Or they would sometimes use a piece of the bread to pickup the object of their choice. They chewed open mouthed, masticating noisily with gusto!

Man, this was not helping! My stomach was already starting to move and protest and I had not had a bite. Well I was just going to have to reach way down somewhere and get through this no matter what. I steeled myself, reached over, took a small handful, rolled it into a ball and popped it in! I avoided watching them eat and chewed away. Well I got that down. Hope it stays. I ate some more, using the bread trying to pick out chicken each time and had a couple slices of orange along with a date or two. I was just starting to feel some confidence starting to build that I was going to get through this after all. Then the agent reached over and offered me the goat's eyeball with a big smile and said something in Arabic. Tashkandy said, "He called you honored guest and to eat." All the other Arabs stopped eating, started smiling and gesturing for me to eat. My stomach started talking to me in a big way.

I mentally transported myself to another place, pretending I had a Martini in front of me and had picked the olive out. The olive was in my hand and I popped it into my mouth and swallowed it before my stomach was aware. Suddenly all was well. The Arabs started talking and eating again and I was off the hook. (Well, maybe.) I still had the feeling of an uneasy truce with my digestive system. A precarious balance.

Eventually the meal was over and we went back to our room. Here everyone lay down on the rug and prepared to sleep. The light was extinguished in minutes. Yes, they did have electricity. A single bulb hung from the ceiling on an insulated wire and was controlled by a pull chain.

I am a very light sleeper and am aware of almost any kind of night noises. All three of them started to snore within minutes and completely out of sequence and in different keys. Man, I could barely hear the dogs bark off in the distance with that entire racket in the room. Out of exhaustion, I dozed off from time to time until one or more of them would stop snoring, then back awake.

About four in the morning, I became aware that I would have to get up and find a place to urinate or never get back to sleep. I remember passing a door way, before we got to the building we are in that might be a "rest" room of sorts. Luckily, I had a flashlight and was able to see well enough to get out of the room and made my way back into the court-yard. After a few false entries, I located the place I had seen earlier. The room was small with nothing in it, except three holes in the floor along one wall. Along side the holes were two "footprints" raised slightly in the cement. They were there as guides to place one's feet on to squat in the right po-sition to defecate. I used one of the holes to relieve myself and made my way back to our "bedroom." I lay down to rest.

No, I do not know what type of toilet facility the ladies used nor where it was located. Although they did have a water source that was plumbed, it was not routed the way our homes were. Here and there was a standpipe with a faucet installed. Buckets were used to transport the water where it was to be used. I don't know if they used water to pour in the holes used as a toilet. Additionally, I never learned if they had a sewer system. I doubt they did.

After about an hour or so, the Arabs started stirring and turned the light on. When they started to dress, I asked Tashkandy what we were doing. He said, "Come we go eat." I thought, "What the hell, it's too early for that, we are not going anywhere." But, I would play the game. After dressing, we filed out and into the "dining room" where all of them had quite a bit to eat. I got half an orange and a piece of bread down. Tash and crew headed back to the room and lay down to go to sleep again. Lights out and I lay there thinking, "What in the hell is going on?" Later I would find out.

Someone had told me this is the month of Ramadan and I should have paid closer attention. Had I done so, some of my confusion might not have occurred.

Ramadan is a big part of the religion of Islam. Ramadan is the ninth month of Islam's lunar year. Devout Muslims are enjoined to maintain a complete fast from sunrise until the boom of the cannon at sundown throughout the entire month. During this period, residents virtually reverse day and night for it is during the night, after the fast is broken, that most of the townspeople will do their daily tasks. During the fasting period, Muslims will not eat, drink, smoke, or have sex. (?)

What had just happened was a part of that observance. All the Arabs got up to eat before daylight to conform to the rules of Ramadan. I had not seen this occur with the crews, because they are usually exempt during their duty hours. Captain Tashkandy (Tash) had remarked to me earlier, this area of Saudi Arabia was very religious and we should be careful not to offend. Meaning me, of course. He too, was being careful it appears. Much later I learned why Tashkandy was so close mouthed, observed all customs to the limit and worried about me more than usual. We were right in the center of Wahabi land. The main tribe in this area of Saudi Arabia was comprised of the descendants of a very strict Muslim fundamentalist named Wahabi. He was recruited by Saud in the early part of the century to back him with his fierce camel riding warriors in conquering and uniting the other tribes to form the kingdom. This area and people remained strict fundamentalist and were treated with care and respect. We were advised they really did not appreciate westerners in their country. We should observe their customs. I would to the letter, if I knew what those customs were. More on this later.

Shortly after daylight, everyone started to stir and we all dressed. Again I tried a dialog with Tashkandy with very little success. I pointed out we needed to contact Jeddah and get some input on what they wanted us to do. Was there a radio in the Village that we could use? He said, "Yes, he would talk to the agent." Within minutes the agent appeared and Tash had a few words with him. Tash and I followed the agent out to the vehicle we had been in the night before and got aboard. The driver started through the streets of the village which were muddy from the rains and pools of standing water were everywhere. Apparently there was no sewer system along with the rather flat terrain and the water had no place to go. There were two dead sheep on our left and opposite those one more. Three more were to the side of the unpaved street in the next hundred yards. I asked Tash what killed the sheep and why they were still there. He said heavy rains had occurred recently and the sheep had been dying for days. Many of those animals were starting to bloat and I knew they had been there a while. "Will they soon come by and move those dead animals?" I asked. He was not sure. "Those dead animals will no doubt be moved soon," I remarked, "as they surely will become a health hazard." He made no comment. Before we arrived at the building housing the radio, we saw many more dead animals scattered about.

We drove down what appeared to be the main street, seeing many people, loaded donkeys, donkey carts, a camel or two, many dogs and some cats. The village was starting to stir.

There was a large number of Arabs milling about in front of the building where we stopped; some were armed with knives and guns. Guards, I supposed. We entered and were led up some stairs to the second floor. The room we went in was occupied by several people and some communication equipment. Initially there was a lot of conversation going on between all of the Arabs in the room. When we walked in, the noise trailed off and all were staring at me as though I was from outer space. Talk about feeling self conscious. All eyes had been on me when we entered the building, but this was worse.

The agent got on the phone to the Emir for a while. Tashkandy said he was asking about the dead animals.

I wrote out what questions I had and Tash added to it, I think. After a lot of discussion, the message was finally sent to Jeddah and/or Riyadh.

My questions were; should we wait for maintenance people to be flown in to repair the aircraft? 2. Would Jeddah give approval for us to fly the aircraft to Riyadh with additional fuel and the gear down and pinned?

When we drove back through the village, we noticed they were busy dragging the sheep carcasses away. That gave me a feeling of relief right along with what I felt when we got out of that communications room.

About two hours later, we were instructed by radio to proceed to the airport, as an aircraft with mechanics aboard were on the way.

The ride in the Land Rover from the village to the airport was just as fast and furious as our night ride had been. At least we could see now in the daylight. There were many places where disaster could strike at any moment and I held on tight. I knew by now the driver had to keep the speed up to keep from bogging down and becoming stuck but that did not help.

When we arrived at the airport, the person in the control room advised us the aircraft from Jeddah had been there but could not land as the clouds were only about 400 feet above ground. The captain on that airplane had advised they would proceed to Riyadh and wait for us to fly there.

We left the gear safety pins in as an added precaution to prevent inadvertent gear collapse when landing at Riyadh. Also added more hydraulic fluid as some had been lost when the leak had occurred. Of course I might have to land with no flaps as we may not have hydraulic power, but that would not be a problem. We had landed at Gassim with no flaps, and that runway was a lot shorter than the one at Riyadh.

The captain on the aircraft that had been overhead and proceeded to Riyadh told me the clouds persisted for about thirty minutes out of Gassim and then it was clear. Knowing that was important. I took off and stayed below the clouds (about 400 feet) proceeding towards Riyadh. Soon we were in the clear and landed with no trouble.

The estimate to fix the aircraft was over two hours, so I decided to go to town and look for a water filter. Our steward, Saife went with me to help with the language. He was not that fluent in English, but he could sure speak Arabic. We had no luck locating a filter.

Saife wanted to go by his home to introduce me to his parents. I thought, why not? They lived in a small mud brick home not far from the center of Riyadh and blended in with all the surrounding homes. His father and brother-in-law met us at the door and invited me in. They were very pleasant and welcomed me profusely in Arabic as Saife relayed their feelings to me.

The room we entered was about 18 feet by 12 feet and rugs covered the entire floor. There were cushions or pillows on the floor all along the walls. There was also a low table about six feet long near the pillows on one side.

Saife's mother and sisters were introduced to me through an open door. They never entered the room nor did I see them. They laughed and giggled a lot. His parents insisted I have some lunch and I could not refuse. Saife brought the food out and placed it on the low table. We sat on the floor and ate in Arab fashion. I ate sparingly and bragged on the bread. The brother-in-law did not stay in the room as we ate because he was fasting in accordance with the precepts of Ramadan. His father did not eat either, but did stay to talk to me via Saife.

When we prepared to leave, his parents asked us to return for dinner. Saife explained we might not be here. His mom gave me two loaves of her bread to take with me. Not knowing the protocol in this instance, I accepted as graciously as possible. Later Saife confirmed I had to take the gift.

The aircraft was fixed when we got back so we took it up for a test flight. All was ok with the fix, but it was getting late and the decision was made to stay the night.

We checked with the Sahara Palace Hotel just outside the entrance to the airport for rooms. They informed us there were no rooms available and none in town.

The crew returned to the aircraft and proceeded to Jeddah with no passengers, arriving much later than we intended. The long two days had worn me down quite a bit and I was some worried about my stomach after the strange meals encountered.

We later learned they had plenty rooms at the Sahara Palace Hotel. The hotel manager was miffed with the airline because they had not been paying their bills. Nothing new about that.

During the night I was stricken with diarrhea and ingested some Entero** Vioforme tablets for relief. This was the accepted remedy for that malady and was readily available at any of the local pharmacies. One could purchase almost any type of medicine without a prescription in Saudi Arabia. Those drugs not available here could be purchased in Beirut, also without a prescription. This malady was to reoccur frequently until I was able to fine tune my intake and change my diet.

Our box lunches were suspect on certain items, which I learned to bypass. I drank no coffee on board; relying on bottled products only and usually carried my own food with me. In the meantime, I lost about fifteen pounds and was starting to appear a bit gaunt.

Later, I would learn some important facts about the people in that area that would no doubt save my life on two occasions. We already were aware the Arabs in that area were stricter in their religion than other areas. I would learn from reading and talking to some of my Saudi pilot friends, those folks were of the Wahabbi Tribe. They were Fundamentalists of that time and a very fierce warrior people who helped Abdul Azziz defeat the other tribes and establish control over the country. They definitely were not friendly to westerners and must be treated with caution and respect.

I was cautioned to never touch a female passenger in any way even to help her. Also, do not accept an ill female passenger unaccompanied by a male member of her family. My memory would save me later in a split second decision on board an aircraft.

MORE ON GASSIM

We landed at Gassim on another routine flight and, as usual, after engine shutdown, I stepped out of the cockpit to observe deplaning of passengers. Selectively, I spoke to some and merely observed the others. A female passenger, covered completely in her all black clothing, approached the stairs and tripped. As she started to fall, I instinctively reached to catch her. At that instant I flashed back to Captain Akkram's warning, "Do not touch a female Arab." She fell all the way down and was spared serious injury by falling into the male passenger at the bottom. Another close one for me.

Another time at Gassim, we experienced a delay loading passengers and I asked my Saudi co-pilot to check the reason. He left the cockpit and went to talk to the agent. Shortly he was back and explained they had a pregnant Arab lady who was very ill. She was lying on blankets under the wing. She was supposed to be transported to Riyadh Hospital on our aircraft; however, there was a big argument going on about who was going to accompany her. Finally the agent came aboard and explained the situation in Arabic to my co-pilot. The gist of his message was starting to form in my mind as I could follow the intent, if not the words. Again my thanks to Captain Akkram! When asked, the co-pilot confirmed that a male member of the family must accompany an ill Arab woman to accept responsibility for her life. After instructing him to advise the agent we would wait for her male escort, if any, as long as necessary, he deplaned. On my instructions, the co-pilot followed him and would inform me when their decision was made. About ten minutes later, he was back and said all clear, we are cleared to go. Before starting engines, I asked him what happened about the lady. He informed me she had died and all had departed along with the body. NOTE: Had she died on board without a male member of her family aboard, I would have been liable for her death. The consequences would be grim.

February 1, 1965, I was to depart on Trip 102, which would be Jeddah to Wedj to Tabuk to Badana to Guriat to Turaif and spend the night. Captain Leroy Johnson would be administering a route check for me.

No problems were encountered en route, and I was kept busy looking for check points on the ground and marking them on my maps.

Guriat has an old Turkish fort on a small hill overlooking the town and airport. The weather was good and the fort was clearly visible. Will make an excellent checkpoint for my map. When we landed at Guriat on their 3500 foot gravel or sand packed runway, I noticed what appeared to be a wrecked airplane off to one side. Leroy explained that was a British Bristol twin engine cargo/passenger aircraft. Saudi Airlines had purchased eight of them a year ago, and one by one they had been wrecked at several other airports.

The Bristol was a two engine, boxcar shaped airplane with twin booms and tail surfaces similar to the United States C-82 or C-119 aircraft. The landing gear was fixed and could not be raised for flight. The remaining wrecks would later be seen as I visited other airports. The wind was blowing just enough to move some of the control surfaces on that wreck and the noise was very strange. The surfaces screeched and groaned as they blew back and forth making one wonder if the deceased crew members were protesting their fate or trying to communicate—-Enough of that!

Ten minutes later, we were on our way to Turaif. Turaif was built by the oil company, ARAMCO, to house the people who would care for and protect the Tapline (oil pipeline).

Turaif reminds me of a small air base that is self supporting. The airport has two four-thousand foot runways, both gravel. There is also a radio beacon to aid in locating the field. They have housing for the workers, a commissary, a rather large building that contains a movie, dining room, recreation room with pool tables, ping pong tables, a shuffle board and a snack bar.

The commissary has a pretty good stock of food including the forbidden pork products. I just might be tempted one day to purchase some and take it back to Jeddah. Surely I have already mentioned pork is forbidden in Saudi Arabia and we soon learned to miss it.

We stayed the night and found our accommodations to be quite nice. Cost me 28 riyals (about five dollars) and another three dollars for dinner and breakfast. Had a very pleasant trip back to Jeddah via Guriat, Badana, Tabuk and Wedj.

Ramadan was over on our return and the three days of festivities had begun. All was gaiety, food and presents for all. Similar in many ways to our own Christmas in that respect.

Before going to bed that evening, I wrote to Marti and David and a letter to my mom as well. I don't have any news of the possibility of quarters or any information on when they might join me.

Woke up with another mild case of diarrhea, meaning I could make it to the toilet with very little anxiety and hardly any panic.

TWA does have a personnel office here in one of the apartment buildings, and I check with them often. The manager remains unknown to me. So far I have not been impressed with his capabilities. He seems to answer your questions at the time, but one comes away with the feeling there was no substance to his comments.

Fortunately, the girls that work in the office know what they are doing and can give you straight answers. They are all wives of employees of the airline. I am particularly impressed with Polly Vincent. Efficiency with a big smile and a pleasant comment anytime. She is the wife of Joe Vincent, a flight engineer on the DC-6's and Boeings. We all learned to see Polly for the straight stuff on almost any issue. Polly and Joe were very nice people and later we would become close friends and neighbors.

Unfortunately, the person in charge of keeping records on the availability and assignment of housing was a devout practitioner of "doublespeak" or obfuscation. Old "foggy bottoms" himself. The answers he gave us on any given day were marginally related to the truth. Even so, I never gave up. He was destined to see me in his office any day I was not on a trip.

February 4th, 1965, we departed on trip #114. The schedule called for Jeddah-Wedj-Al Jouf-Badana-Turaif-Guriat-Amman. (Jordan) Another "route check" for me and Bob Wells. Captain Leroy Johnson was again the instructor or "check pilot."

Later, I would make many trips in and through Amman. We almost always stayed in the Philadelphia Hotel, just across the street from the old Roman ruins of a theatre. Most of the steps were reasonably intact with pieces of statues here and there. The city was quite picturesque, with the hills on either side festooned with quaint houses, apartments and greenery with colorful flowers. We very much enjoyed walking from the hotel to the souk, a distance of about two miles, and then in the sometimes narrow winding streets of the stalls, stores and eating places. Sometimes we would stop in one of the restaurants or bars and imbibe a cold one. There was very good beers available, even though this was a Muslim country.

The leg from Wedj to Al Jouf is worth mentioning for its surprising beauty in one area. About twenty minutes out of Wedj we pass over an area that is very much like our own Painted Desert north of Flagstaff in the United States. When the sun is at the right angle the colors of the cliffs are many and bright. This area was in sight for about twelve minutes and then back to the bland desert, looking for camel trails or oasis. From Badana to Turaif, we ran into a band of solid heavy rain and were buffeted about for a long five minutes before bursting into bright sunlight. Turaif was fine with no problems. So was Guriat. Thirty minutes from Amman, we could see the clouds approaching and obvious rain ahead. The field elevation at Amman is 2,550 feet and there are surrounding hills above 3.500 feet.

Leroy told me the radio beacon which would normally be used for an approach was very unreliable under these conditions and we would be more likely to find the airport by staying under the cloud deck. Leroy knew the terrain and provided the headings to fly. We descended to 3,700 feet and stayed a little north in an attempt to find the valley entrance

PORT SUDAN TERMINAL, 1966   Captain Porter, Pilot

Arriving Hajii's (Pilgrims), Jedda, SA 1966

towards the airport. We got past the hills to the left and turned towards the field on a heading of 240 degrees (actual runway heading) and flew down the valley through the rain. We spotted the runway, and were cleared to land straight ahead. I made the landing in about a twenty degree cross-wind of thirty five knots gusting to forty five. Not bad. At least we walked away from it. The weather on the ground was wet, windy and seemed quite cold. The passengers and crew were not dressed for those conditions.

The Saudi agent provided us with transportation to the Philadelphia Hotel where we would spend the night. The hotel is across the street from the ruins of a Roman Amphitheater built in the second or third century A. D. The next morning I would go there to investigate the Roman ruins previously mentioned and take some pictures.

My room at the hotel cost me 1750 Fils (about $5) including breakfast. Dinner next door at a night club was 850 Fils.

The hotel had picture postcards in the lobby, and I sent some to my folks and Martha. Also bought two souvenir spoons for Mom Kilcrease (my mother-in-law). She liked to collect them.

Departure time at the airport the next morning found us waiting for the weather to improve enough for takeoff. The temperature was about 38 degrees F and the wind was still gusting. Low ceilings were moving by about every thirty minutes. After about an hour delay there was an opening and we were cleared to depart. After takeoff we leveled about six hundred feet, reversed course and flew back out the valley to the northeast, past the beacon and on course for Guriat. Soon we were in the clear.

The arrival and departure procedure was not exactly my idea of a proper instrument approach and would not have been acceptable in the states for an operating airline. Leroy was a good pilot and that was simply the way he and others had been doing things for years. Only Dhahran, Riyadh, and Jeddah had a published instrument approach along with the radio facility to support it. Some of the other small airports we transited had a radio beacon that could be used for an approach under weather conditions, BUT were neither always operational nor reliable. We drew up our own instrument approach and used it as an aid to find an airport under adverse conditions. One example of non-operational radio aid would have to be Wedj. About the time of my arrival in the country, a radio beacon was installed at Wedj. The beacon was battery operated and checked out very good. Two weeks later the beacon was off the air. Maintenance people were sent to check it out. Investigation revealed the local Sheikh, or the airline agent had found what he judged to be a better use for the battery. Future batteries were destined for a similar fate.

Obviously this young and growing airline had many problems to overcome. Even so, the airline had an excellent safety record and would continue to have for many years. One has to attribute this to the skill and resourcefulness of those early pilots. Many were experienced "bush pilots," instructor pilots, and those with military backgrounds and all had many flying hours. Additionally, the aircraft were very well maintained by a dedicated and skilled cadre of mechanics sent over by TWA. In addition to doing the actual work, they were also trying to train some of the local people how to maintain the fleet. This would prove to be a very difficult task.

Bob Wells would make the landing at Guriat. The surface wind was about twenty degrees off the runway heading and gusting to 38 knots. He made a very good landing on their 3,500 foot gravel runway. Not exactly an easy thing to do.

The return trip was without incident and I got another good look at the "Painted desert" between Al Jouf and Wedj. The colors were not as spectacular as the sun was too high.

Our one hour delay out of Amman caused us to be late getting into Jeddah and it had been dark an hour before our arrival.

The posted schedule called for me to depart early the next morning on another trip, but due to our late return had to be changed. OK by me, I was tired.

Bob Wells came by about 11 a.m. Saturday morning driving Bill Clarke's Volkswagen and asked me to go with him to see about a car. He headed for the Volkswagen dealership and we learned they had no new cars, they were still in Customs. Same story as last week. The dealer does not take trade-ins but does sell customers cars on a contingent basis. Bob was going to try for one of those.

Bob dropped me off at the entrance to the souk where I would get a haircut. This would be my second since arrival. The barbers were Palestinians, Egyptians or Lebanese and seemed trained, except for their hygiene. I was getting a little tense about this and decided to look into the possibility of cutting my own hair. Later I did just that.

After the haircut, I went through the drug souk and bought some more Entero Vioforme for my loose "stool."

One might wonder how we were getting by without speaking Arabic. Most, perhaps all the merchants spoke English or there was an employee or relative who did. All the barbers spoke English. Even so, we were already learning some words and or sentences to help in the bargaining process. Numbers I had already learned; however, dialect sometimes made understanding somewhat difficult. Everyone seemed to want to help and were very patient.

Monday the 8th of February, Jim Money and I would go with Leroy Johnson to Riyadh via Medina, Hail and Quasim. After departing Medina, I took two pictures of some strange markings on the ground from about nine thousand feet. The markings were not all alike and had to be quite large to be seen so clearly from our altitude. Leroy was not clear on what they were and neither was our Arab Steward or the radio operator. I will look into that later. Note: Much later I did learn those markings were from antiquity and were made by laying rocks in a chosen pattern to mark burial places. Why they were so large and laid out on the ground so they could only be viewed from the air was never explained.

While on the ground at Hail, refueling, etc, I took two pictures of a local Turkish Fort and one of the "palaces."

We would stay the night in Riyadh at the Sahara Desert Hotel. After checking in, we took a taxi to the MAAG house and were welcomed to use their facility by Lt. Colonel Lelbach, the Air Force chief. We joined them for a dinner of pork chops and appropriate trimmings, followed with cherry pie and ice cream. Best meal I had since arrival in Saudi Arabia! After dinner and a few rounds of table tennis, we walked about two miles back to the hotel.

Sleep did not come easily, but apparently I did doze off, as I awakened to a chorus of the nearby feral dog packs. They gradually slowed to an uneasy ending, just in time for the roosters to begin trying to out crow each other. Soon the darkness was fading to gray, and now the Muezzins began their call to prayer from the minarets of the many mosques in the city. A far off one began the call joined by others within seconds or minutes. Each voice was unique and some were really unusual and very musical. Rather an eerie, exotic and not unpleasant awakening call. Just wish I had achieved some rest before the "wake up."

This was the first of many wake-up prayer calls I would experience before returning to the United States. I would hear it in Amman, Bahrain, Beirut, Damascus, Baghdad, Cairo, Shiraz, Tehran, Tripoli, Karachi, Isfahan, Kabul and many other places.

The return flight through Quassim was routine and then on to Hail which had visibility of 2 to 3 miles in suspended dust. The dust had risen to about 10,000 feet and was with us all the way to Medina. Jim Money made the landing here. We both took note of two hills which stuck up about 500 feet on the approach end of runway 36. They were just far enough apart one could stay between them and be clear. They could be a little tricky at night and in low visibility. There was also a raised lava bank to cross before reaching the end of the runway. About a half mile west of the field was a prominent peak to keep in mind as well. All the terrain surrounding Medina was rough and not at all suitable for an emergency landing. We continued to Jeddah.

I had two letters from Marti waiting for me on our return. One was postmarked January 29, the other, February 1. Not bad for regular Air Mail. I wrote to her after dinner, relating some of our latest adventures. Naturally, I left some out as there was no need to make the situation appear too primitive or dangerous. My writing skills were too weak to relate some of the incidents without leaving too much room for interpretation or speculation.

A check with operations revealed there had been changes made in the short time we had been gone. First, I would report to Convair ground school tomorrow, second we learned MacDougall had lost his job as DC-3 Supervisor and Goodman, Johnson and Lorenz would assume duties as co-supervisors.

Convair 340 ground school began this morning (Feb 10, 1965) with fifteen young Saudi Captains from the DC-3s and three Americans including myself. We found the class to be rather slow paced and had to shift gears to keep any interest. The language barrier for the Saudis created the need for slow going. They had all read the technical manual for the Convair and had many questions as the class progressed. The slow pace was not due to lack of talent or brains on the part of those young men. They were excellent, very diligent students. They could and did quote word for word any of the instructions in the manual, but had much trouble with interpreting what was written. The Americans understood because each had a long history of exposure to technical material and the experience to interpret the written word. We knew one did not always do exactly as the manual decreed, but applied that guidance to the set of circumstances we found ourselves in. Experience would eventually bridge that considerable gap.

We understood the problems they were facing and the reasons back of them. American youth grew up in the mechanical world of bicycles, motorbikes, cars, and later, airplanes. These young men knew nothing of those things. They grew up in a desert environment with goats and camels or at best in small primitive villages. The brightest and luckiest of the young people were sent abroad to learn English and enter into education to prepare them for the career the government had chosen. Their government had very limited young people resources and had to allocate them to all the various areas of need.

The class was very good and was of great benefit to the Americans to get a feel for the status of the young Saudis. We were better equipped to cope with their needs when we exposed them to operational flying. We knew we could not take anything for granted and would have to be prepared to offer explanations for many things done during the course of any flight.

After class that first day, I went with Bob Wells to pick his car up from the dealership who kept the car to have it registered for him. He could drive the car, but the registering did not quite "take." Something had gone wrong. Maybe he could come back tomorrow and all would be OK.

When we started back towards the hotel, it was after sundown and rather dark. Shortly after turning north off Mecca road onto Airport Road, we saw a bicycle lying in the street and Bob had to swerve to miss it. Objects were strewn around and there appeared to be broken glass on the pavement near the bike. Looked as though someone had been hit by a car and knocked off his bicycle. There was no car around and no person or body, so we continued on. We were already aware it was not prudent to be involved in any way with an incident or accident. Had we been observed at the scene or reported it, we would have been arrested and transported to a jail. An investigation would then ensue and we could be held until they were satisfied with the results. Not a good plan.

Convair ground school continued on a daily basis and so would my daily routine. Most of the time I walked to school and back, not that I really had to. I could take a taxi or hitch a ride with one of the other guys. I could use the exercise and observe Saudis going about their daily routines as well.

After arriving back at the hotel, fixing me a bite to eat in the room or preparing to go to someone's home for dinner was usually first on the agenda. Many times one or two of us would proceed to the souk after a bite to eat just to wander through the streets filled with the local populace, the aromas and the constant plethora of sounds. Really very interesting! We also practiced our "skills" of "bargaining" with rather poor results. These guys were way ahead! We found out early on that you could end up with a price, not to your liking or unsure if you really had a bargain and leave. Then come back the next day thinking you could start off with that same price and attempt to bring it down. Not so, it was an altogether new ballgame. The starting price might be even higher than it was yesterday. Anyway, it was fun.

Convair ground school continued and so did our daily routine of investigating the city of Jeddah and all it had to offer. Each day was a new adventure and some were embarrassing as well as possibly very troublesome. One day I ventured to town alone carrying my camera very discreetly so as not to bring attention to it. Like I previously mentioned, picture taking of the local populace and or locations that might not reflect well on the Saudis was forbidden. Advice from my English speaking Arab friends was to be very discreet when taking pictures. Get permission to take a picture if possible and do not let the Matawa (Religious Police) observe you in the act. So far this advice had worked very well. Not this time.

I was walking down Abdul Assiz Street nearly across from the entry to the drug souk and observed two Yemen "street sweepers" in their native dress busy working on a dusty roadway. The "brooms" they were using were unlike any I had seen or perhaps only in pictures of many years ago. They appeared to be "handmade" and perhaps they were. They had a short handle, maybe eighteen inches and the "broom part" was perhaps two feet long. Later, I saw loads of brooms just like them in the Old Souk. Thinking this might be a pretty good shot, I looked around carefully and not seeing anyone observing, I clicked off a couple of frames.

No sooner than done, I heard a shout from across the street and saw a Saudi running towards me shouting in mixed Arabic and English. I did not understand the words being shouted, but did understand the threat. Moving quickly, I retreated about a hundred yards and entered the Kodak shop. A few minutes before all this started, I had been in that shop and knew the proprietor spoke and understood English. The irate Saudi citizen skidded in right behind me and was still shouting in an angry manner. The proprietor took over and sorted the whole thing out. He explained that the angry person was thinking I was taking pictures of those Yemen and would go home and tell people those were Saudi workers, thereby demeaning his fellow citizens. "Not at all, I explained, quite the opposite." The pictures were intended to illustrate how clean the Saudis tried to keep their city streets by having Yemen laborers sweep daily. Somehow this seemed to soothe the very angry young man and he calmed down enough to apologize for mistaking my intentions, but did admonish me not to take any demeaning pictures while in his country. I assured him I would be very circumspect and would only take pictures that portrayed his country in a respectful manner. When the formerly irate person left the shop, the proprietor and I exchanged grins and farewells. Whew!

I carried my camera openly, but was very careful to either wait for a hopefully unobserved candid shot, or ask permission to take their picture. I learned the phrase for that request in Arabic and was successful most of the time. Once when we were in the souk, I had taken several shots with and without permission. On one of the busy streets, I noticed an old gentleman whom I thought would make a good photo and he looked amenable. After asking for and receiving his permission, I set up for the photo and looked through the view finder to compose the shot. Just before I clicked off the shutter, his hand flew up and in it was a big rock. I was startled as the shutter clicked and I ducked.

Everybody in the picture and those in proximity were getting a big laugh out of the incident.

Twentieth of February brought me some good news. There were some changes at the MAAG house and they were definitely to my advantage. Colonel Keefe and Major McKaig were both transferred to Dhahran. Lt. Colonel Harms was the new commander and would prove to be more amenable. Colonel Harms authorized me use of their small Post Exchange facility and approved the use of the APO (Army Postal Service). I bought some U.S. stamps and would get a letter in the mail quickly to advise Marti to now mail everything to me via the APO.

We found out soon enough their communications system left a lot to be desired. Very few people in Jeddah had phones in their apartment or homes. Only the essential personnel had phone service, and that did not include pilots or most others. However if one wanted to pay the tariff, they could have a phone installed. But who to call? No one else had a phone, you might know. If one had a need to call outside the country, there was a central phone service facility for accommodation. One could place a call, and then wait patiently for a connection. This could take quite some time, even days. See picture for a possible reason the system was faulty.

NEW CAR

Sunday the 28th of February, I made ready to go to the Volkswagen dealership to start a dialog concerning an automobile. After entering a taxi I proceed to King Abdul Aziz Street and on to the square where we follow Harbor Road for a few blocks to the Ghazi I. Shaker Bros. Volkswagen dealer. When I enter, I was faced with speaking to an Arab who does not speak English. After some attempted conversation with no understanding, I am introduced to one who speaks passable English, whom I ask if I may see Sheik Shaker. Not knowing if he is a Sheik, I opted to err on the plus side, not wanting to offend and lose a point or two right off. The young Saudi did not correct me and I was led to Ghazi Shaker's presence where upon he greeted me with quiet manners and considerable charm. He spoke good

English and we passed the time of day and of course I was offered "shei" (a warm, very sweet tea) in a small cup. This tradition occurs even in some very small shops and it would be very rude to decline. Just go ahead and take your chances. One hopes the tea water was boiled but fear the worst.

I explained to him I was a pilot with the airline and had recently arrived in his country and was trying to become acquainted with the local people. I did not want to offend and felt if I could get to know some of the customs my stay here would be more enjoyable. This seemed a little thin to me, but it didn't seem to bother him. Currently I was using taxis for transport, but would soon consider buying a car. More shei was poured and he seemed in no hurry to discuss cars or to get rid of me. After more talk, I remarked I must really leave. Actually I had to go after all that sweet tea! He escorted me to the door and invited me back tomorrow. I readily accepted as Akram had predicted that might happen.

My plan is to go see Sheik (Mr.) Shaker the next day right after Convair class is completed for the day. Another taxi ride from my hotel down through town, and on to the Volkswagen dealership. This time, I am pretty well familiar with the drill and have little trouble being ushered into the presence of Mr. Shaker. We exchanged pleasantries and accepted the inevitable cup of shei. Small talk ensued long enough to have to endure two more cups of shei. I could find no** nearby place to pour the contents of my cup with any degree of secrecy. After what seemed a very long time, Mr. Shaker asked me if I had any trouble finding a place to park upon arrival. "Well no, I replied, I had not yet had a chance to purchase my own automobile." "Would you consider a Volkswagen?" he countered. The remainder of the "negotiation" centered on when, how and what color would I like. The price was not negotiable (I had previously been advised on this) and would amount to 8,690 riyals (about $2,095) and how would I like to pay? Personal check? That would be fine!

Mr. (Sheik?) Shaker suggested I might come back the following day if I chose and pick up the automobile. In the meantime, he would send one of his employees with me to go on the lot and pick out the car I wanted. The lot was not on the premises and the employee drove me through several blocks of "Old Town," flying through blind cross streets with a blast of the horn and taking corners with a swirl of dust, with me hanging on best I could. He eventually pulled over in front of a gate into a walled area. We got out and entered the walled in lot which I could now see was almost filled with many Volkswagens. My first act was to relieve my about to burst bladder in the observed Arab way. This was a must after all the shei we drank and that wild ride. I was thankful I had not done the act in the car. My first choice was a white car, but there were none. My limited choice was a blue one with a "moon roof." I never saw a white Volkswagen in Saudi Arabia. Why were there none? Beats me.

The ride back to the dealership was just as terrifying as the first trip and my knuckles were white and almost locked on the door handle. I would return the following day to pick the car up.

The car was ready for me upon my return about 1700, March 2, 1965. Mr. Shaker was ready for me with a glass of shei and a ready smile with the traditional Saudi greeting. My check covered registration, city sticker and plates. The bad news was, I cannot register the car and get plates until after I receive my permanent resident visa. That will be about a month from now. Anyway, I accepted the vehicle and drove back to the hotel. No more taxis for a while! Sigh and a deep breath along with, "Thank you God (Allah)!"

March 4th brought me another small adventure. Friends advised I would need a city sticker for the car, so I started out to get one. Driving through town and on to Harbor Road was a bit sticky through all the car honking, dashing traffic but I managed to make it to where the road forks to go out to the pier. There an Arab was seated on a table at the side of the road and two police were stopping traffic to check for stickers. When it was my turn, I handed the policeman fifty riyals and pointed towards the windshield. He started to get me a receipt and then pointed to where my plates should have been and wanted the plate number. I tried to explain in a halting manner about, new car, have to wait, all that to no avail. This started a real hubbub, as good intentioned Arabs started a heated dialog with the policeman. He held his ground, but the crowd continued to grow and after about twenty minutes of that, he gave up and with a flourish, finished the receipt and gave me a sticker. This brought cheers from the haranguers with much laughing and good natured hand slaps on the car, bid me on my way. The whole incident was, I believe, mutually rewarding for all the participants with the possible exception of the defeated policeman.

VIVIAN'S GIFT

My well intentioned sister, Vivian, provided me with another adventure I could have done without. She learned through letters I was preparing some of my meals in my room. She took action to help out without my knowledge and sent a package through regular mail for me. One day I received a notice that Customs was holding a package for me. Omar, the desk clerk told me where to go for the package and what to do. "Go to the Customs shed on the pier," he said, "and get a Saudi to negotiate for you." That wasn't too difficult and all went rather well once I was able to locate the "shed." Almost immediately, help was offered by an Arab who spoke some English. I presented my notice about the package and he took over. First to a desk where an Arab was being besieged by many others, all talking at once. My "helper" asked me for "Baksheesh," and slipped it into an open drawer of the desk. The "official" now stamped the notice, initialed it and the helper picked it up and motioned me to follow him. Now, I thought, we will go get the package. Not so fast! We entered another room filled with chattering Arabs and several desks with attending "officials." Almost the repeat of what occurred previously. It was a hot day and the building was not air conditioned. That and the anxiety and frustration helped to increase the uncomfortable feelings I was experiencing. Now my guide motions me towards another room. About to give up, I followed anyway. This did look a little more promising. This time there was only one desk, and the Arab behind it looked more official, although there were a lot of "hangers on" lounging about drinking shei and chatting. His desk drawer was open part way also. This time though, my guide held up five fingers for the "baksheesh." Now I rebelled! "La la" (No no), I remarked, "not until I see (shuf) the package!" That caused quite a stir! A good bit of chatter followed and concluded with the official ordering the package brought in. The package had suffered damage in transit and I could make out what appeared to be a hot plate sticking out. Well, I certainly did not need that and was not about to invest any more "Baksheesh" in this debacle. My response was to inform them they could keep the package and donate it to a good cause, then turned and strode out. Two Arabs, including my "helper" followed me, saying I could not leave without the package. I must take it! That did not work for me and I continued on back to the hotel. My hot plate was still in my room where I had left it. I had purchased one in the souk.

Convair School was completed on the tenth of March and I would resume flying soon. Actually I found out the next day I would take a trip to Riyadh and back on Saturday. Just routine, except possibly for the approach and landing. We were advised approaching Riyadh the wind had picked up and dust was starting to blow and to be advised there would be a wind shift on frontal passage. We could look down and observe the desert on the move and knew the field might soon be obscured completely. We added a little speed and started an early descent in an attempt to beat the desert. Soon it became apparent, we were losing the "race," so I asked for and received clearance for a straight in approach and landing on runway one nine. Frontal passage and we arrived at almost the same instant and that old DC-3 touched the runway left wing down with the wind switching from left front to left rear simultaneously. Things were a bit "sticky" for a few seconds until I was able to slow to a walk. The blowing sand was so dense by this time it was difficult to see while attempting to taxi in to the terminal and the wind blowing against that big rudder did not help either. We stayed the night and the desert continued to blow until the next morning.

The annual Hadj (Pilgrimage) of the devout Muslims from all over the Arab world to Mecca and Medina was now in full swing. On twenty March I flew a shuttle from Jeddah to Medina transporting Hajjis to and from their second most holy city. I made two trips lasting all day.

My next trip was rather routine, but does deserve a comment or two because of the area which may provide an insight to the remoteness of some of the places we fly in and out of. The route was from Jeddah to Medina to Hail to Qassim to Zilfi to Riyadh. Zilfi was a small mud brick walled village (or oasis) located about one hundred fifty miles north of Riyadh. The route to Zilfi from Qassim was mostly over rolling sand dunes with very few identifying features for the inexperienced eye. However, as I surveyed that vast desert, my attention was suddenly riveted on a very green small area nestled amongst the dunes. Looking closer, I could make out a small grove of palm trees and a few mud brick buildings. I was looking at my very first bona fide, right out of the movies, oasis! What wonders a little sub surface water can provide. The thought comes to mind, "In the middle of nowhere." This is the type of terrain usually portrayed as "desert."

Later approaching Zilfi, we were searching the area for the "airport." The village stood out pretty good even though the buildings were all constructed with "mud" bricks, not to different in color from the surrounding area. The date palm groves in and around the village really were the first things we saw. The bright orange wind sock was the tip off for location of the airport. The runway was simply compacted sand, outlined to be identified as a landing strip. The "terminal" was a canvas tent. Near the runway, about midway of its length, was a "wind sock" which shows pilots the direction of the wind and can give an idea of strength as well. Very interesting. Zilfi's reason for being here was also due to subsurface water and should be classified as an oasis, although it was not located in the sand dune area. There were many other small villages scattered about the vast areas of desert in Saudi Arabia, including hundreds, perhaps thousands of "watering holes" used by the Bedouin in their treks across the country. All of these villages and watering holes were dependent on sub-surface water.

Another of the villages that were transited occasionally was Majma which was located about midway from Zilfi to Riyadh. It was about the same size village as Zilfi and was located on one of the numerous dry wadis (dry riverbeds) crisscrossing the country side. During the winter, numerous heavy rains replenished the underground water reservoirs.

During the month of March, 1965, I flew well over one hundred hours. Hours flown in excess of seventy five were paid as overtime and most welcome. During our entire stay in Saudi Arabia, we used overtime pay to cover living expenses. I volunteered for any and all flights that came up, as I had no need for the time off and I enjoyed the flying anyway. We simply had to stay within the FAA guidelines for maximum flight time in a given month and for three month periods.

FIRST HAJJ

The first part of April, 1965 brought us to the beginning of the annual influx of Hajjis for their pilgrimage to the holy cities of Medina and Mecca. April 3 started a series of very long duty days for me. We took an empty plane from Jeddah to Port Sudan which is across the Red Sea, returning full three times, logging nine hours and thirty minutes of flying time. Actual duty time was over thirteen hours. This schedule was repeated on the fifth and seventh of April. Once the arrivals of the Hajjis began, the airport would be busy day and night bringing them in. Our fleet would be busy and so would the fleets of all the surrounding Arab countries. Planes from Iraq, Lebanon, India, Pakistan, Iran, Libya, Nigeria, Ethiopia, Syria and many others would be landing and taking off every few minutes. Many other thousands would travel by bus, trucks, private automobiles, camel train, etc. All available parking areas around the airport and city would be full and the passengers in those vehicles would be "camping" out. They would sleep in and around their conveyances, prepare food, etc.

The area immediately adjacent to the airport terminal was turned into one immense bazaar. Food venders brought in carts of food, others erected tents with all kinds of merchandise, there was even a bank facility opened up right on the side walk. Across from the terminal, there was a wide tiled area used for foot traffic that was covered with rugs and other items for sale.

The Hajji's brought items with them to sell in the hopes of covering the expense of their trip. Bartering was rampant daily up into the late evening hours. The whole thing was very entertaining for all the westerners. We went there often just to see all the different types of Muslims arrive in their sometimes very colorful costumes. Yes, we entered into the bartering as well. Some gorgeous Persian rugs could be bought at bargain prices if you were capable, knowledgeable and quick. Monkey skins? Lots of them! Live monkey? Some of those too. Fancy an exotic parrot? There were many brought in and a good many of them could speak. Not English though. There were a large number of snake skins, some as long as twenty five feet. Additionally there were leopard skins brought to Jeddah from the "Painted Desert" mountain area north and east of Wedj. The Arabs say there are many leopards in that area.

There was a lot more they brought with them and some of it was not good. Cholera was always a threat and when there was a load of Hajjis' arriving from a Cholera area; get ready for another shot. Head lice and other body dwelling varmints were also imported. The Saudi approach to that was to fog all in the vicinity with DDT dust. We stayed very aware of the location of the roving foggers and gave them plenty of distance. My shot record logged a large number of cholera shots even though I made every effort to avoid possible contact. I had so many cholera shots; I think my blood could have been used for shots.

When the ceremonies in Mecca were completed and the visits to Medina wound down, the exodus would begin. The airport would be busy night and day until all were transported back to their homelands. Our fleet would also be running full time along with the regularly scheduled flights to help get the Pilgrims home.

Marti and David did not get to see this first Hajj but did the second one the following year.

During our visits, we never observed any resentment towards us or any other westerners. We were careful about taking pictures and tried to stay very much in the background. I believe that indicates the character of those Muslims who were making this very important pilgrimage to their most holy places. Altogether a very interesting and exciting time. We can not imagine what it must have meant to those Muslims participating. I saw many grinning constantly just for the pure joy of being there.

CAR REGISTRATION

My resident visa was approved, and I could now pursue a title and license for my car. There was a young Saudi, named Achmed attached to Base Operations that would help we Americans through some of the difficulties associated with mundane tasks of licenses, etc. He generated the necessary paperwork for me prior to actually applying. All forms in Arabic, of course. Achmed accompanied me to the vehicle registration office located just off Airport Road in a very large old style building. There were wide concrete steps leading up to the entry and the inside was quite spacious. The first stop was very near the entrance and was similar to other official offices I had seen. One desk occupied by a harried Saudi deep in ignoring several other Saudis all talking at once waving paperwork and trying to get his attention. My helper joined the fray. After a few minutes of doing the same as the others, he sidled around where he could drop a couple of riyals into the partly open top desk drawer. About a minute later, the official grabbed his (my) paperwork, stamped it vigorously, initialed it and passed it back. Achmed motioned me to follow him and we went down a hall and through a doorway into another hubbub around a desk attended by another "official." Same drill as before and about the same amount of time. Next we headed down another longer hallway and entered a quite large room, possibly fifty feet by sixty. Near the only windows in the room was a Saudi Officer in uniform of some kind seated behind a very large wooden desk. To his left front about fifteen feet away were a bench and some folding chairs. I was directed to one of those chairs and sat along with others already there. Along the wall to the officer's back was many Saudis squatting, Arab fashion, chatting while drinking shei and /or "Gahwa" (Arabic coffee). The floor was all marble and looked pretty good except for one area about three feet in diameter close to the front of the desk. That area was somewhat concave with chips of marble in it and around the edges. I was wondering what on earth caused that. Within seconds I found out. A policeman in an ill fitting wrinkled winter uniform entered the room and marched across that marble floor, his hobnail boots ringing out with each step. He halted, British like, in front of the desk and slammed his right boot in place, raising his left boot and slammed it back down with force enough to cause the bits of marble floor to fly as his right arm whipped up in a vibrating salute. (That sure explained the broken marble in front of that desk.) I almost laughed out loud, but was able to contain myself for a while. Note: The winter uniform the policeman was wearing must have been very uncomfortable. The temperature in that room had to be over a hundred.

After the soldier was dismissed, the officer made a motion and Achmed went forward and slipped some riyals into the partly opened drawer, simultaneously laying the documents on the desk. The papers were quickly initialed and we were on our way. Getting a driver license was a very similar process, but not as easy. It took several tries. While waiting for a Saudi license, I purchased an International Driver's license in Beirut. It was written in Arabic with my photo in it, and there was a good chance it would be accepted if necessary, I was told.

One had to purchase their own license plates in the souk and they were rather puny and not very well constructed. Later when we visited Beirut, I had a set made out of cast aluminum, with raised numbers, painted and complete with the Saudi crest of crossed swords and palm trees. We still have those plates.

My daily routine continued, with trips to the souk, flying as much as possible, visiting with new friends and generally investigating my new home. By now, I had flown trips to almost all the villages and towns supported by the airline. Learning the ground check points on the routes was becoming easier and my "comfort" zone was growing. That is, except for my diet. My weight had lowered from about one hundred ninety pounds to a svelte one hundred seventy. Not a healthy sign as the weight loss was due to diarrhea and poor eating habits. The onboard lunches were suspect, so I had stopped eating them some time ago, along with any opened beverage such as coffee. I carried my own lunch and bottled water.

Another trip with a little excitement occurred on May 14th. We departed Amman for the Tapline stations starting with Turaif, Badanah, (did not land Badanah due sand storm) on to Rafha then a landing at Quysumah, where I found out after touchdown we had lost our brakes on the left side. Just a bit sticky for a few minutes, but got the aircraft under control. After shutdown, we inspected the brakes and found a leaky fitting on the hydraulic line. After removing the fitting, it was discovered that it had been cross threaded and could not be used. There were no parts available, so I asked one of the Tapline maintenance guys if he could machine a part to fit. He did that and threaded it back together. Pressure held and we continued on to Dhahran, where I landed again with no brakes. We waited there two days for a wheel and brake assembly to be flown in from Jeddah.

Nearing the middle of May, there was still no available housing in sight for my family and I was continuing dialog with the housing and personnel offices. I spoke mostly with Polly Vincent in the personnel office, as she was the most knowledgeable and reliable person there. Housing had pretty much a "closed door" policy and was considered by most as not very helpful. Political might better describe their policy.

MARTI AND DAVID ARE COMING

Continued dialog elicited a proposal to provide my family with adequate space in the hotel where I was staying to allow Marti and David to proceed to Jeddah right after school was out for him. Polly took care of all the necessary paperwork, and Marti was duly notified by TWA to proceed with preparations for travel.

Marti had already planned for the items to be shipped to allow us to set up an apartment for living. On her list were a freezer, washing machine, portable dishwasher, iron, toaster, and other "must haves" for our style of living. Oh yes, add a set of golf clubs to that list as they were not available in Jeddah. There would be some things available in the souk, but those listed above were considered necessities. She had made contact with the shipper and would soon have the shipment on the way. Additionally, she had to make arrangements to store our 1963 Pontiac Grand Prix. Before my departure, I had stored our 1960 Sunbeam Alpine sports car, with the proviso we would soon add another vehicle. Even so, that was just one more hurdle for her to overcome.

The travel order was dated June 21, 1965 and it directed her travel to begin June 29, 1965. Not very much time to pack all the bags and boxes she and David would have to look after on that long flight to Jeddah, changing carriers and planes numerous times. She was authorized to bring 100 pounds each for her and David. All of that was crammed into twelve separate bags or cartons. The itinerary was attached to the travel order showing the following: American Airlines, San Diego to Los Angeles, TWA, Los Angeles to New York, (JFK) thence to Cairo, then Saudi Arabian Airlines, Cairo to Jeddah. The actual route turned out as follows: San Diego to Los Angeles, to New York to Gander (Newfoundland) to Madrid to Algiers to Tunis to Tripoli to Cairo. Total en route time was twenty-four hours. Marti and David arrived in Cairo about 9 p.m. on June 30th. Everyone off the plane separated in two lines, returning nationals and foreigners. She joined the foreigner's line and got visas for both. Actually she did not need a visa since she had to stay in the hotel on the premises because she was a "through" passenger. There was no one there to tell her differently, though, due to the late arrival. David checked and found all the bags and cartons. (Small miracle.)

Right after that, a small energetic Arab appearing person showed up and said, "Sorry I did not meet you on arrival, the schedule was messed up due to the late arrival. Let me have your passports and I will get you a room here in the Airport Hilton so you will have a place to stay until your flight tomorrow." Marti did not know who he was, but he seemed to know what he was doing so she handed over the passports reluctantly. They finally got checked into the hotel, both completely worn out. Marti said her legs were swollen and her back hurt from the long trip in such a confined space.

The small Arab person's name was "Chico," at least that is what he claimed. We later learned he was employed by TWA to facilitate movement of TWA personnel through the complications of Cairo airport. He knew all the in and outs and was well known by frequent travelers who appreciated his help.

The day Marti and David arrived in Cairo, June 30, 1965, I was on a Royal Charter flight with Captain Jim Bird to Riyadh to pick up many members of the Royal family to take them to their summer palace in the cooler climes of Taif. Taif is located about ninety miles east of Jeddah, but at a much higher elevation, and is drier and cooler. Our passengers were the family and servants of Prince Satum. All went well and we received some gold coins (baksheesh) for our endeavor.

Neither Marti nor David could sleep at first, and David was worried about their baggage being untended near the baggage claim area. He went down to check on it and soon returned with several small Arabs each carrying a bag or two. Marti was somewhat surprised and chagrined to realize she had to pay each of them some "Baksheesh." She later complained, "Why couldn't they have carried more than one or two pieces each?"

The next morning they prepared for departure and were soon waiting in the lounge for their flight to Jeddah which was to depart at 12:30 local time. Yes, she had to pay those little guys baksheesh again to move her bags to the proper area. While waiting they observed the comings and goings of many people, including various flight crews, some of whom wore Saudi Arabian Airlines uniforms. All appeared neat and they wondered which might be part of their crew. Later they observed one Saudi captain (an American) who did not fit the mold. He was a little on the fat side, had skimpy reddish hair and a scraggly red-blond mustache and goatee. His uniform was ill fitting, wrinkled, and his pant leg on his left leg was caught in the top of one of his seven inch scuffed up black boots. Altogether a much disheveled appearance. Nervously they glanced at each other, thinking surely this will not be our captain. Neither voiced their concern to avoid jinxing themselves. He was Captain Scot and was actually a very competent pilot. Scot was just indifferent to his appearance.

Marti was becoming increasingly nervous about their passports, as they were missing and no one could help them. Their flight was eventually called for the boarding process and within seconds, Chico showed up with the passports and all was well, that is, except for the lingering anxiety.

The flight was soon airborne and they were on their way to Jeddah at last. The bad news was, the flight proceeded to Dhahran on the east coast first and then would backtrack to

Riyadh for deplaning passengers, loading others and then finally on to Jeddah.

Their plane landed Jeddah about 1500 local time July 1, 1965 and I was there to greet them. The temperature was about 101 degrees and the soggy heat added to pressures of arrival in this new strange country. I was able to get into the Customs area just far enough to help keep track of the luggage and get it outside to the vehicles for transport to the hotel.

Finally, we were all together again and attempting to relax in our "rooms." The airline had reluctantly agreed to our having three rooms. One for our living room, one for our bedroom and the third across the hall for David. Marti and David were exhausted from their long ordeal of travel and were simply coasting on the dregs of adrenaline.

Marti said, "I brought you something," and rummaged through her handbag and came up with a miniature bottle of Beefeaters gin. That was a surprise! And a shock! The Saudis forbid anyone bringing in many things and alcohol was a big no-no, right up there with pork. Lucky for us, Customs had not adequately checked her handbag.

My big plans for taking them for a tour of the wonders of the souk were dashed by their condition. Neither had any enthusiasm for seeing anything but the bed and a good long rest.

The next day we did take a tour of the souk and they were duly impressed but not yet up to enthusiasm for further adventures. We went to one of the local food stores and picked up some items so Marti could fix a bite to eat in our quarters. Supermarkets they are not, but one was using that name.

The following day I was gone all day on a flight, and David was busy investigating the hotel to learn where the fun places were located. It didn't take him long to learn there were some interesting possibilities inside and out. Marti used the time to good advantage by resting.

The next couple of days were utilized in regrouping sightseeing and generally getting used to the new surroundings. Monday evening we were invited to one of American captain's quarters in the "Old Zeiben compound" or known by most as "TWA compound." They were very gracious in their hospitality and provided us with our first good meal. This was the first of a series of invitations from those who had been in Saudi Arabia for a while. We thought it was a nice gesture for so many to be willing to help make us welcome.

Not only was it a "nice gesture," but for some of the newly arrived wives, it would prove to be absolutely essential. The cultural shock of all the strangeness they were encountering was almost overwhelming. They got to see first hand that others had adjusted and were coping quite nicely. Most rose to the challenge and adjusted their thinking and actions to fit in rather well. Some just could not adjust, and the entire family would return to the states. In other cases, the wife (and children) simply returned alone, leaving the husband to earn a living in Saudi Arabia.

One of those couples that entertained us would turn out to be very good friends indeed and remain so for the rest of our lives. Polly and Joe Vincent lived in the Kraji building and had a very nice spacious apartment. They had two sons, Scot and Randy, plus a big cat named Smokey.

Joe was a flight engineer crew member on the DC-6's and the Boeing jets. Polly was the number one employee in the personnel department and the "go to" person to get things done. We were fortunate to meet them and so early in our tour. Polly and Marti hit it off from the beginning and Polly clued her in on lots of the "do's" and "don'ts."

Marti was well equipped to cope with her new surroundings and entered into the daily routines and adventures with enthusiasm. David too was well seasoned, and was eager to investigate all of the areas that might lead to new adventures.

Our "living room" window looked out over what would have been open gravelly desert but for the tin walled compound directly across the road from the hotel. The several hovels that were erected inside that approximately seventy-five yard square were constructed of a variety of cast off materials. Corrugated tin cut and flattened large tin containers, cardboard, pieces of shipping crates, whatever. Large pieces of cloth or cardboard might be placed or draped over the entry of each of the hovels to afford some degree of privacy. A large space was reserved in the approximate center of the compound for communal washing, drying or possibly space for a donkey and or other small animals. These people were the "homeless" of Jeddah. They were also all immigrants. A mix of Pakistanis, Indians, Yemeni, Sudanese, etc. Each of these varied groups had their own compounds of course. The men worked if at all at the most menial of tasks to make enough for the daily bread. It could not have been a very "good" life.

We did take advantage sometimes by watching their activities and comings and goings. We were to see many such "compounds" scattered through out Jeddah. Some of those were quite large. Two of those I can think of were as large as a small square block as we know it. We even saw a few two-story "hovels."

Marti and David were observing the compound across the street one day from the security of the hotel window and were to see a puzzling act. A female came out of the closest abode partially dressed. She did not have a head and face cover and her breasts were exposed. She proceeded with some sort of work activity and was quite unaware she was being observed. Suddenly she scurried to the entrance of her dwelling and disappeared. Marti and David wondered what that was all about and looked around to see if there was a reason. They noted there was male, dressed in a similar manner to the occupants of the compound, approaching from about a half block away but discounted his presence as a factor as she had been shielded from his view by the corrugated wall. However, they watched as he made his way to and into the compound through an entry off the street. He made his way through the labyrinth to her location. She had reappeared wearing a head cover and her face was obscured by a veil; however, her breasts were still exposed. He entered her area and they apparently had a short conversation before he turned and exited the area.

There were two questions voiced by Marti and David and remained unanswered to this day. One: How did she know he was coming? She could not see or hear him. The wall protected her area from view at street level and there was no visual or audible way she might have known. Two: She took care to cover her hair and face but left her breasts in full view. Why?

Earlier, I had mentioned "wild dogs." An explanation is more than likely required. Throughout the city, one could find packs of wild dogs almost anyplace there was an open area of any kind. Invariably there would also be a small refuse or garbage dump nearby. They were of a medium size, medium length hair dogs and could be different in coloring, depending on the pack. Blacks and tans predominated.

When a "westerner" passed by a pack, they would stand and acknowledge your presence by wagging their tails, fawning, and generally expressing obeisance as you passed. The puppies were cute and without fear. They would approach you with joy. It was not wise to exhibit any act of aggression, however, as the leader would immediately issue an unmistakable warning. Friendly, ok, but don't mess with us.

The presence or passing of a Saudi would generate a quite different response from any dog pack. As one, they would stand, with bristled hair, stiff upright tail, bared teeth, and low warning growls could be heard.

Why the different response? I don't know. We do know, however, the Saudis generally did not like dogs, considered them unclean and could not appreciate them as pets. The dogs apparently understood their feelings and responded accordingly.

Many Americans (and westerners) adopted the puppies and raised them as house pets with great success. They were friendly, loving, and loyal pets. Most were also very good guardians of the premises.

One had to be careful in their choice, however, as many of the packs were diseased and could pose a threat to humans.

The "wild" cat population also deserves mention. There were thousands of "wild" housecats throughout the city. They came in all the varied colors one sees in housecats. Some were quite beautiful and desirable, but none were of a friendly nature. Unlike the dogs, the cats were truly "wild." They, too, thrived on the garbage disposal system of the city.

The disposal system appeared to consist of priorities. The dog packs seemed to have first priority, followed by the cats, and then the local goatherd would come by with a pretty good flock of "garbage disposal" goats. They would eat a lot of things left untouched by the dogs and cats. They even ate the glue from the cardboard and part of the cardboard as well. Perhaps finally, a truck would appear with peon loaders and remove the residual.

The local kids had great fun messing with the cats. Arabs and all others as well. They loved to throw rocks or objects at the trash piles to scatter the cats. In later years, "dumpsters" were added here and there to the mix. Of particular glee was to chuck a rock at one of the dumpsters. The cats would boil out of there like you wouldn't believe! I thought it was fun, too, and so did David. The Arab boys didn't mess with the dogs though. They were truly afraid of them. The dogs did not like them either.

By July 6, almost all my flights were in the Convair and I shared each flight with another American captain. Very few Saudis, if any, were checked out in the Convair at this time. I had already flown with Lee Curry, Jim Bird, Orton, Fred Wright, and the next flight on July 6th was with Captain Fox on a Royal Charter flight. He had flown these charters previously and was in command due to the special circumstances. The flight would be departing Riyadh for Taif and would fly under "special rules." There were forty-four seats on this aircraft, and we ended up with sixty nine passengers, mostly women and children. The children sat on their mom's laps, and seat belts were "optional." Not a good plan! The "baggage" aircraft was REALLY overloaded. Taking off with an overweight aircraft on a hot day (108°F) was not something one should do. Possibly even worse was landing that aircraft at a relatively high altitude airport where the air is much thinner and provides less lift. The field elevation at Taif, where they were to land, is in excess of forty-five hundred feet. Don't remember the crew on that one, but very happy I was not part of it. Baksheesh does not make up for that!

My first flight to Asmara, Ethiopia occurred on July 8, 1965 with Captain Jim Bird. (Asmara, once the capital city of Eritrea, is again back in that capacity due to a revolution.) The itinerary was Jeddah to Port Sudan thence to Asmara. Asmara is located on relatively high ground, and the surrounding area presents a beautiful sight from the air. The runway itself is paved and plenty long, but does present a bit of a challenge on takeoff and landing. Each end is higher than the center causing one to land the aircraft downhill from either direction. Quite a surprise to any pilot on his first landing and sometimes on subsequent ones as well. The whole thing is compounded by the 7600 feet plus field elevation. That construction and the thin air causes one to land a little further down the runway than he would like or drop onto the runway without warning. Either is not a good thing.

The terminal was small, but very nice and well kept. The people were very friendly and quite comely. A very large percentage of the natives had fine features and were, for the most part, medium in color. There were variations, of course, as there are in other races and countries. Some of the women were indeed beautiful, attractive too! Not to worry, I was well married. Still, they really were attractive! We were to learn later, these attractive features were shared throughout Ethiopia, at least in the cities.

We had lunch in the café while waiting for refueling and passenger loading. The food was good and very reasonable. Admittedly, there was a very strong temptation to imbibe a liter or two of the cold beer available (this tasty beverage not being available in Jeddah). But abstinence won over desire. Barely.

Takeoff was a little strange on that concave runway too. The aircraft picked up speed rapidly on the downhill run, tapering off a little in the middle then swooping up towards the far end.

After a brief stop at Port Sudan to offload and load passengers, we continued back to Jeddah. The entire flight, including ground time, was eight hours.

July 10th I would fly the first of many "teacher flights." This trip would be shared with Captain Ted Hunt. The entire passenger load would be to take school teachers on the way back to their homes after the school year. Almost all teachers in the kingdom were from other countries. They would be on their "teacher break" for several weeks, and then fly back for the new school year. We would, of course, reverse the flights. The route for this first outbound was Jeddah, Medina, Amman, Damascus, Jeddah, the entire flight at night. The night landing and takeoff at Damascus was quite an experience. Upon arrival, the evening was moonless and appeared very clear as we could see the lights of the city from miles away. The lights of the city appeared very bright and seemingly sparkled like jewels, especially against the dark background of the very nearby mountains. The effect was quite beautiful. The city is surrounded on three sides by some pretty impressive jagged hills. The "downwind" leg must always be on the south side of the airport and the turn on "base leg" must be of sufficient height to insure proper ground clearance. For takeoff, climb quickly with a turn to the south to avoid the "hills." Really not a very comforting area to require an "instrument" approach. Later I was to make flights into Damascus for overnight stays. Very interesting!

Bob Wells' wife, Ruth, arrived from the states and she was duly ensconced in the Al Haramain Hotel with her husband. They had a suite one floor up from us and we were to join them many times for meals and sightseeing. There was another Bob staying in the hotel. He, too, was a captain and I had flown with him a couple of times. His name was Robert Majors and his young second wife, Murphy, along with Bob's fourteen year old son, Bill, had also just arrived in the country. They were located in a suite two flights up and at the west end of the hotel. Young Bill was to become an almost constant companion of our son. He was a mischievous rascal and was in constant conflict with his young stepmother. His father tried to keep the peace, but had to mostly take her side against the little rebel. Bob had a bit of an explosive nature to begin with and when he had a few drinks, little Bill had to be quick on his feet. Fortunately he was.

David and Bill roamed the hotel and knew all the crooks and crannies, including some storage rooms here and there, where they rummaged from time to time. They acquired some "bean shooters" and were soon blowing beans or whatever at unsuspecting "hall boys." The "hall boys" were unofficial bellhops and were at your beck and call at all times. Most, if not all, were from Yemen and were working for almost nothing. They depended for the most part on the generosity of the guests of the hotel. They were on station on all floors and if a person wanted an errand performed, just open the door or ring a bell from inside and there would be an instant messenger at your beck and call. Of course, there was a bit of a catch — you had to express your wants either in Arabic or sign language. Some could speak rudimentary English, however, so the system worked after a fashion. To get back to the "bean shooting." At first the hall boys were surprised, not aware where the shots were coming from, but they soon learned and then the chase was on. Up and down the stairs, the length of the halls in and out of some doors, etc. A great game!

Shortly after the Majors set up in the hotel, Marti, David, Bob Wells, his wife Ruth, and I were invited to their apartment for drinks before dinner. Bob had acquired some "sadeki," the very alcoholic drink I had described earlier. Each was offered their drink of choice. Marti does not drink so that was easy. She settled for a soft drink. Bob Wells and Ruth both asked for Coke and Sidiqi. A comment on the "Coke" is appropriate here. There had been a Coca Cola plant in Saudi Arabia until the Saudis were led to believe the company was Jewish-owned. Saudi Arabia then ordered them to leave the country and took over the processing and bottling plants. They continued brewing the same formula and renamed the product, "Kaki Kola." My choice was a martini. Bob Majors then brewed himself a unique mixture that was to become a topic of conversation for many months, perhaps years. There was at that time a flavored colored product on the market the size and shape of an Alka Seltzer tablet, named "Fizzies." Bob mixed his "sadeki" with a little water and threw in a Fizzie. It fizzed and dissolved just like an Alka Seltzer. Bob liked that! After a few of those, Bob's lips would take on the hue of the colored Fizzie he had imbibed. Looked like he really smeared his lipstick!

When Billy was really a bad boy, Majors would lock him in his room while they went someplace. Billy at first opened the glass doors which opened onto the balcony, then inch his perilous way across a narrow ledge to the next balcony, enter that room and on out to the hall. A slip of foot and he would have fallen four floors to the pavement! Later, he filched a key from one of the hall boys and would simply unlock his door and away he would go. Once Majors came home early and became aware Bill had gotten out. He was furious and when Billy tried to sneak back in, Bob was waiting for him. He would have beaten the #*%$ out of him, but Billy was fleet of foot and was able to stay head of him down all the stairs and out the main door. Can't remember how long Billy stayed out, but it was hours.

A PRINCELY GIFT

My trip on July 13, 1965 started out very routinely, but ended with a "prize" I would cherish. We departed Jeddah for Taif in the early morning, arriving about sunup. Along with several others, a prince of Yemen boarded along with his entourage. He was Prince Abdullah al Hassan. The prince was slight of build and I judged about five feet, four inches in height and quite young. He appeared to be in his mid or late twenties and quite handsome, along with a very out-going pleasing personality. He had flown with me before, and we acknowledged each other with friendly greetings. I took the liberty of inviting him to the cockpit after reaching cruise altitude and he readily accepted. Within minutes of leveling out, he knocked on the door and asked permission to come in. He obviously was a different kind of "royal." He spoke excellent English with very little accent, and we were able to chat about many subjects. I asked if he had lived in Saudi Arabia or Yemen. He explained he had been visiting his cousin, Hussein, in Germany for about a year and had only recently returned to help his native Yemen in the war against Egypt and political forces in his country. He was a cousin of the Imam of Yemen, Mohammed El Badr. When I started the descent for landing at Bisha, the Prince went back to his seat in the cabin. After a brief sojourn on the ground at Bisha, just to let a couple of passengers off and three more on, we departed for Najran. After reaching cruise altitude, the prince was back, again knocking on the door and asking permission. The prince told me some of his soldiers would meet the aircraft to greet him on his return. He told me not to become alarmed if they shot their weapons repeatedly into the air to exhibit their enthusiasm for his return from Taif. That was normal. That prompted me to ask him about the weapon he was carrying in a holster around his waist. He quickly withdrew a pistol from the holster and presented it to me for inspection. I released the magazine, extracted it and drew back the slide to check it out. Sure enough it was loaded. He laughed about that. The pistol was an Astra model 800 "Condor," nine millimeter, semi-automatic man-ufactured in Spain and was of excellent quality. I admired it with enthusiasm, professing the desire to own one just like it. Actually that was a faux pas on my part, as I had tem-porarily forgotten Arab protocol. One should not admire a possession of another in such a manner. That person is then obligated to give it to you. Most certainly the prince's edu-cation and savvy allowed him to ignore my rudeness, but he did not forget my feelings. Soon we could see the greenery ahead which grew along the stretches of the Najran Wadi, tipping one to the fact there was subsurface water along that old river bed. Beyond the wadi about two miles was the country of Yemen. The airport did not stand out against that arid desert landscape, as there were no paved runways or buildings. The terminal was a tent, and the only other artificial items in abundance were scores of empty and full fifty five gallon fuel drums, plus a few discarded shipping crates and of course the orange "windsock." The runway was compacted dusty desert, marked at both ends and aligned southwest-northeast and about five thousand feet in length. Best to land to the southwest as there were low rugged hills close by north and east.

The prince asked if he could stay in the cockpit until we were ready to land. Permission was readily granted. We circled the field about a thousand feet above the ground at his request, and he pointed out the large group of soldiers waiting to greet him. I was impressed.

After the prince returned to the cabin, I initiated the approach for landing and all was well until just before flare (round out) for landing. Seemingly out of nowhere, three camels appeared directly in our path. Very quickly, I applied full power, upped the gear and skimmed the backs of those errant beasts of burden, narrowly averting a disaster. (There were numerous clumps of small trees or "shrubs" growing on and around the area and the camels had a want for browsing amongst them and they were very well concealed.)

We circled and landed without further incident. We taxied back and shut down even with a line of barrels and close to the terminal tent. Prince Hassan came forward and laughingly congratulated me for not killing one of the local camels and thanked us for the flight.

The soldiers were lined up several deep about fifty feet from the aircraft and stretched for over a hundred yards. The "soldiers" in appearance were unlike any we might expect as they did not wear uniforms as such. None wore trousers, of course, and each had his own preference for color of drab, but all had the ever present decorated curved dagger or knife ("sakeen" in Arabic) in a unique scabbard with its curved or angled tip. The scabbard was attached to a belt and worn almost directly over his belly button. The belt also served as his "money belt, etc." and part of his ammunition storage. The weight of all this was relieved by a strap over the shoulder not much different from that worn by many Kansas Highway Patrol Officers.

When the prince emerged from the doorway, a mighty cheer went up and rifles were fired repeatedly into the air (I sincerely hoped). We watched as he greeted several of his commanders with hugs and kisses on each cheek. He got up on one of the nearby barrels and made what I assumed to be a very rousing speech as there was a lot more cheering and gunshots. He, along with two of his ranking commanders, made their way through the throng of fighters to be greeted by Prince Khalid al Sudairi, the Royal leader of that southern Province. Prince Sudairi was a younger brother to the first king, Abdul Azziz ibn Saud, and an uncle to the present King.

About ten minutes later as I was exiting the aircraft, a Yemen soldier came running   and held out a box, offering it to me, along with a short speech. Turning to the steward who was nearby, I asked, "What is this about?" He responded, "He is offering you a gift from Prince Hassan, you must take it." Yes, there was indeed a brand new nine millimeter CONDOR semi-automatic in that box. The weapon was factory wrapped in wax paper and coated with protecting grease. The gift was received with many mixed emotions. First, I remembered my faux pas of expressing my desire for his weapon and regretted my method of expressing appreciation of his possession. Secondly, I had an immediate thought it may not be legal for me to have such a weapon in Saudi Arabia. What to do? The decision was an easy, difficult one; I concealed it in my hand baggage and kept it. The sticky problem would have to wait until I was better informed. While waiting for service and reloading, I tried talking to some of the Yemeni soldiers with little success. Of the three I was talking to, one was really small, thin and appeared quite wiry. He had the usual curved dagger in his scabbard and it appeared to be decorated with gold coins. I asked him about it and he said it was given to him by his father who in turn had received it from his father. Each of them had placed a gold coin on the handle. "Mighty Mouse" (my label) was small, wiry, quick and had a good sense of humor. (See photos) I asked him if his Sakeen (knife) was sharp. His response was, "Shuf" (look) and handed me the knife. I gingerly tested the blade with my thumb as was the custom and realized it was indeed sharp. Both he and his buddy started** laughing and looking at my finger. I looked down and observed the blood running down and dripping on my shoe.

The return flight was uneventful from Najran to Bisha to Taif then on home to Jeddah. The possibility of going through Customs on our return was very unlikely, but always a possibility. Ninety-nine percent of the time, upon returning from a flight from inside the kingdom, we were allowed to bypass the customs inspectors, but the thought was there. Needless worry, we waltzed right on through.

About a week later, I had a chance to question Captain Akkram about possessing a hand gun or any other type of weapon. He let me know a foreigner was not allowed to have a weapon without a permit, and it was unlikely one would be issued. Sometimes a prince would present some notable for-eigner with a permit for a shotgun for the express purpose of hunting small game or birds in the kingdom. The question then was, who could issue a permit for other than a shotgun and what was the procedure? He explained that only a prince or the king could issue such a permit and very likely that would never happen.

Should I be discouraged and give up? Well, maybe not. About ten days later, I realized I was on schedule for trip to Najran, departing on August 2. A hazy plan began to circu-late in my thoughts. Perhaps I will have another opportunity to meet and talk to Prince Hassan. If so, I will broach the subject of a permit for the beautiful gift he had given me.

Typical decorated Arab Truck

Tin shack area near MAAG House. Jedda. SA. 1965 .

TWO YEMENI WARIORS, MIGHTY MOUSE ON LEFT, CAPT. PORTER, 1965

Pistol Presented to
Capt. Porter by
Prince Hassan

That made sense up to a point. Just how likely would I run into him again? Not very! What then? Well, maybe Prince Sudairi will be at the airport again, and I will definitely summon up the courage to ask him for a permit. Maybe.

Just before daybreak on August 2nd, we departed Jeddah en route to Khamis Mushayt for a landing with passengers to offload and others to board for the one hour flight on to Najran. (Khamis Mushayt was built as a military airport, was paved and located in the southern mountains. Field elevation was sixty five hundred feet.) Just at round out for touch-down at Khamis, a camel ran on the runway right in front of us and turned straight in line with our direction. FULL power, Go around and pray! Allah, where are you? I just know we scraped the hair on that camel back. Phoooeee! That was another close one. Talk about an omen! Reminded me of a similar mishap at Najran when the Prince was with us. We circled and came in for another approach and landed, trying to avoid the camel crap on the runway. Would you believe that I would have had to pay the owner of that camel for its loss had I hit and killed it? About six to eight thousand dollars worth! They told me that after the last near miss at Najran.

We departed Khamis after a few minutes on the ground and within an hour were landing at Najran. No camels or other impediments this time.

Shortly after shutting down, I proceeded to the terminal tent to ask the agent, Aiadi, if Prince Hassan or Prince Sudairi was around. Aiadi surprised me with a gift! He handed me a small piece of cloth tied into a bundle with something inside. After untying it, eight nine millimeter cartridges were revealed! He did not speak much English, but the gist of his attempt was this was a gift from him to me for the pistol Prince Hassan had given me. Luckily I had taken a picture of him two months previously and just happened to have a couple of prints of his picture for him. He was very pleased.

He then informed me Prince Sudairi would be here soon to see a Sheikh depart on my flight. As soon as they arrived, Aiadi let me know. Here was my chance.

When I saw the Prince arrive, I walked over to him. He was accompanied by his constant companion who apparently was his assistant, scribe, bodyguard, whatever and the sheik. When he acknowledged my presence, I introduced myself in what I hoped was the correct manner for addressing a prince. Then continued with the story of Prince Hassan presenting me with a pistol. (Neither seemed surprised by my announcement as though they were already aware of that fact.) "Not being sure if I was allowed to have the pistol, I asked one of my Saudi friends what I should do. The friend advised me it was illegal to own and I must seek a permit to keep the weapon. My friend advised that only a prince or the king could issue a permit for the gun. My immediate thought was Prince Sudairi is the closest to being a king and certainly the most powerful prince I had met." Both he and his assistant laughed amusedly about that statement and I smiled broadly. Then I asked, "Would your Excellency honor my request for the necessary permit?" There was no doubt from his manner he was about to deny my appeal, hesitated a moment, then apparently changed his mind and uttered the Arabic equivalent of "Why not!" Then looked at his assistant, who shrugged and smiled with the prince. The assistant handed a clip board to Prince Sudairi who then scribbled out a few sentences in Arabic, signed it and handed to me. Without further ado, I expressed my thanks in Arabic the best I knew how and retired from the scene. Even though I was aware the Prince spoke English quite well, I spoke to the assistant at all times as I had been briefed. The assistant pretended to interpret but the prince did not require it to understand. When I thanked the prince in Arabic, he responded in English, with "You are welcome."

NOTE: Later, I learned for sure Prince Sudairi was already aware Prince Hassan had presented me with the pistol before I brought it up. My name in the body of the permit reflects my full name, including my middle initial which I had not revealed.

This really should not have been a surprise. Admittedly I was more than just a little naïve. First, Prince Hassan met with Prince Sudairi immediately after greeting his men and he most certainly would have informed him of the gift. Second, news for these people had been word of mouth for centuries, and they loved good stories. Telling of events was their life and pastime. After the fact, I have little doubt the entire population of Najran knew of the gift within a day or two. Possibly including my name, rank and serial number. Prince Sudairi and or his secretary would surely have told the story to their circle and the agent, Aiadi would spread the news to the rest.

The story would have grown with the retelling, of course, and I would not care to speculate on the course of their imagination. No doubt there were bets on how soon I would be arrested in Jeddah for possessing the wonderful pistol given to me as "Baksheesh" by the prince.

Now, Prince Sudairi would have another story to tell about the naïve American who boldly asked for a favor of that magnitude. He most certainly would have put the proper "spin" on the story to assure maximum hilarity. On the other hand, perhaps the story took another turn and the American was described as a naïve but very clever person, who was successful in obtaining an almost unheard of document for a foreigner.

Whatever, I had just become part of the lore of that part of Saudi Arabia and possibly the story is still told on occasion.

Sometime later I was at the MAAG house when the Commanding General was visiting from Riyadh. He had an Arab interpreter travel with him at all times and of course he was there that evening. Taking advantage of that, I asked the interpreter if he would read and write out an interpretation of the permit.

After reading the document, He looked up and asked "Where did you get this?" My response was, "Prince Sudairi wrote it out for me." He then said, "This is his signature all right, how much did you pay for it?" My answer was, "Nothing, He just gave it to me, after I had asked him." He was absolutely incredulous and said, "People pay as much as ten or twelve thousand riyals for these permits!" (Enough to buy a Volkswagen car.) Now I understood why the prince and his assistant were so amused by my request. Ignorance is worth a lot!

Reproduced here is the word for word interpretation written out for me by the general's interpreter and later verified by another Saudi friend:

"TO WHOM IT MAY CONCERN: CAPTAIN LEONARD V. PORTER IS AUTHORIZED TO CARRY A PERSONAL PISTOL WHICH WAS GIVEN TO HIM AS A GIFT BY PRINCE ABDULLAH IBN AL HASSAN."

11-5-85
Signed by: Khalid Al Sudari,
Prince of Najran, Saudi Arabia
(The date shown above reflects the Arabic calendar.)

The way the permit was worded, I would be entitled to wear the pistol in a holster or have with me any where in the kingdom. The idea of wearing a holster with the gun was certainly an intriguing one, but I did not deem it prudent and did not.

NOTE: Prince Khalid Al Sudari was one of seven brothers whose mother was Hussa bint Ahmad Sudairi, and their father was the founder of the Kingdom of Saudi Arabia, King Abdul-Aziz Saud. King Fahd, one of Khalid's brothers, died in 2005 and was succeeded by another brother, King Abdullah.

(Note: In June of 1968 Prince Hassan would become the Prime Minister of Yemen after him and another cousin, Mohammed al Hussein, ousted Imam Al Badr. Thirteen months later, he, Prince Hassan, was shot while at prayers. He was thirty years old. (The identity of the gunmen was not known.) NOTE: Copy of the actual document is on last page.

ADEN

July 16th, I would make my first trip to Aden, located on the southern tip of the Arabian landmass, just south of Yemen. The town of Aden was about one hundred twenty kilometers beyond and west of the entry to the Red Sea. This country, with its indeterminate, elusive border was under a protectorate provided by the British. The people were Arab, but were being influenced by the Communists and it appeared the British had a tenuous toehold at best. Not really a very safe place to hang around. Captain Bill High had been there before and would provide guidance for me on this trip. We made plans to go to town after arrival to a duty-free store and purchase some tape recorders. Prior to landing, Bill had called ahead and requested transport for us to go into town.

The approach and landing was not really a very "fun time." The surface wind was from 210 degrees at twenty knots gusting to thirty five and the visibility was only about one-half mile in blowing dust. Bill High made the approach and landing, doing a great job of sticking it on the runway. Not an easy thing to do under those circumstances!

After taxi in and shutdown, the passengers deplaned, we then inquired about transport. A British major approached to offer us a ride to the duty store and let us know we would have to ride in an army two and a half ton truck along with him and an armed escort. Things had gotten a bit sticky the last couple of days, he explained, and there had been a few shooting incidents.

Bill and I piled in along with the soldiers and commenced a rather tense, rough ride through a large section of town to reach the duty store. Once inside the store, things seemed almost normal. We did our shopping in short order. I purchased two reel to reel Akai tape recorders at a real bargain price and Bill did the same. One of the two I bought was for me and the other for a friend.

Soon we loaded our purchases and piled back into the army vehicle, along with the armed guard, and raced back through town to the airport. Nothing untoward happened, but the tension was certainly high. The soldiers were very alert and quite wary. That uneasiness was transmitted to us and, if anything, we were almost as goosey as they were. Probably lucky we were not armed.

Once back on the airplane, we stashed our purchases in a place where the Customs agents were most unlikely to look. If they were tipped that we might have Customs liable items on board, they knew where to look. When first I was* talked into buying the equipment in Aden, I understood, although it might be illegal, it really was an accepted practice. Customs would just ignore it if the Americans brought items like that in for their own use, and not for resale. Now that I was being told to hide those items, I was not so sure. On the way back to Jeddah, I brought this to Bill's attention. He said not to worry, he had made arrangements for one of the maintenance men to offload the packages after we departed the aircraft, and he would deliver them later. Did it often, he said. Just routine and not to worry. The worry part was not so easy to put aside and was not over even after I received my tape recorder.

The tape recorder provided us with many hours of great music for years to come, surviving a trip back to the states and a return to Saudi Arabia in 1971. In nineteen seventy five the machine made another trip back to the states with us and served us well for several more years.

COPING

Marti and David were still coping, mostly marking time in between my trips.*

David kept himself amused rather well scouting out the hotel and surrounds while attempting to resist the mischief

Donkey drawn water barrels being filled for delivery elsewhere
1965 Jeddah

Kraji Building, Our Apt. 2nd Fl.

Marty-Living room, Kraji Bldg, Jedda, '65
Cocktail table from Marble Factory
Bedouin tent rug from Taif

stirred up by the active imagination of Bill Majors. David had a very active imagination as well, but possessed much better judgment, thank Allah.

When I was available, we spent a lot of time investigating mysteries of the souk. The sights, sounds, aromas and hustle bustle of the crowds of people provided an almost never ending source of awe and entertainment. The dress or costumes of the shoppers (or sightseers) varied greatly depending, in part, on their origin. We were also seeing many Yemen soldiers sightseeing in the souk along with us. They were "in uniform," that is, a knee high garment, usually khaki in color, but otherwise similar to the Saudi thobe. They wore the belted dagger along with one or more bandoleers of ammunition and many carried their rifles (no doubt loaded). Most wore a head garment, but a few were bare headed showing off their shiny black curls. All seemed friendly enough, but we deemed it best to stay clear. We learned they were here on "rest leave" or just a break from the fighting in Yemen. Later in Najran and Gizan, I would see Yemen soldiers in a variety of shades of drab in their dress unlike the uniform khaki observed in the souk.

Our sojourns to the souk were mostly in the evenings, as daytime shopping was just too uncomfortable. Additionally, the car sitting in the sun would be unbearably hot when we returned from shopping, and that Volkswagen was not air-conditioned. The steering wheel would be so hot I could not hold on and had to carry a towel in the car for that use.

This time of year and for the rest of summer the daytime temperatures were, on average, one hundred eight degrees Fahrenheit. The proximity of the Red Sea also added humidity to make it much more difficult. By evening, the temperatures would moderate to about eighty-five to ninety degrees. We gradually acclimated to that and accepted it as normal.

GOLD

From the beginning, Marti was fascinated by the souk and David and I were intrigued. Each of our visits had to include walking through the Gold Souk. The shops were side by side for a short block on each side of the narrow street and the windows were full of gold jewelry of all types. On display would be literally hundreds of bracelets, chains, and other adornments of many descriptions. All were of high quality gold, and some would be of such a rich mixture of gold as to be inappropriate for daily wear. The craftsmanship of those pieces was sometimes exquisite. Even so, everything seemed too be sold by weight. After many such visits, Marti pretty much narrowed her preference of shops to just the one located near the end. The owner was a fairly young, handsome Arab, named Ahmed Hasan Fitaihi. He spoke good English, was charming in manner and was amenable to fair bargaining. We did not buy often, but did develop a good relationship. Once Marti really admired a pair of "rectangular" bracelets there. One was yellow gold, the other white gold, but otherwise, identical. She initiated the bargaining and progressed nicely to the point where he weighed them separately and quoted a different price for each. The white gold one was more money. This precipitated a semi-heated discussion about the relative values. Generally gold jewelry consists of an alloy of gold, with silver and copper added for strength and hardness with a karat as the measure of that mix, fourteen karat gold being fourteen parts gold and ten parts silver and copper. White gold is a mix of gold and silver, leaving out the copper. Arabs do not appreciate white gold; therefore there were almost no other pieces of white gold jewelry there, if any. Ahmed's stand was that white gold was rarer, and that was why it had to cost more. Marti said, "Not so, no one wanted it, therefore it should cost much less." Marti was closer to the truth in terms of desirability, but not in the facts. Ahmed's point was also wrong. Anyway, we departed amicably without a sale with the belief no Arab was going to buy them as a pair anyway, so she could try another time. One week later, we returned and Marti started the process with an offer she knew to be too low. Ahmed countered and the dealing continued until he finally weighed both bracelets together, followed with a new price for both. (For the record, each weighed twenty grams.) Marti countered, he accepted, and the deal was done. Both saved face by grouping them as a pair and both were pleased with their astute handling of the matter. We most certainly would return and departed on the best of terms.

Sometime later, on another visit, Marti spotted a multi diamond ring with a total of eleven diamonds mounted in white gold. There was one fair size diamond with four smaller ones on each side and two much smaller ones. She noticed they were old cut and so was the mounting, but admired the overall effect. After taking a look with my loupe, I agreed they were old cut, but not bad. For some reason, Arab women were not fond of white gold and not especially enamored of diamonds. This one had been owned by a princess and been discarded for the glitter of other jewelry. Marti asked about a price and made a counter offer, but the deal never got off the ground. She admired the ring, but felt she really did not need it, so reluctantly passed on pursuing the deal. She talked about it for days and wished the price was much lower. One day while she was at the beauty shop or a bridge date with the ladies, I went to the souk and started working on Ahmed for a better price. After three more trips of haggling, I caught him in a weak moment and bought the ring at a substantially discounted figure. We went to the MAAG House for dinner that evening and I gave Marti the ring. After I told her what I paid for it, she was even happier. Women love a good bargain!

Sequel: A few months later, Marti had to make a sad trip back to the States to attend her father's funeral. While in San Diego, she went to Jessup's Jewelers to have the ring sized to fit her for it was much too small. While there, the ring was also appraised. The ring was appraised for many times what I had paid for it. Further the mounting was Platinum, not white gold as we thought.

Through the years we enjoyed Ahmed's banter and steered many a customer to his shop.

REMARKABLE

Trip # 312 on July 20 in a Convair with another American captain was remarkable in that we made it back, in spite of the almost complete lapse or lack of proficiency on the part of the captain who was supposed to show me the way. I had not been on this route and he was supposed to give me the benefit of his expertise.

Captain "Al" and I departed Jeddah at 0545 GMT bound for Taif, thence to Bisha, Khamis Mushayt, Gizan (Jizan), then on to Riyadh for an overnight stay in the Sahara Palace Hotel. We would return to Jeddah the next day on a reverse route.

On approach for landing Taif, the nose gear light indicated "unsafe" when the gear was extended. I had noted in the maintenance log a previous write-up concerning this and that it had been ground checked ok. After a recheck, I decided to continue the approach as I would be landing the aircraft from the right seat. After landing, I allowed the nose gear to settle in gently. After shutdown, I checked the nose gear well and noted the cam lever on the solenoid was bent a little. No maintenance was available here so with the use of a pair of pliers, we bent the cam lever enough to engage the solenoid and the light came on as it should. Taif to Bisha was uneventful although we saw and went around a lot of "dust devils" on descent and again I made the landing from the right seat. "Dust Devils" are miniature tornadoes, generated by the rising heat of the desert and can be very dangerous. Avoiding them is the prudent thing. This area and south is the perfect breeding ground for thousands of them daily. Watch out! Landing, deplaning passengers, boarding five more and departure was routine with Captain Al making the takeoff and climb out. He would also be doing his own navigation using maps and identifying features on the ground

55 FOOT BY 8 FOOT ENTRY HALL OF APARTMENT IN KRAJI BUILDING, MARTI AND DAVID

Talbot, our houseboy with Yemen headdress. 1972

Majmah, S.A. Airport and Terminal, N. of Riyadh

Capt. Porter and Gen. Fedama of the Yemen Army

to maintain the proper track (pilotage, we call it). He would also make the landing at Khamis Mushayt. If he found it.

Within minutes of leveling out at cruising altitude and supposedly on track, I noticed a deviation. From my view, we were already off track to the west. Immediately I brought this to his attention. He denied being off course, stating he knew exactly where we were. Thereafter, I kept my own counsel and tracked us on my map. When our ETA (estimated time of arrival) was up, he was peering in all directions trying to locate the town or airport. When he asked me if I saw the airport anyplace, I said, "No, we are ten miles west of Khamis, suggest you turn seventy degrees to the east." Fortunately, he did or I would have been faced with insisting.

His approach was a bit erratic and he allowed the aircraft too descend much too low on final and tried to make up for it by adding power. My thousands of hours of instructing came in handy once again as I stood ready to take over and either land or go around as needed.

After landing and shutdown, he attempted making excuses for being off course, but none of them registered with me. It was quite obvious we had picked up an unexpected wind from the east and he had not corrected for it.

After takeoff from Khamis, he turned on a compass heading for Gizan and before we reached cruise altitude was again drifting off course to the west. Keeping track of the drift was easy and when we reached the coast of the Red Sea, I knew we were several miles north. Al was again looking all directions trying to determine where we were in relation to Gizan. When he asked, I advised him to turn south and follow the coast line. Several minutes later we spotted Gizan straight ahead. Suggesting that I make the landing as I had not previously landed there seemed the prudent thing to do. Fortunately, he concurred.

Our ground time went smoothly, and within twenty two minutes we were airborne and en route to Riyadh, about three hours and fifteen minutes to the north and east from Gizan. We could safely climb on course as there would be time to reach sufficient altitude to clear the mountain range ahead. Within about twenty-two minutes we could make out the King's Retreat (or hunting lodge) built at the top of the escarpment at an altitude of about nine thousand feet. We would fly over this mountainous area for another twenty minutes or so before reaching the down slope to the true desert area. From that point, we would have to exercise great care in visual navigation as there would be no more villages to aid in keeping on track. Only camel trails, wadis, (dry river beds), changing color of the terrain, and small Jabals (hills) rising up out of the desert here and there. Definitely not a good area to lose track of one's position. My log was very detailed as I kept track of every item that might now or later provide a clue as to our whereabouts. Later I would transfer those possible clues to my navigation map if they proved useful. Two hours later. we would spot the two thousand foot high ridge, with a mental sigh of relief, that ran south from Riyadh for hundreds of miles, deep into the Empty Quarter. Now we could pretty much parallel the ridge line and be assured of locating Riyadh without much difficulty.

Al would make the approach and landing and again, he allowed the aircraft to get too slow and low. When I felt the margin was getting a little too thin, I suggested with authority, "Put some power on and get back on a proper glide path," while standing by to take over if he did not react. He did as told and continued the approach to make a halfway decent landing.

Our overnight stay in the nearby Sahara Palace Hotel was normal. I listened to the wild dogs howl at each other for hours; followed by roosters all over the area voice their penetrating "wake-up" crowing, then at dawn, the Muezzins started their call to prayer from numerous Mosques encompassing all areas. Well rested? Not exactly.

After a breakfast, difficult to describe, we completed all necessary preparations and were airborne for Gizan right at 0505 GMT. Beautiful day and still quite moderate, but soon to scorch the eyeballs as we strained to identify landmarks through the wavy heat rising from the desert floor. Some two and a half hours later, we reached the rising mountainous area of the Aisr District. It was wondrous to see those patches of bright green scattered through the peaks and ridges of those mountains. The natives tilled every possible area to plant vegetables, grains, grapes, etc. All tilling was done by hand, of course. Due to the mountains, this area of Saudi Arabia received much more rain and there were many streams to be used for irrigating the crops. They had developed intricate means for saving and directing the flow of water for many hundreds, perhaps thousands of years.

Several years later, when Marti and I were able to visit this area, we were astounded to see the variety of food grown locally. On market day. the food stalls in the towns of Khamis Mushayt and Abha were overloaded. After seeing the rest of Saudi Arabia, I never would have guessed.

Landings at Gizan and Khamis were routine, but arrival at Bisha in the middle of the day provided a challenge and old Al had his hands full. The area from Bisha to Taif in the summer can be very turbulent and today was no different. Even at twelve thousand feet we were bouncing around and things only got worse as we descended for landing. The passengers were losing their cool and their morning meals. The steward could stand it no longer back there and came forward to the relative relief of the cockpit area. At least the air we breathed was much less upsetting.

On base leg, Al kept moving the flaps from up to twenty degrees down to up, etc., due to the speed fluctuations caused by turbulence. This was no help of course, it only served to further distract. On touchdown, the right gear hit first, we skipped, hit left gear, skipped, right gear again then hit firmly (jarringly) with both gear and stuck for the rollout.

The climb out en route to Taif wasn't much fun either. The landing at Taif was accomplished by me, from the right seat, and so was the final landing back at Jeddah.

Did I mention earlier, this trip might be labeled "remarkable?" There might be a better term for it, and I can think of a few, but I shall leave it to the imagination of the reader.

Some of the shortcomings mentioned above were discussed at length with the Convair Supervisor and the Chief Pilot. A written report was also submitted.

The shortcomings of the pilot pointed out in the above by no means reflects the competency of the rest of the pilots. Some of them might not always follow all the rules, mostly because of the nature of the country, but they were competent pilots. There were also some who might very well be labeled "exceptional."

This might be a good time to discuss survival in the desert. The large expanse of desert we had flown over between Riyadh and Gizan could easily be described as "the trackless" wasteland and probably has been. What would happen to us if we should crash land in that area and survive the impact? Some of us had been trained in survival tactics in various parts of the world, including desert areas. That training and knowledge would no doubt be helpful, but we would be no match for those treacherous desert sands.

When we landed in Riyadh, the temperature was 110° Fahrenheit. The desert would have been several degrees higher, making for a very harsh environment. We might make it, in the short term, but most likely we would depend on one or more of our passengers. Usually there was at least one passenger who had lived the Bedouin life and would be privy to the secrets of survival in the desert. We would be wise to let them lead.

Our large, two thousand pounds, shipment of household goods was overdue, we thought, and Marti was anxious to retrieve some items she needed to make day to day chores easier. The oven in our apartment in the hotel used bottled gas and was a most unpredictable thing. That's not what she called it on occasion, but I deem it best not to repeat comments from a lady in the heat of passion. In particular she wanted an electric skillet, purchased especially for use here. One day I spotted our shipment in their storage area and started making waves to get one or more of those crates opened to search for the needed items. Eventually someone reluctantly sent two Arab workers with a crowbar to the area with the proviso I am there to supervise. No problem, I intended to be there anyway. Marti had made out a list and I rummaged around till most of the items were located. The difficulty lay in transporting those things to the hotel. The distance was only about a city block, but things did not fit in the Volkswagen very well. Why not a truck furnished by the airline? Well, actually our request was a bit out of the normal routine of things and didn't fit the schedule of priorities. Marti was very pleased with the items I brought back and especially happy she would not have to mess with that @%*&$ stove anymore.

HAIRDRESSER

There was a serious requirement for hairdressers in Jedda to accommodate the needs of the ladies. Women could not own and operate regular commercial shops there, consequently the void was filled by qualified wives of the many employees of western companies. They set up shop in their own homes and advertised by word of mouth. Finding a good hairdresser was very high on Marti's list and was one of the first questions asked when we were entertained by others. When I was available, it was one of my chores (or opportunities) to drive her to an appointment and pick her up after. While I was away on trips, she would have the hotel clerk obtain a cab, escort her to the car door, and give instructions to the driver. Women were not supposed to ride in taxis alone, but necessity required some kind of compromise. The same procedure would be used on return to the hotel. The hairdresser would have her houseboy go find a taxi, bring him to the door and give proper instructions to get her safely back.

One of these appointments did not work quite as planned. The hotel clerk flagged down a taxi, escorted Marti to the vehicle, gave good instructions to the driver in Arabic and closed the door. The taxi drove off. Marti knew the way and additionally had learned the Arabic words for left, right, slowly and stop. When she recognized the street to turn on, as usual, she uttered "yameen," Arabic for "right." The driver went right on past the turn, not even slowing. She now shouted at him and using hand signals, got him to stop. The situation got worse as she began to suspect he did not understand Arabic and certainly not English. Anyway, with many hand signals and shouting, along with some degree of panic, she was able to direct him to the hairdresser's villa. The driver was newly arrived from Africa and had not yet learned rudimentary Arabic or had been instructed in a slightly different dialect.

KRAJI

Two weeks later, we were estatic in the news of an apartment opening for us. We would be moving into the Kraji building, a large multi-story home built by a local wealthy Arab. (He was also the Mayor of Jeddah.) He had intended the home for two of his wives, one living in each wing, but for some reason unknown to us, he deemed that plan a failure. He leased the building to the airline, who then converted it to generous apartments. Note: He built two large multi story homes directly across the street, built a wall around the two of them, and moved his wives in, one to each home. Our building was also walled completely, as was the custom, leaving room for a bricked courtyard surrounding the building and servants quarters which were located in the south portion.

Trees were all around the wall inside and out, providing shade and color. There were two trellises in the courtyard that supported rose vines to form an arch over stone benches. Just inside the main gate was what I suppose could be called the gatekeeper's quarters. The person who inhabited that building was a Pakistani and he dressed in a very exotic fashion. He wore a multicolored skull cap that was shaped around his ears. His long skirts were bright colors, usually

Roman Amphitheatre Ruins in Amman, Jordan

Lother Meyer, wife & two of his children after Red sea rescue. Wedji, Saudi Arabia, 1965

U. S. EMBASSY GOLF COURSE, JEDDAH, LT. COL. RANSTEAD

red or purple, and his vests were solid color with beads and sequins. He wore open toed leather sandals, no doubt good ones from Pakistan. Just what his actual duties were we never learned. We did not see him do much of anything except stroll regally around in his finery, especially on weekends when he entertained his men guests. Weekdays, he discarded the fancy vest, leaving him bare chested. Very likely he was not a threat to the women. Perhaps he really was just a guard. The massive iron double gates were never closed, and we drove freely in and out, parKing our vehicles inside the walls off the street. There was also a set of double iron gates that could open onto northbound Medina Road. These gates were never used, to my knowledge, as that was the rear of the building. Medina Road split into north and south one way roads for safety just about fifty yards south of the Kraji Building. The north and south corridors were separated by other buildings and walls for quite a distance. About a hundred yards north in between the two roads was Prince Faisal's Palace (later to become King). Possibly one could make a case that Prince Faisal was one of our neighbors. We did see him often as he rode by in one of the official automobiles and wave to him. He would respond likewise if he should see you.

There were two smaller apartments on the ground floor with a huge "lobby or reception" area plus a stairwell and the entry to the elevator. Above the ground floor were large apartments on each side of the elevator for three floors and a "penthouse" on the top floor, center. Here the elevator door opened directly into the apartment. Our apartment was on the second floor and very spacious. The entry hall was fifty five feet long and eight feet wide. All the floors were marble and the ceilings were ten feet. The furniture provided by the airline was very sparse and of poor quality, hardly a match for the quality of the building. Marti soon learned it was going to be "make do" time and dug in.

The city water system was very poor and quite limited, so most dwellings, including our building, depended on cisterns. One large cistern was near the entry to the courtyard and had to filled by water trucks almost every day. The water was then pumped from the well up to the top of the building and into a holding tank, thereby providing pretty good pressure at the faucet. I did have a picture of the truck and process, but decided not to print it. The truck itself was grimy and junky. The "nosepicker" that languidly watched as millions of bacteria were emptied into our cistern would only appall.This was not a very sanitary method, consequently Marti boiled all our drinking and cooking water. We then stored the good water in a five gallon crockery container which also had a filter installed, along with a tap. On occasion, we would learn something would go wrong with the delivery schedule and the water level in the tank would go below the intake. When this happened, if one were alert, you could hear a gurgling from above and realize the import. The response was to rush to the bathroom and turn on the tap to attempt filling the bathtub before the water was gone. While on this subject, I must mention Marti washed all dishes and vegetables in water purified with Clorox.

The city did have a water distribution system, but it was old and covered only a small portion of the growing city. Sometimes there was water and pressure in the lines, but very little, and besides, the furnished water was always suspect anyway. Most of the sprawling city had cisterns or tanks for storage and pressure as the Kraji building had. Many of these storge facilities were filled daily by donkey cart or by unsanitary water tank trucks. The donkey cart tanks were constructed with two steel fifty five gallon barrels welded together. These carts were refilled at various wells or access points on the city water system. Some photos are included to show carts and methods. Our system was, of course, by cistern and pump method.

The sewage system was of porous concrete, old, leaky and hampered by the near sea level drainage.

Our by now good friends, Polly and Joe Vincent, lived in the apartment directly above and that was very good news. The day we moved in, Polly brought down a loaf of her homemade bread and cemented the friendship forever. Our neighbor across the hall was Captain John Rich and he lived there alone as his wife could not acclimate to this environment. John also had a full time "house boy," a Palestinian who did the house work and, we learned later, also tended the fermenting mix destined to become "Sidiqi." John was a "bootlegger" in addition to his regular job as a pilot for the airline. He produced a very good product and had a thriving business. He even went a step further by adding coloring along with the proper flavoring to produce Scotch, Bourbon, Gin, Crème De Menthe, etc. We both liked John, but Marti was never comfortable with the thought of living next door to a "Bootlegger." She could not keep from conjuring up the image of the police raiding his apartment and connecting us with the operation. John admitted he made much more money from selling Sidiqi than his salary as a pilot.

Within two weeks we were moved in along with our entire household shipment. Marti was busy making drapes for the windows and otherwise improving the livability of our quarters while I was on trips. Later she would use her skills to produce some interesting additions to our seating arrangements by using orange crates, padding and colorful fabric.

Our move was very timely for David to enter the eighth grade in the local school provided by TWA. The curriculum was borrowed from the San Diego school system along with the requirements and grading system. The female teachers were, for the most part, wives of TWA employees or other large American companies in the area. They were very well qualified and well suited for jobs they performed. The male teachers were hired specifically for their qualifications and some of those had qualified wives who taught.

We were very fortunate to have such a quality school for David to allow him to maintain his place in the educational system.

David's friend from the hotel, Billy Majors, was shipped out to Rome, Italy to attend Notre Dame for his first year of high school. Jeddah did not offer classes beyond the eighth grade. Other students his age and older were attending schools in many far off places, such as Geneva, Paris, London, Berlin and places in the United States. This arrangement would prove to be very difficult for parents to keep tabs on their children. The parents were not fond of the situation, but Jeddah was where the job and "home" was located. What was the alternative?

Bob Major encountered a problem with young Bill's Notre Dame (Rome) schooling he had not anticipated. For some reason, he had opted to send by mail, Bill's room and board, tuition, etc, monthly. After two months, he received notice from the school that payment had not been received. Immediately he mailed two more checks to catch up on the payments. This situation did not improve for three more months. Bob was getting desperate as he did not want them to expel Billy for nonpayment. He got time off and flew to Rome in an attempt to straighten the mess out, taking with him whatever skimpy records he had. His bank records did not show deposits of the checks he had written, so he wrote a check for the entire delinquent amount. After returning to Jeddah, he talked to the owner of the hotel, who then initiated an internal investigation which soon revealed the problem. Bob had been turning his outgoing mail into the hotel desk for group mailing as was the custom. One of the individuals entrusted with receipt of the mail had been removing the stamps which he would later sell and was ditching the envelopes, along with the enclosed checks. Bob changed his method of payment. This was not an isolated incident and was not completely resolved for some time.

Fifteenth of August, 1965, was the first of several very long internal trips we flew in the Convair. The time involved required a third pilot, so I would join Captains Dew and Wright on this one. The route would be Jeddah, Medina, northeast to Quassim in the desert north of Riyadh, thence to Dhahran on the east coast, then turn back and proceed to Riyadh. From Riyadh we would head for Quassim again, and here we would pick up some very tasty "hub hubs" (wa-

termelons) for our own consumption. Who would have
thought this presumably arid desert area could produce large
quantities of fruits and vegetables? They did though. The
"hub hubs" were the round variety and probably weighed on
average about ten pounds, and were sweet and juicy. They
were as good as or better than any I had ever tasted. Better
yet, we only paid about a dollar each and bought some extra
for our friends in Jeddah. From Quassim, the flight continued to Medina then on home to Jeddah. The landings at
Medina and Jeddah were at night and I made both. The total
flight time was ten hours and fifty minutes, but the "duty
time" totaled eighteen hours. A very long day.

HOUSEBOY

There was some good news on my return. Polly had located a "house boy" for Marti. He was a medium colored
Sudanese, slender, about six feet, named Omar. He spoke
good accented English, had a very nice friendly quiet manner
and was neat in appearance. His duties would consist of
normal daily house cleaning along with washing the dishes.
No cooking involved. After our prompting, he told us he
had learned English in a Christian school while growing up
in the African country of Sudan. He had come to Saudi
Arabia as his country was very poor and there were no jobs
available. It was not made clear just how long he would be
with us, as his former employer had returned to the states
for a leave of some sort. When those people returned, he
would go back to them as agreed. Polly's house boy was a
Yemen and he had a good friend back home he would get in
touch with and ask him if he would come back and work for
us when Omar left. That sort of communicating took considerable time as the postal service could not be utilized. The
usual procedure was to get a "letter writer" in the souk to
write their message in Arabic, and then find one of their
countrymen who was going home to hand carry the letter. A
time consuming and dubious method of communication.

Omar, our first houseboy, was with us for about six weeks before his former employer came back. Within a week, our new house boy, having received his friend's long distance message, arrived and showed up one morning at our door with his friend as "interpreter." Unfortunately, the "interpreter" could not speak much more English than he. With a little outside help, we were able to understand and get the salary, duties, time, etc. settled. The new house boy was a small (five feet five inches tall), well built young Yemen about thirty years old or so. Pretty hard to tell about his age, and we felt sure he did not know how old he was either. His name was "Thalbot" to be pronounced with the "h" from far back in the throat. Not an easy thing for us foreigners to do. We settled on calling him "Talbot" and he accepted.

Talbot did not speak any English, and Marti at this time knew only a very few Arabic words, and none of them were helpful for communicating his duties and or shortcomings in properly completing his work. My Arabic was much better, but more work related and not very helpful in this area. There would be an awful lot of frustration generated in this arrangement on both sides, it turned out. However, we learned Talbot was honest, diligent, trustworthy, and pretty much had his own way of getting the job done. A sometimes uneasy and unspoken truce ensued, and the situation would endure on both sides. He never did understand the need or use of Clorox in the water for washing vegetables, the table top or dishes. Marti had to keep a close eye on that.

Marti had shown Talbot how to use Clorox in the white load while doing the laundry and had stressed, white only. Do not use for colored clothing. Everyone knows "Murphy's" law, I am sure. And, of course, it applied here. One day I returned home to be confronted with a livid, almost incoherent, wife. Disconnected words flew as I patiently weathered the mini storm. Those words began to connect as she held up the new plaid shirt she had bought me in the states. The plaid was gone, replaced by various sized polka dots of indeterminate origin. Talbot knew he was getting "what for" and why, and he kept angrily repeating,

"Madame say, Madame say." He was right in his way. The details were just fuzzy. Summoning up patience and limited Arabic, I was able to help him understand and for him not to worry about it. We parted on good terms and he returned the next day exhibiting his usual workmanlike demeanor.

SECRET

August 18, 1965, I would depart Jeddah at 0600 bound for Gizan, a port town on the Red Sea, located near the Yemen border. This was the original "slave port" for the lucrative import of slaves from Africa. One could still make out the outline of the pens or compounds where slaves were kept awaiting transport to various destinations in the Arab world. One of the stone "lookout towers" just west of town appeared to be in good repair. The tower was multistoried and appeared large enough to hold several men, and left me with the impression it was a mini Castle of sorts. There were some who hinted the trade was still practiced in a small way. Perhaps.

From Gizan, we would continue on to Najran for offloading passengers and supplies. It was necessary to deplane during the short stay on the ground to supervise refueling, check in with the agent in the passenger tent for information on the outgoing load, plus engage in a little PR. The "soil" in this area was about the color of grayish khaki and the consistency was about the same as talcum powder. Little puffs of this "dust" would arise as one walked, leaving the residue on shoes, trousers, etc. Even a moderate breeze would pick the desert powder up and deposit it on your person. This "stuff" could not be casually brushed off, and remained there the rest of the trip. The shine on my shoes was ruined each time, requiring cleaning with soap and water before attempting a coat of polish.

Thirty minutes after landing at Najran, we would depart for a "secret" airport located about two hundred sixty miles on a heading of about eighty degrees, flying over an unmarked desert. We would hope our "dead reckoning"

MARTI AT SILVER SOUK, JEDDAH, SA

Normandy Hotel, Beirut, Lebanon, 1966

Normandy Hotel Bar, Anoir on the left, 1966

navigation would prove to be accurate enough to enable finding the village of Al Sulayyal and the nearby newly built airfield. Finding the "ridge line," which is marked on maps as "Jabal Tuwayq," that runs south from Riyadh for hundreds of miles should be fairly easy, as it can be seen from a distance. The village should be just beyond the ridge line at an altitude of about two thousand feet. However, if we should miss it due to drift, which direction should we look for the village or airport? Actually, as it turned out, we found both with very little effort and only a small amount of anxiety. Allah with us again, I suppose. The airport belonged to the military and consisted of a ten thousand foot paved runway, complete with all the necessary facilities to support an air wing. The airfield was indeed classified "secret;" however, they decided the time had come to start using the national airline to supply their needs and rotate military personnel. Later, I would fly with other captains and help guide them finding the elusive checkpoints across the desert.

Possibly I am repeating something, but it is important to realize there are no radio aids for our use in navigating the desert stretches of this country in those times. When we became comfortable with knowledge and checkpoints for any route, we many times deliberately flew off course and parallel to locate and identify areas on the ground. These areas would be marked on our map to be used in the event we were sometime in the future blown off course during low visibility conditions and had the need to establish our current location.

Our trip was continued on to Riyadh where we stayed overnight in the non-plush environment of the Sahara Palace Hotel. The return trip to Jeddah the next day was uneventful. My shoes and trousers were a mess.

FEDAMA

My time with Marti and David was cut short by a knock on our door in the very early hours of 20 August. The young Arab lad from operations informed me I was needed for a special trip scheduled to depart in less than an hour. The "special" routing was Jeddah, Gizan, Najran, Sulayyil, and then Riyadh where we were to remain overnight, returning the following day on a reverse route. We departed exactly one hour after I was notified. During takeoff, I noted low fuel pressure on number two engine, circled the field and landed. We performed the necessary checks, regaining proper pressure, and resumed the flight. This time all was well, and we landed safely at Gizan almost three hours later.

As usual, I deplaned to oversee refueling, loading, and checking with the agent for any information that might prove useful and follow up. The airline agent informed me, when asked, there would be a full load of passengers and ten bags of salt weighing about four hundred kilos. Therefore, with passengers, baggage, and salt, we would be at maximum takeoff weight when we departed Gizan for Najran on that temperature day. While watching the wiry Yemen workers load the bags of salt, I noticed they were straining a bit handling those supposed forty kilo bags (one kilo equals 2.2 pounds). That did not look good to me, so I stopped the loading. The agent came over to ask what was going on, so I asked him to lift one of those bags for me. He declined, so I turned to my co-pilot, Ludwig Sigurdson, a strapping six feet one inch Icelander in his twenties, to pick one up. Ludwig struggled in his attempt as it weighed, not forty kilos, but eighty. No wonder the Yemen were having a bit of trouble handling those bags! Had I allowed that load, I would have been about fifteen hundred pounds over our maximum gross weight for takeoff.

I ordered all the bags removed. The agent immediately attempted negotiating to take half the bags. No sale, remove them all. There is little point in attempting to interpret the Arab words and phrases he was uttering as he turned and stalked back to the terminal.

The passengers were soon on board and we taxied to the end of the runway for takeoff. All seemed well as we ran through the checklist and the engine "run-up" procedure, and were soon rolling down the runway for takeoff. Just before reaching a good speed for takeoff, fuel pressure started dropping on number two engine and the power declined. We promptly aborted and, after clearing the runway, initiated an engine run-up. Fuel pressure was not good. We returned to the ramp where we would off load passengers, while I called Jeddah Operations on our long range radio to inform them of our problem. Within a short time, Jeddah advised they would send another aircraft with a fuel pump and a mechanic. The aircraft and crew on the way would replace us and continue with our original schedule, as we would not have sufficient crew duty time to complete the trip. We would wait for the repair and return the aircraft to Jeddah. Armed with this information, I proceeded to the terminal to brief the agent and inform the passengers of the change in plans. My briefing was short, but my hope was to give them as good an educated guess on the delay as possible. It appeared they would have at least four hours' delay, possibly five. After letting them know they were free to return to aircraft and retrieve their hand baggage, I followed them out.

While standing near the bottom of the stairs from the aircraft, I accidentally bumped one the passengers as he deplaned. Without thinking, I immediately responded with, "Excuse me!" in English. His response was, "Not at all," in a definite British accent. That response coming from a person with his appearance was a complete surprise! He appeared to be about five feet six, a little on the heavy side, possibly forty to fifty years old with blue black curly hair. His dress (uniform) ended just below the knees in the typical Yemen soldier look, complete with dagger on a wide black belt held up with the traditional shoulder strap. He wore leather sandals with ankle length black socks. Even with the surprise, I managed to respond with, "Your English is excellent." He returned my smile with, "Thank you very much," in that amazing British accent. He continued on to the terminal and I vowed to seek him out later during our long wait for the rescue aircraft arrival.

After insuring all baggage, freight, salt, etc. had been removed, I secured the aircraft and returned to the terminal.

There, I located my British speaking acquaintance that I had bumped. He was seated at a table with another Yemen who appeared to be a teenager. Upon introducing me, the older person identified himself as Brigadier General Salih Fedama of the Yemen Army and the young man, his son, Farook. They were drinking sodas from bottles and asked if I would join them. With pleasure, I assured the general. After explaining a little about myself, I asked about his background, specifically mentioning where he was educated. He let me know he was Yemen and was in Cairo near the beginning of World War Two attending the university. Some of the professors were British, which partially explained his accent. The Germans were all over Egypt and when the war began, he, along with most of his peers, was involuntarily added to the German fighting force. They were sent to Germany for training, most returning to Egypt to fight the English and Americans. He stayed and fought with the German army for two years. He gained a commission while in German Army, achieving officer rank, but that part was not clear. He returned to Egypt after the war to continue his education.

In the early 1960's, war with Egypt appeared imminent, which prompted him to return to his native country of Yemen to offer his services in defense. He became the leader of a very substantial fighting force and was given credit for defeating the Egyptian Army in the mountains of Yemen. Our long wait for the aircraft from Jeddah allowed him time to explain in part how that was accomplished.

The Egyptians invaded Yemen about one hundred twenty miles south of Gizan and a little north of Al Huydadah with a very large force and were allowed to advance with ease for a few miles. Soon, they entered a valley that would eventually lead them right on up through that mountainous area to the capital of San'a. General Fedama deployed small forces each side of the invading army and began harassing them with hit and run tactics daily. When the invading force was well into the mountains, in the area where he wanted them, he waited with his small army. One night when the moon did not light up the very dark sky, his forces surrounded a large contingent of the Egyptian Army and waited for the soldiers to settle down for the night while their fires grew dim.

When the time seemed right, he and all his men crept into the Egyptian tents with their very sharp daggers in hand and quietly slit the throats of every soldier they could locate. When daylight finally came, Fedama and his men were gone and the entire Egyptian camp was quiet. There were no survivors. They were found later that morning by scouts sent forward to find out why they were not moving. When the word got back to the main force, they seemed to lose interest in the advance and soon started a retreat. That part of the war was all but over.

It is impossible for me to write this story the way it was told to me. General Fedama was a very charismatic individual and a quite a story teller. He held me fascinated with his recounting of their creeping in under the cover of darkness, knives drawn, his hundreds of men moving stealthily over rocky ground making not a sound, and later, his sound effects of the slitting of throats. He also was using very dramatic gestures and grimacing as he simulated the slaughter. Not good stuff for the weak of stomach or heart.

My throat was dry and I raised my bottle of orange soda to have a deep swig. As the liquid started to flow, I saw a black object enter the neck of the bottle heading for my open mouth. Knocking over my chair as I headed for the open door, I attempted closing off my throat. When I reached the outside I spewed orange soda and I hoped the fly along with it. The General and his son tried their best not to laugh, but when I joined all the others in laughter, they too joined with great amusement.

It was at this point when someone shouted with alarm and pointed to the east. There, was a huge black cloud approaching quickly just over the foothills. The ominous roll cloud preceding that storm was already picking up clouds of dust as it bore down on the airport. Realizing the DC-3 was facing the wrong way to make it through that storm without damage, I shouted for my co-pilot and raced for the aircraft.

Quickly boarding, I looked around for Ludwig, realized he was nowhere near, slammed the door shut and ran forward. No time for a checklist this time. Quickly starting both engines, my first option was to take off ahead of the storm and wait it out. Even with a suspect fuel pump, I felt it an acceptable risk with an empty, light aircraft. That option was quickly removed by the sudden wind direction change, as evidenced by the wind sock. Just ninety seconds more and I would have been out of there! Now, in order to save the aircraft, I would have to "fly" it through on the ground. I waited for the storm to hit. Already I was nosed into the approaching wind and intended to keep it that way. A portable stairway used for boarding larger aircraft started moving from my right front and it was picking up speed as it flew past. Seconds later, the storm engulfed the aircraft and we began to buffet badly. Almost instantly, visibility was zero in blowing dust coupled with the darkness of the cloud itself. By this time, I was using engine power to keep from being blown away, literally "flying" on the ground. The dust was now long gone and we were being pounded by heavy rain. Luckily, I had turned the instrument lights on. It was now so dark I had to use instruments and feel to keep contact with the ground. Fortunately the huge storm was a "fast mover" and soon passed with bright sunshine now in my face. That procedure should never be a pilot's chosen method to save an airplane. After engine shutdown, I departed the aircraft and looked around; there was not a single piece of equipment left on the airport. Running water and puddles were visible everywhere. All the passengers and airport personnel were safely inside the concrete terminal and welcomed me back.

But where was my co-pilot? The agent then told me, Ludwig had borrowed his motorcycle and went to town shortly after we deplaned, hours ago. Ludwig was a very likeable guy, but a bit of a "free spirit" and inclined to be a tad adventurous. His absence came as no surprise, but I viewed his long stay with considerable apprehension. The people in Gizan were described to me as religious fundamentalists and not overly friendly to strangers. They were possibly even "slave traders." The general's son pointed out an object leaving town and remarked it looked like a person on a motorcycle. Much too far for us to make out, but yes, there was a moving vehicle of some sort coming this way fast. Much to my chagrin, the motorcycle pulled over to a camel caravan heading in our direction. The caravan stopped and the agent became very agitated as he explained with his limited English, those people were not friendly and he was in danger. The general confirmed that, but pointed out there is nothing we can do. We waited and watched. After what seemed a long time, but actually only a few minutes, the motorcycle was on its way again and soon Ludwig came roaring in with a flourish, stopping right on the mark. He got off and came towards me with his usual big grin, like, "what a wonderful world," saying, "That was some storm," and, "I got some good pictures." My god, what else has he done? How did he get out of town alive, taking pictures of those people? Later, I learned he stopped and had the Arabs on the camel train pose. Ludwig's charm is engaging but his luck is phenomenal. What to say? Deciding that nothing was more appropriate, I said, "Welcome back, and stick around."

The aircraft from Jeddah with our new fuel pump and mechanic soon arrived and within an hour, the pump was installed, checked and ready to go. After escorting the general and his son to the aircraft that would take him through Najran and Sulayyil on to Riyadh, I returned to our aircraft. Our return to Jeddah was uneventful.

Luckily, I would see and talk with the general many more times before my return to the states. Either he would be a passenger on my aircraft or I would see him on the ground someplace and chat a bit.

SAD NOTE: Shortly after my return to the States in June of 1966, I read a dispatch from the AP in Aden. The news was tragic. In part it read as follows: "One of Royalist Yemen's most outspoken leaders, Sheik Ali Salih Fedama, has been ambushed and killed in foothills near Mudieh, 200 miles from here, British intelligence said today. A British spokesman said guerrillas, acting on Egyptian army instructions, laid the ambush yesterday. Four persons died with the Sheik, including his eldest son. Another son, Farook Fedama, 16, is in chains in San'a, Yemen's capital, where constant torture has robbed him of the use of his legs, says British intelligence.

The Sheik was forty-five years old, and in WWII won an Iron Cross while serving with the German army on the Russian front. He subsequently became Governor of Mjubah province in Yemen."

The "general" was dead. His young son, Farook as good as dead from the constant torture. No reason to torture him except for their twisted pleasure. That part of the world was and is a very dangerous place.

Captain Cruse and I departed for Aden on August 27 in a Convair with passengers and cargo. Aden was as usual hot, windy, and dusty. We entertained thoughts of the duty-free store across town, but a British Army major advised things were a bit touchy these days. He would have truck load of soldiers take us, but he would not go. We did not have to give that problem much more thought and preceded with preparations for return to Jeddah. The Egyptians were constantly stirring the pot, here and through out Yemen. They wanted to control the whole area. Our return to Jeddah was routine.

MARTI'S FATHER DIED

The following day, August 28, 1965, we received word through TWA sources, Marti's father had died suddenly the day before. Steps were already being taken for the necessary travel passes, exit visas, routing, etc. Personnel needed to know who was going and when. The decision was a little difficult. David had already announced intentions of attending the local school, which would commence in three days. We wanted to get him started along with his peers so he would not have to play "catch-up" when he returned. What arrangements could we make for him while I was gone on trips? The answers were not good. In the end, we decided he must go with Marti. He would be of great help to her on the long arduous journey back to San Diego and support while there. Those suppositions proved out in the end.

Both were provided with positive space tickets and the visas came through with unusual dispatch. Within two days they were on the way and I was on my own again. Marti and David would not return for a month. Attending to all the problems associated with his death and related matters stretched their stay beyond Marti's original thinking.

While Marti and David were gone, I continued flying as many trips as possible. When they needed a pilot to replace another, I was ready. Extra trip scheduled? Count on me. One such extra trip was to take Prince Hassan from Jeddah to Najran for some kind of meeting. He came up to the cockpit right after takeoff and we talked for three hours. The prince was an interesting young man and extremely bright. The prince was a very active participant in planning the course of defense of his country against the Communist insurgents trying to topple the Royalist government of Yemen. He was very open in his discussion of the difficulties, probably telling me more than I really wanted to know. There was no doubt in my mind the information was really classified. It would not be a good idea to repeat any of this to my friends, as even a hint to the Saudis I might know something could get me in serious trouble.

When we taxied in, at least a hundred of his troops, maybe many more, were there to greet him. Prince Sudari's secretary escorted him off the plane. He also recognized me, offering the usual Arab greeting and I replied in kind.

We stayed on the ground waiting for almost two hours. The prince did not return, but one of his commanders, along with ten of his soldiers, arrived to go to Jeddah for some R & R. The agent checked them on board after announcing to all, weapons must be unloaded before boarding. As the first man started to step up, the agent took his rifle from him and rapidly worked the bolt flipping cartridges out onto the powdery soil. The rest got the message in a hurry and were working their bolts, being careful to catch each cartridge before it fell in that powder. The first man was still on his knees searching frantically in the sand for his precious ammunition as the others started boarding. Oddly enough, they were very good natured about the situation, laughingly chiding their compatriot, still busy in the sand.

The return flight was routine, arriving back in Jeddah after a ten hour duty day. My shoes and trousers were coated with desert dust as usual, requiring some attention later on. The hotel room would be lonely. Not in the mood to fix my own dinner, I opted to drive over to the MAAG house for a drink or two with the Air Force folks, followed with a decent meal. Maybe I would stay for a movie or, better yet, see if I could join in a table tennis game with some decent players.

September 18, Captain Fred Wright and I would depart Jeddah for Taif, the first of many flights required to transport the Royal family members, their servants and luggage back to Riyadh. The summer season was officially over. Transporting these people was always a big hassle. The usual loading and flight rules were bent or simply ignored for the most part. We had to consider safety of flight, however, and had to be ever vigilant against outright overload. Many times I stood under the aircraft and counted bags, estimating weight as it was tossed out of the trucks. When my estimate reached what I considered the limit, I would enlist the aid of a nearby worker and start moving bags under the plane to the other side, leaving them on the ground. When one of the trucks had unloaded, I would direct the driver around the aircraft to pick up the excess for loading on the next flight out. Luckily, I was never challenged on this. Had I allowed those bags to be loaded and then calculated we were overloaded, we would have been in deep #%*." They had the idea that if there was room, then it must be alright. We would have had an unenviable confrontation. Royal flights were a Royal pain, Baksheesh notwithstanding. After an uneasy ground time of one hour forty minutes, we proceeded to Riyadh, where the passengers and baggage were deposited. We wasted no time loitering in Riyadh and hastily departed for Jeddah, empty.

KHARTOUM

Khartoum, a place of mystery, adventure and history, especially for the British in indulging in misadventure, intrigue and disaster. My next trip, September 20th, 1965 would take me there.

Captain Money and I departed Jeddah in a Convair for Port Sudan. Several passengers deplaned there and we picked up ten more for the two hour flight, south and east to Khartoum. The city of Khartoum was located at the confluence of the Blue and White Nile rivers. Certainly was not difficult to find. There was some problem picking out the airport itself as everything seemed to blend in rather well, under somewhat hazy conditions.

My anticipation of seeing the fabled city close up via a taxi ride through the streets was dimmed, then quashed by the news there would be no time for that as they wanted a fast turnaround. In less than an hour we departed for Port Sudan with thirty one passengers. During the climb out, Khartoum called on the radio, relaying a message from Port Sudan. Port Sudan requested we over fly them and proceed to Jeddah. We contacted Port Sudan as we neared the area to see if they had changed their mind. The agent there told us he had thirteen passengers for Jeddah, but knew we could not take them all for lack of seats. He knew the ones that could not get on the aircraft would rebel at the news and a riot would no doubt ensue. We had witnessed demonstrations of that nature and gladly flew on, appreciating his good judgment. Maybe some other time I would get to see Khartoum close up, on the ground.

Three days later, I would see another of those situations where an overload would cause serious problems. This flight was through Port Sudan to Asmara, Ethiopia, where we would deplane passengers, refuel, pick up more passengers and return through Port Sudan to Jeddah. This airport was high elevation and on hot days, the gross weight of the aircraft for takeoff could be quite limited. This was one of those days. The agent knows how to calculate how much load the aircraft can take and adjusts the number of passengers and cargo accordingly. However, it is to his personal financial advantage to put on board as many as he can (baksheesh). He allowed a thirteen hundred pound overload. Naturally, I counted the number of passengers, checked his figures and disallowed the load. He must remove passengers or cargo, to reduce the weight. His arguments to me fell on deaf ears. He now was frantic and wanted me to pick the ones to get off. My answer was as polite and firm as I could make it. No.

Before it was over, he and three of his helpers, along with six passengers, were injured in the melee. I had locked the cockpit door after ushering him out. The whole mess lasted an hour and we finally blocked (departed) out an hour and a half late.

The way the agent worked his little scam was as follows. He informs the waiting passengers there is no more room after checking in the required number and allowing them through. Suddenly he has some of the unlucky ones approach him with very generous offers to get them on that flight. There are empty seats of course, because we are limited by weight, not number of seats. Then he slips them on board at the last minute, does not bother to add their weight, and steps forward to inform the captain all are on board, ready to go. He hands the release to the captain for signature, retrieves it and departs the aircraft. (To thwart that possibility, I had alerted my steward to let me know if any passengers were added after I had done the count.) The previous flight two days earlier he had gotten away with it. The captain on that flight had not done his homework and was remiss in not questioning the number of passengers on board. That flight was overloaded on takeoff. Luck was with him.

During the month of September, I had flown one hundred thirty hours, the maximum allowed under the rules in force. Saudi Airlines abided by ICAO rules and had adopted the United States FAA rules as well. Pilots were also limited to three hundred thirty hours in any three month period. Those limits were really stretched during the annual Hadj when the pilgrims were being flown in and right after on the outbound portion.

All hours above seventy five hours a month were paid as overtime at a very nice hourly rate. I continued to fly as much as possible the rest of our time there. That pay covered all our expenses each month. We were able to save a rather nice nest egg in those years.

Marti and David arrived back in Jeddah right after the first of October, and I was there to meet them. They made it through the chattering, gesturing, and shoving babble of the Customs lines without injury or incident. Ushering them out through that entire moving mob was not a simple job, but we got through. Two of* my* friends with cars were outside waiting to help load all the extra luggage they had brought back. Marti took the time to shop while gone and now having a pretty good idea of the things she would need, had stocked up. The vehicles were full as we proceeded "home" to the Kraji building.

The following two days were rest up time for the both of them. Going "straight through" on that long arduous journey is debilitating. David popped back without difficulty, but Marti took a little longer.

The third day, the bus picked David up in front of our building and he was off to school. We were anxious to learn how he was accepted and what impact that very late start might have on him. David was not easily daunted, and seemed to fit right in. There was little doubt in our minds; it would be difficult for him, entering a new school and a month late at that. When he returned from school that afternoon, he was upbeat and remarked the school was ok and he felt he would like the teachers. If he was carrying a heavy load, it did not show. That was a relief.

STRANGE STORY

On the fourteenth of May, 1966, we were called out for a Royal Charter flight to Wedj located on the Red Sea shore north of Jeddah. First Officer Rasheed would be the Trainee Pilot. There were eight passengers waiting to board, six of whom had a very strange, exotic tale to relate. There was a man, Lothar Meyer, his wife, three small daughters, twelve, ten and one and a half years old. They were accompanied by a nineteen year old friend. The other two passengers were Saudi Secret Police sent up to Wedj to accompany them back to Jeddah. Their story was they had left Egypt in a small sail boat with the intentions of sailing through the Suez Canal, on through the Red Sea, around the horn at Aden and on to India. They had made it through the Suez and part way down the coast of Arabia before a storm broke the mast and took away their sail. They had drifted helplessly for days until spotted by some local fishermen and towed into a small port at the village of Buwaydah, several miles north of Wedj. They were out of food and water and were not in very good condition when rescued. They were viewed with suspicion by the Saudis, hence the escort by the Secret Police. They were held in Jeddah several days for questioning and checking of their story before being allowed to proceed. It must have seemed weird, stupid and suspicious for that man and wife to subject those small children to such a hazardous attempt. So the Saudis had to check it out.

They were held in Jeddah for quite some time before release. I am not sure if they ever got their boat back to continue their ill fated voyage. See photo page.

SADDAM?

Most of the flights I went on were just routine, but there were a few that turned out to be very interesting and or very dangerous. One of those "very interesting" and quite possibly very dangerous started out on April 14th, 1966 with a routine flight delivering passengers to and through Medina, on to Beirut and a turn around back to Jeddah.

The aircraft was a Convair 340, HZABD and my first officer was N. Alloush, a Saudi National. Too bad I have forgotten the name of my radio operator, as he played a crucial role in the outcome. Without his input, this story would have had an entirely different ending and could have ended in disaster for me.

Shortly after our arrival in Beirut and while I was making preparations for the return, I was called to a meeting with the airport manager. He advised me there was a change in itinerary and there would be a short delay as they were waiting the arrival of some VIPs that were to be flown to Baghdad. The request seemed reasonable to me. I asked about the number of people involved to allow me to figure the load and add extra fuel if necessary.

The manager told me there would be seven passengers and they were all important military officers and that I should not speak to them. That was all right with me. I usually had no reason to talk to the passengers anyway.

Luckily, there was further delay as the passengers were still in Beirut and would be driven to the airport as soon as possible.

Alloush was working on a flight plan, so I went back out to the aircraft to check on the refueling and provisioning. When I went on board, I spoke to the radio operator and told him of the change of plans that we were to fly to Baghdad. He had his headset on and removed them to listen to me. That is when he related the startling news that the President of Iraq had been killed in a helicopter crash right after takeoff and there was fighting going on at the airport and in Baghdad. He had been listening to all that on our long range single side band radio, unaware we were to fly there. His English was not good and the extent of my Arabic was too limited to be sure I understood the alarming message. Immediately I returned to Operations to advise Alloush and asked him to go talk to the radio operator to clarify that disturbing story. Then I proceeded to the airport manager's office to question him about the situation. He was very cagey and reluctant to answer any of my questions. My consternation was mounting.

First Officer Alloush came in about that time and confirmed the story the radio operator had related to me. Then he and the airport manager entered into a rather long conversation in Arabic. Shortly the manager spoke to me and agreed there were difficulties in Baghdad and it was very important these Iraqi Army officers return immediately. I must go, he said.

Thereupon I informed him I was a retired United States Air Force Officer and carried identity to that effect. Therefore, I could not fly into a country where military operations were occurring, possibly even a coup in progress. This could place me in a very dangerous position and could embarrass the United States. The Iraqi government could accuse me of spying and or a part of any coup in progress, if I were a party to returning opposition officers. I did not relish becoming a principle in an international incident.

The airport manager was not pleased and ordered me to take the flight. Upon hearing that, I returned to the aircraft and, using the long range radio, called Jeddah and asked to speak to the airline operations officer. Captain Awliya, a Saudi National, formerly an active airline captain soon answered. Captain Awliya spoke very good English and was able to think for himself and make decisions. He understood the problem immediately and concurred with my analysis of the situation. He asked me to remain on standby and he would get back to me shortly. Later he told me he had contacted the Beirut airport manager and had made alternate arrangements. Ten or fifteen minutes later, Captain Awliya called me back and asked that I return to Jeddah.

We returned to Jeddah without incident, although a wee bit off schedule. First Officer Alloush confided in me he was very happy we did not go to Baghdad as things were not good there.

Note: Had I not specifically asked Alloush to confer with the radio operator and relay the information to me, he would not have offered any input, nor would he have intervened with the airport manager on our behalf. That's just the way it was. (Much later, Alloush had upgraded through the smaller aircraft and became a 707 captain shortly after my return to Saudi Arabia in 1971.)

Years later, I read a newspaper account of a partial history of Saddam Hussein, including his imprisonment in Iraq for political reasons and his actions after release. That caused me to investigate a little to learn if it was possible he was one of those seven Army officers I had refused to fly to Baghdad. In 1964, Hussein was jailed by some "rightist" military officers who opposed the Baathist takeover. In 1966, Hussein had escaped from prison and set up a Baathist internal security system known as the Jihaz Haneen. Through political influence provided by his older cousin, General Ahmad Hassan al-Bakr, Hussein became deputy Secretary-General of the Baathists in 1966.

The time frame fits and agrees with what I was told at the time of the incident. I believe he was indeed one of those seven.

WARNING: An irrevocable curse has been sworn against the person or persons revealing the name of the pilot involved in leaving Saddam behind in Beirut. ☺

Leonard V. Porter, Captain TWA

DAMASCUS

This was to be my first trip into Damascus, Syria. There were many such flights as ours to various countries and cities in the Middle East taking school teachers to their respective homes for "vacation." (barak in Arabic)) Most schools in Saudi Arabia previously had taught only the Koran, and those teachers were all men. No Saudi women were allowed. And the men were not certified. In recent times the Saudis had allowed foreign teachers in to teach almost a regular curriculum. They came from Syria, Egypt, Lebanon, Pakistan, and India, among others. We had already returned many and would continue to do so. When school reconvened, reverse flights would be necessary.

We departed Jeddah in the afternoon, proceeding to Medina, thence to Amman, Jordan then on to Damascus, arriving about eight PM. It was a very clear evening with enough moonlight to light the nearby partially snow covered mountains. The city lights sparkled in that crisp clear atmosphere. Captain Ted Hunt made the approach and landing, while I observed and tended to co-pilot duties.

We only stayed on the ground for an hour to offload passengers and refuel, and then back to Jeddah direct, landing about 1:48 A.M. Rather an uneventful flight this time, unlike some to come.

Another flight to Damascus in January, 1966 was very interesting and would result in a mini crisis before it was over. This time we departed at 4:30 a.m., transiting Medina, Tabuk, Amman, and arriving Damascus at 11:07 a.m. The crew was transported to a nice hotel in downtown Damascus. We would stay here overnight and return to Jeddah the next day.

We knew it was not prudent to assume all was safe in the city. There were many demonstrations often, and a good many would be anti-westerner. There was a Syrian in the city that had lived in the United States for twenty-five years. He had returned and opened a small bar in the city. He spoke excellent English and was pro-American. After checking in and cleaning up a bit, I called him to learn the present atmosphere in the city. All is well, he reported, and invited us to his bar for a drink, food and a chat.

About five o'clock, we hailed a taxi and went to see him. He was delighted to chat with two Americans and insisted on free drinks. Joe was a very interesting person and certainly had his finger on the pulse of the city. The first important message he had for us concerned security. He wanted us to know just how serious things could be. Just last week, he related, a British crew stayed overnight in our hotel. He had warned them not to leave their rooms, as a very dangerous group was preparing to demonstrate in the streets. The crew could hear the terrible noise of the demonstrators roaming in the streets just after nightfall. One of the pilots went down to the lobby to find out what he could. Just after he arrived in the lobby, the crowd was passing in front of the hotel. They saw the pilot, recognizing a westerner through the plate glass windows, and rushed into the lobby, grabbed and dragged him out to the street. Before it was all over, they had beaten him to death. Joe said he did not want to tell us about that incident over the phone. He knew we would be safe tonight, so just waited till we arrived to brief us.

The food Joe later prepared and offered was a bit strange to my palette but I had to admit, quite tasty. I don't remember the Arabic name of it. He briefed us on conditions in town and advised we would be safe to go to the souk and browse. Joe reminded us before we departed to be sure and call him the next time in town for a rundown on local situations. He had certainly given us reason enough to heed his warning.

After thanking Joe for his generosity and friendship, we proceeded to the souk in a taxi. Just outside the covered portion of the souk were many tables and stalls covered with all manner of things for sale. There were fruits, vegetables, and many different kinds of nuts, figs, dates, etc, covering every bit of space. The pistachio nuts were very large, cheap, and too tempting to pass up. I bought five pounds! We moved on to the entry of the covered souk, taking in all of the usual busy sounds coming from all sides. There were many different modes and styles of dress evident amongst the shoppers and browsers indicating area or tribal affiliations. Some of them were from other nearby countries along with a smattering of westerners and all were busy. We were careful not to offend as we weaved through the crowded shoppers. No one seemed to pay much attention to us for which we were grateful. A street sign in English sure got my attention. The sign read; "A Street Called Straight." My first thought was, "Could this be the biblical street? Much later, someone confirmed that really was, "The Street Called Straight." Anyway, it wasn't straight at all. We followed it for a short distance, but soon turned and retraced our steps to avoid getting lost.

There was so much to see and hear that later I had trouble sorting it all out. My intentions were to return as often as possible to help me remember all the many interesting sights. It was not to be. Our schedule simply did not work out to allow many more visits to the souk. I think I may have eaten too many pistachio nuts.

The next morning, we departed for return to Jeddah via the same route we covered the day before only in reverse order. As we climbed out after takeoff, I got a good view of the surrounding area and realized an instrument approach to their airport would be tricky. The mountains encroach on their space on three sides, not allowing any room for maneuvering. The city is only open to the south. I immediately made an entry in my log to that effect. The return to Jeddah was routine except I ate too many pistachio nuts last night.

About a month later, I took another flight into Damascus that did not turn out as well as the described above. The weather was good; the city was again a beautiful sight as we entered the pattern for a landing. Again we stayed overnight in the same hotel, but with a difference. When I called Joe to learn about the current situation, he warned the city was not safe for westerners any place. Do not leave the hotel and do not appear in the lobby. It was best to stay in our rooms all night. Don't leave until the crew bus comes for us in the morning. We, of course, followed that advice. We remembered our previous briefing about the British crew that had stayed in the hotel and the captain's brutal murder by rioters.

Shortly after arriving at the airport and while preparing for departure, the steward came to me with the news that Customs had lost our passports. I went to see the agent in charge, and he reiterated the passports could not be found. Having experienced something of this nature before, I said, "When you locate them, let me know. If they are not found by 0500, we will return to the hotel and stay until the passports can be located." This "lost passport" situation had all the earmarks of a hustle to pressure me into handing over some baksheesh. I had simply countered with a bluff of my own. They apparently soon decided the dumb captain did not know the rules and might as well "find" the Passports. The agent waited until about ten minutes before my imposed deadline, and then produced the stamped and cleared documents. He did not want to be found responsible for a delayed or canceled flight. One has to be ready for almost anything while flying in this part of the world.

ETHIOPIA

My first flight to Addis Ababa, Ethiopia was October 13, 1965. I would be sharing command with Captain Parker who had been there a time or two. The route would be from Jeddah across the Red Sea at an angle from north to southeast, intercepting the coast of Africa at the town of Assab to land and refuel. The flight time to this point was five hours. Assab was just above sea level and shortly after takeoff the ground rose slightly as we climbed. Inside about twenty minutes we approached a very prominent escarpment several hundred feet above the plain. We would see a considerable rise in elevation as we progressed towards Dire Dawa, a small town which would be our major checkpoint. Navigating in Africa was much different than Saudi Arabia. The terrain was a mix of greenery and flowing rivers for a considerable stretch, becoming a large area of grass lands for miles and miles. Thirty minutes later, one might be looking down at desert land almost like Saudi Arabia with the accompanying dry river beds (wadis). All of this was just as "trackless" as where we came from. Trackless for now, but after this trip we will have noted many features that will make the next one much easier. One better pay close attention to his maps. Those who do not fly for long stretches over terrain like Africa cannot appreciate how the thrill of flying is enhanced by being "lost" for much of the flight. It would take about four hours on this portion of our flight. As we progressed, one could look ahead and to the right and make out a good sized river. Checking our map, I found it was the Awash

MARTI SHOPPING IN HONG KONG

ASMARA, ETHIOPIA, 1972

River. It wasn't too long after that the river meandered to the left and appeared to empty into a very large lake. Later I was informed the lake was indeed the end of the river's journey. Approaching Dire Dawa we could see a range of mountains to our left and that jibed with our map. Not long after that one could make out a river crossing our path from left to right. A quick check of the map identified it as the Awash River again. Three hours forty-five minutes out of Assab found us looking for Addis Ababa. The ground now rose abruptly in front of us to over eight thousand feet. There just ahead a few miles lay the fabulous city of Addis Ababa. The runway at the airport for Addis was about 8,200 feet elevation and demanded careful attention to airspeed on landing as the air was considerably thinner and provided less "lift." The same would be true on takeoff. Visibility was good and we found the airport with little difficulty.

Our cargo was two Pratt & Whitney piston engines for overhaul in Ethiopian Airlines facility on the airport. Trans World Airlines operated the facility and trained local people in that type of work. Our cargo to go back to Jeddah the next day would be two overhauled engines.

The crew bus took us to town and the hotel. The hotel was very good and the service was excellent. We took a cab to the souk and found it different from Arab souks, and very interesting. The shops were located door to door much like some small town in the U.S. The streets were paved and the row buildings were in very good repair. Fairly wide sidewalks gave one ample room to stroll and shop. The shops contained local handwork of all kinds. Some crafted from ivory, some from different exotic woods. All kinds of knives, spears, shields, masks, carvings, clothing, jewelry, etc., in various degrees of artistry.

It seemed each shop had its own appeal in the variety and beauty of their offerings. There were animal skins of many kinds with lots of monkey skins, and a good many snake skins of different kinds. Almost, if not all, of these items were illegal to export and to import to your country of origin. Lots of exotic stuffed birds of many colors, including many live ones in cages. We were repeatedly assured by shop owners all these items were "legal." Fortunately we knew better. We were the only white people in the souk at that time. It made one feel at bit obvious. I bought two sets of spear heads and a "Dicky Stick" That was the local name for a tapered wood club with a straight slender eight inch stiletto secreted inside. (The items I bought were "legal," sic.) The club was about eighteen inches long and an inch in diameter at the large end. The proprietor told me it was patterned after the "Swagger Sticks" favored by British Officers. My question to him was; "Aren't these things illegal?" He grinned and said; "Well yes, but they are still carried with discretion." Those items are mounted on a board in our family room along with several other such souvenirs. We could not stay as long as we would have liked due to sunset fast approaching and were reluctant to remain after dark. I vowed to come back when I could browse a bit longer.

The next morning we worked on a flight plan on another route neither of us knew. We would fly from Addis Ababa to Asmara, Ethiopia direct. The flight time should be about four hours. Our load back was two rebuilt engines that would slow our climb considerably as we approached the mountain range about two hours forty minutes out of Addis. Some of those mountains were at least ten thousand feet high and most likely higher.

The takeoff was fine even with our weight and thin air. Within minutes, we were beyond the escarpment and started descent to fly at a lower altitude over the four to six thousand foot elevation plain that stretched for many miles ahead. There was evidence of human habitation for miles. There were several kraals, huts and many types of "fences" all along our path, along with people tending herds of small animals. They appeared to be goats and sheep mostly. Those fences were apparently constructed with either slender limbs cut off, stripped of leaves and planted upright in a circle, or branches of trees with prickly thorns stood upright in a circle. The people seemed friendly enough as they waved as we passed over their heads. One of them even waved his spear at us. Of course that might not have been a "friendly" gesture as we were flying lower than normal to see the sights and his herd of goats had bolted and run.

Further north we would see herds of wild animals and, as we approached the foothills of the mountains, there were many "tribes" of baboons to be seen. They were very aware of our progress as they scampered about amongst the rocks.

We later had to climb to eleven thousand feet to penetrate the mountains ahead. The real bad news was clouds were obscuring the mountain peaks and it became very difficult to find the "saddles" to fly through. Our aircraft was not pressurized and there was no oxygen for us, so it was not prudent to climb much higher. Luck was with us and we proceeded to Asmara, refueled and proceeded to Jeddah.

My second trip to Addis Ababa was not to be until January of 1966. My First Officer was Achmed Korban, a Saudi captain.

Our route this time would be from Jeddah to Gizan, Saudi Arabia (the old slave Port), land, refuel and proceed across the Red Sea to Assab for refueling. From there we would fly our previous route across Ethiopia to Addis Ababa. Navigating was much easier this time as I knew what to look for.

After landing, securing the aircraft, doing necessary paper work to deliver the engines for repair, we took the crew bus into the city and hotel. When we were in our rooms and cleaned up a bit I asked Korban if he would like too accompany me to the souk. He declined, saying he would go visit a friend in town.

The doorman got me a taxi and I departed for the souk. The taxi went where I wanted to start and parked while I began shopping from one store to another. Actually I was more browsing than shopping as I had nothing in particular in mind. Everything was so interesting! After about thirty minutes one of the shop keepers alerted me with his body language something was not quite right. I noticed his attention was drifting to the windows, something had his interest. I too looked and all I saw was two men standing outside apparently talking to each other. I had seen enough here and proceeded out of the shop and on to the next one. I took another look at the two men as I passed them and neither looked at me. By this time I was more than half way around the square and decided to pass up a shop or two and looked back as I entered another shop. The two men came around the corner in back of me just as I opened the door. The shop owner came to greet me and I held up my hand to indicate wait a minute. Sure enough those guys came to a stop a few feet outside and, I thought, were trying to appear casual. The shopkeeper again asked how he could help. I asked him who those two were seemingly waiting outside. He appeared startled and mumbled they were not nice people. Here I was in an all native community, sunset was not far away, and no police in sight. Now, it seemed, was a good time to conjure a plan of some sort. Looking through his knife assortment, I picked out a mean looking seven and a half inch curved blade knife and asked for the price. As I paid the bill, I heard the shopkeeper softly say, "Be careful." After paying the small price he asked, I removed the scabbard, and holding the knife in my right hand, walked out the door, looking at the two as I turned and walked briskly towards my taxi. Strangely, I could hear some of those others on the street chattering excitedly, and one or two clapped their hands. Later, I interpreted that response as if they knew those two intended to rob me and were glad to see them thwarted. I urged the taxi driver to get the hell out of there now! I think those guys were surprised when I burst out of that door with a knife. Their indecision gave me just enough time too reach the taxi and go. They were already moving in my direction. Arriving safely back to the hotel, I was finally able to take a deep breath. That knife is still with me and is currently hanging on a wall in my family room along with several other souvenirs.

When I arrived back at the hotel, I talked to a native manager there and recounted the incident. My main question was, should I report this to the police? His explanation and response was, "No, the shopkeepers would not want that, because to them the police could be troublesome. That is the reason one of them did not call the police when they realized what might happen. They simply had to choose. They are really good people and would not want you hurt. The odds are pretty good they would have pitched in and helped if the two did attack you. It is best not to go there without some one with you." Now he tells me!

Our return to Jeddah was relatively routine and safe.

ASMARA

Marti and I, along with Chuck and Betty Frey, planned on a short vacation and picked Asmara as a suitable destination for a short trip. Asmara is the second largest city in Ethiopia and is quite modern. They have a thriving business district and a large very nice residential area. Of course not all of the residential area is "nice;" they also have their share of poverty. The streets are wide and clean and traffic flows nicely. The "souk" area covered several blocks, and Marti and I on a week's visit covered all of it. The United States has a Communications Base there. There was a nearby "antenna farm" installed by the U.S. that was an integral part of their worldwide communications network. We were allowed to use that facility, eating at the Officer's Club, using the PX, and enjoying a movie or two with Chuck and Betty. Chuck was also employed by TWA and was a ground school instructor. The employees in the Officer's Club were all natives, spoke English and were excellent waiters. Their features were much finer that most other Africans and they had medium dark skin. They served some great shrimp cocktails with very hot sauce. I had to order another martini or two to cope.

On our walks around the residential area, we observed all of the nice homes and villas were walled with seven or eight foot high stone or brick. On top of all was broken glass set upright in the concrete covering. This would make a formidable deterrent to a casual burglar. Professional burglaries did occur, however, and we understood residents were advised if they awoke in the night and observed a stranger in the room to lie quietly until the intruder departed. Authorities had noted that in several cases of an interrupted burglary, the assailant had killed the inhabitants. Most were armed and, if seen by the victim, would attack.

Marti is an avid shopper and she really had a great time visiting all the intriguing shops. She did buy several items of jewelry, including an elephant tail hair bracelet and matching necklace. Each of these pieces was several strands of tail hair worked into a circle and held together by silver or gold bands at strategic points. I would think that would be risky business taking hair from the tail of an elephant! She also acquired two rings, one silver and one gold, each entwined with zebra tail hair. Each piece she bought she still has, and can tell you where and when it was acquired. Don't remember what else she bought; I didn't have much say in the purchase either. And yes, she did use her skills in bargaining as sharpened in the souks of Saudi Arabia.

I was to make many trips to Asmara during our stay in Saudi Arabia. Almost all were either in transit to another further destination or a turnaround and back to Jeddah through Port Sudan. The good news was we could eat lunch in their very nice restaurant in the terminal while we waited for refueling and loading of passengers for the return. The bad news was they also served cold beer. Cold beer was not an option in Saudi Arabia, which increased the pull even more. The temptation was great but duty won.

About a year and a half after my retirement from the Air Force, I was in the process of climbing after taking off from Asmara for return to Jeddah when I experienced an unusual event. I overheard a MATS (Military Air Transport Service) pilot call Asmara on the radio asking for landing information. Before I retired from the Air Force in 1964, I was a MATS pilot as well. The information they relayed to him was not up to date and could affect his landing. I listened to him confirm what they had given him. Knowing it was wrong; I called him and informed him, "This is Saudi Air HZAAB. I am departing Asmara and will advise you of up to date info if you like." He answered yes, he would, so I told him about the unusual characteristics of the runway first. I pointed out no matter which direction he landed, the first part of the roll would be downhill. That is not easy to deal with, even with favorable winds. The actual runway winds were thirty degrees off runway direction and gusting to about 25 knots as opposed to their report to him of 10 knots at 15 degrees from runway heading. Further they reported scattered clouds at 2000 feet, where actually the cloud cover was more widespread and should have been reported as "broken." When I finished with my report to him, there was no answer for several seconds. Finally he said, "Saudi Air, I know this sounds silly, but is this Colonel Leonard Porter talking?" I confirmed that yes, this is he. He came right back and said, "I was just sure that was your voice, but had no idea where you were, what are you doing in a Saudi airplane?" After my explanation, we chatted a bit, I asked him to convey my regards to my friends still remaining at McGuire AFB in New Jersey and wished him happy landings. We parted with the same thought; this really is a small world.

HAJJ

The "Hajj" was the pilgrimage of Muslims from all over the Arab world and from any other country with Muslims to Saudi Arabia. Their intent was to visit the holy cities of Mecca and Medina. Mecca was a must, and Medina was desirable in addition. The Hajj was performed once a year and all Muslims were intent on being a "Hajji" at least once in their lifetime. They came by individuals, by groups, by families, some with small children. They came by almost any means of transportation. They arrived by boat, airplanes, trucks, camel train, automobile, buses, and there were some who walked. They brought large amounts of baggage as they would have to be very self sufficient while here. Many brought with them items to sell to help defray the cost of this expensive, perilous journey. Those from Africa brought parrots, many of them the desirable Gray Parrot which could be easily taught to talk. Some brought snake skins, mostly large constrictors as long as twenty five feet. Monkey skins of different kinds, many of the black and white variety. Almost all of these were illegal for export. Those from surrounding Arab countries brought rugs of many patterns and colors. All of these were available for sale just across the street from the airport. Every day, large crowds gathered on the plaza area and hawked their wares. Rugs and other items mentioned above were laid out by the hundreds on the pavement by merchants. Many of the snake skins were strung across limbs of the small trees in that area, rugs too along with birds in cages. An awful lot of noisy trading went on there daily until it was time to proceed to Mecca. We joined them from time to time and I took a lot of photos. Altogether a very interesting happening.

Those that arrived by truck and buses congregated in a huge open area near the Red Sea, close to the entry to the town. Their baggage was piled high on these vehicles, lashed in place by many ropes. Lots of pots, pans, water containers, and other necessaries were hung from the sides. They had to be prepared to care for themselves on the long rigorous journey they had just endured. At that time there was no highway to the north, only trails. I still marvel at their feat of accomplishing that journey across all of that desert area. What trials they must have endured. They were still mostly on their own and still had the trip to Mecca ahead and possibly worse yet, the perilous liturgy in the crush of humanity in the desert heat of Mecca. If they survived the ceremonies, the trip home across the desert might easily result in the death of many. The years we were in Saudi Arabia accounted for much loss of life. Hundreds died in many ways, including sickness, old age and countless accidents. Reports at the time were sketchy, but foreign papers reported hundreds, sometimes thousands, of worshipers were trampled to death by stampedes caused by failure of ramps or bridges. Accidents of this nature still happen almost every year as the crowds continue to grow.

CROWN PRINCE SHERIF OF BEIHAN

MARTI AND RUTH WOODS AT KING'S PALACE IN JEDDAH

Our part in all this was to transport as many as possible from their origin airport to and from Jeddah. We would fly the maximum each way. For example, on the 3rd of April, 1965, we flew three round trips from Jeddah to Port Sudan, Sudan, empty one way, full on the return, logging nine hours, thirty minutes of flying time, plus six hours of "duty" time for a total of 15 hours and 30 minutes. We would do almost the same thing the next day, possibly more, depending where we were scheduled to go. I might be headed for Medina for an all day shuttle back and forth or Asmara. Within a month on the "outbound" portion of the Hajj, the reverse travel would be necessary.

We were but a small part of this movement of in and out. Many countries' airlines were involved in the Hajj. On any given day, one could see many different Russian made air-craft on the ground from countries such as, Iraq, Iran, Afghanistan, Egypt, Pakistan, India and many African coun-tries. Of course there were U.S. aircraft involved too; car-riers such as those from Lebanon, Turkey, and France. Very large numbers were air transported.

THE ARAB WAY

The beginning of this saga was certainly innocent and routine, but the proceedings were to take a very strange and dangerous turn in the next twenty-four hours. My crew con-sisted of myself, First Officer Ashemimry and Steward Saife. January ninth, 1966, we flew trip number 314, a Convair 340 from Jeddah to Riyadh, arriving at 1005 local time. We were to remain overnight and stand by for a possible royal flight the following day or whenever. Actually, we were at the whim of any one of the royal family members who might decide they wished to go somewhere.

We proceeded to the Sahara Palace Hotel, located just outside the grounds of the airport. This hotel was our usual "crew" rest abode and was not too bad. Certainly was not a "star" hotel, but reasonably comfortable. The "night noises" were a bit of a bother for me, as the lack of air conditioning was normal and open windows were the prime means of moving air.

Soon after checking in, Ashemimry came to my room to inform me I would have a car with a driver waiting for me when I decided to go someplace. Somewhat startled by this announcement, I could only mumble something like, "Who ordered transportation for me, and what do you mean?" He answered, "My uncle has provided the car and driver and was pleased to offer any further assistance desired." The tendency to blurt out some dumb rejoinder was very strong, but fortunately, I was able to come up with some stilted phrase like, "Thank you very much for your uncle's generosity." Those are not my exact words, but certainly along that line. Saudi Arabia was not finished with surprises for me. Later, I would learn Ashemimry's uncle was the commanding General of the Army.

Now made responsible to use the gift of car and driver, I had to make plans to go somewhere. Having failed at explaining to the driver where I wanted to go, I was reduced to directing him by using my, at this time, quite limited Arabic. We proceeded to the MAAG house where I persuaded Lt. Col. Raider Ramstad, the Commanding Officer, to go for a sightseeing tour of Riyadh. He was duly impressed with my "gift." We soon tired of this, but enjoyed the visit and after returning him to the MAAG house, proceeded to the Sahara Palace.

The next day was uneventful right up until about 3 p.m. Taking Ashemimry with me, we proceeded to the Operations office on the airport to find out if anything was pending. About thirty minutes later, I was informed Prince Sudairi wished to go to Najran (Najran is south of Riyadh on the Saudi-Yemen border about three hours, fifteen minutes by DC-3) and we should prepare to take him. Checking the time, I informed Operations we would have to depart within an hour and fifteen minutes to arrive before sunset. At that moment, I had no feelings of urgency. My comment was purely informative. NOTE: The airport at Najran was not equipped for night landings and it would be illegal for me to make an approach there except in an emergency. There were no navigation aids there, such as radio beacons or lights. We would have to rely completely on visual navigation. The airport was the same color as the surrounding desert and difficult to find even in daylight. Trying to find it at night was not a good option.

After informing Traffic to insure refueling and food for the flight, we went to the hotel to change clothes, pack and return. Here I learned only partial fueling had been done and no food had yet been placed on board. Realizing time was running out on me, I went to the agent to hurry things along. He then informed me Prince Sudairi was not to go, but this was a "secret military mission" and that I must go, never mind the time. This was the first indication things were about to heat up.

Immediately, I headed for the tower to use their single side band radio to call Jeddah direct. After contacting Jeddah, I asked for and got Captain Awliya (the Airline Operations Officer) on the radio. He was a Saudi National, spoke excellent English, and was well versed on proper procedures in addition to knowing the right thing to do. He was trustworthy. After explaining the situation, I asked him how the airline might respond if I had to proceed to Jeddah after departing Riyadh. He grasped the extent of my problem immediately, and responded with "You handle it; we will concur with any decision you must make."

When I returned to the line, Ashemimry informed me the airport manager wanted me in his office immediately. Ashemimry explained the manager was a very powerful sheik who held his position due to family ties and was appointed by the king. He asked if I wished him to accompany me to face the sheik. He confirmed the sheik could speak pretty good English, but I might need help on what he says in Arabic. My response was thanks, but I think it best if I can feign ignorance of some of the things he might say. Besides, I did not want to put Ashemimry in a precarious position.

Entering the manager's office was a bit imposing. The room was about fifty feet long by thirty feet wide and filled with a large group of Saudis in their full Arab dress. About twenty were along the left wall, seated on a long bench which was padded and covered with red material. Several "pillows" with the same color material were used as back rests. The entire wall was covered with drapes. The opposite wall had several windows, which were also hung with drapes. The floor from the entry to beyond the manager's desk was almost covered by many Persian rugs. The remaining Saudis (about ten) were standing behind the sheik who was seated at his massive desk, situated about two-thirds the distance from the door to the back wall. The whole set-up was expected to impress and put me at a disadvantage. Which it did.

Sensing the disapproval, I ignored the entourage and proceeded directly up to the sheik's desk and announced, "Your Excellency, I am Captain Porter. May I talk to you?" When he gave permission, with a wave of his hand, I began speaking. I said, "Sir, I need some help getting things ready for the flight to Najran. They have not refueled the aircraft as I instructed and there is no food on board for the passengers. Also, the passengers must be on board within thirty minutes to allow us time to arrive in Najran before darkness prevents us from landing." Almost before I could get the last word said, the sheik was on his feet. He turned to one of those behind him and spoke rapidly in Arabic. I assumed he was giving instructions to go chew some ass and get things done. The "gofer" left the room in a hurry. Then it was my turn. He started out by saying, "Never mind the time, Prince Sultan has directed you to take these people and go. If you do not depart immediately, we will not hire you!" I cannot describe his accent, but I can assure you, I understood that comment. Never mind the syntax. He had a few more things to say, but I don't recall them. The die was cast. From this point, the rules would follow "The Arab Way." My last comment was, "Yes, your Excellency, I will wait for the passengers."

Turning to depart, I was aware of the entire group, smiling and congratulating each other and the sheik about how he had really put me in my place. I must have really gotten an "ass chewing" in Arabic and didn't even know it. It wasn't over yet.

Ashemimry was waiting for me and anxious to learn what happened. But first he had news for me. He knew who the passengers were to be. He said they consisted of a Yemen sheik, who was a military commander, and six of his "officers." All were armed and in their native dress. Prince Sultan had decided they had been there too long and wished them gone. That was bad news indeed. It would be almost impossible to fool these guys with the change of direction I had planned. Now it was imperative I enlist the First Officer's help. It was then I told Ashemimry about the threat the sheik had made to fire me if we did not go. He was really upset! Then I informed him there was a way we could do what the prince had directed, and do it in a possibly safe manner, but it rested entirely on his help. He was anxious to learn what he could do.

My first plan was quite simple, but out of the question now after learning the type of people we would now be transporting. These people were armed Yemen warriors and very dangerous. They would not take kindly to an attempt to confuse or fool them and I knew one or all would know if I attempted to change direction from the course to Najran. After all, they had spent many years of their life navigating the desert by the stars, sun, and the type of terrain. They had been over this route before and I had no doubt at least one of them would be looking for checkpoints. More likely though, all of them would be following our route. That belief forced me to alter my plan to make it more believable.

Ashemimry was smart, resourceful, had a good command of the English language and, I believed, trustworthy. Now for the plan. We would take off and establish a course for Najran as usual. After about thirty minutes of cruising at altitude, I would initiate a gradual turn to the west, perhaps twenty, twenty-five degrees off course. If the sheik did not ask to speak to me or come to the cockpit within a reasonable time to inquire about the change, Ashemimry would go to the passenger compartment with an explanation. The explanation being that we had information via radio of a storm between us and Najran and we were turning to go around it. We believed if he accepted that thought without objecting, the rest of the plan would get a big boost. The remainder of the plan was laid out for Ashemimry and when I finished, he was delighted and could hardly wait to get started. I did admonish him not to be too glib, but to take it easy and try not to allow the explanations to appear rehearsed. Then I added, it would not be a good idea to inform Saife, our steward, as he might inadvertently say or do something to alert the Yemen.

When we went to the aircraft to check on progress, workers were swarming the plane, refueling was just completed, and there was more food on board than required. They were even sweeping the interior.

Twenty minutes later, several vehicles approached with sirens and flashing lights. Our passengers arrived. The prince really wanted to get them out of here and was putting on a display to impress and insure their departure.

When I saw those fierce looking warriors come aboard, my spirits sank a bit. This was real. The sheik was carrying the traditional curved knife (dagger) in a scabbard across his middle and an automatic pistol in its holster. The rest of the men also had their super sharp knives (sakeen in Arabic) in place with dual bandoleers of ammunition hung around their necks and crossing in the center. In addition, each carried a rifle. Not an ounce of fat in the lot. Just bone and muscle. I knew about those sharp knives as I had just touched the blade of one previously and was not aware my thumb was cut until the blood ran into my palm and onto the ground. These people had been fighting in the mountains of Yemen for almost two years against the Communists and Egyptians. Their tendency was to react instantly to any threat and sort it out later. Not a good thing for me. Attempting to fly with my throat slashed would not be easy. Was I having second thoughts? Well, certainly I was reviewing my plan. Was there a better way? Not that I could think of. The whole thing depended on Ashemimry's skill doing his part. I would try to control his approach and be prepared to back off if a threat became imminent.

Takeoff and climb out was normal. We leveled out at our chosen cruise level and began to review our actions. Twenty minutes later, I changed course twenty-five degrees right (towards Jeddah) and waited. Fifteen minutes went by and I was thinking of calling for the steward when he arrived in the cockpit. He said the sheik was coming up and turned to go back, bumping into him. Both the first officer and I greeted him. Me in English, the First Officer in Arabic. The English greeting was to let him know I did not speak Arabic and to encourage him to use English if he understood. He acknowledged my greeting, but only in Arabic. He spoke to Ashemimry in a questioning manner. Ashemimry then told me the sheik had noticed our heading had changed and wanted to know if anything was wrong. Well, here goes. "Tell him about the storm," I replied. The two chatted for several minutes while I pretended to be relaxed and comfortable. After what seemed a very long time, the sheik looked out the front for a bit, turned and smiled just a little and departed. The First Officer had a big grin on his face and said, "He understands and thanks you for your concern for them." That really relieved the pressure considerably. Now I felt like we just might pull it off. "Ash" (FO) still had a big grin and was really enjoying his role. How lucky to have him on board! Most of the Arab First Officers could not or would not be trusted to act this out in a believable manner.

Meanwhile, I began reviewing the rest of the plan. We could not delay the next phase too long, as we were already off track to Jeddah and I wanted to stay as close to route as possible as we had to rely on pilotage. That is, we needed to see the ground to identify checkpoints to compare with our map. We were already out of sight of familiar objects and getting further off every minute. Remember, we had no radio aids available to help us navigate. Further, the last one-third or more of the flight would be in darkness.

My feeling convinced me it was necessary to make one more apparent effort to proceed to Najran. Accordingly, we continued on course for another ten minutes. Then I turned another twenty degrees west. I rang the bell for the steward, Saife. When he came to the cockpit, I asked him to go back and ask the sheik if he would like to come forward or have the FO come and talk to him.

The sheik elected to come to the cockpit and was actually right behind Saife at that moment. This part was critical! I still remembered that strange little "smile" he had given me after our first briefing. What had it meant? Was he already suspicious? No doubt about it, we (Ashemimry) had to convince him, or our very lives could be in jeopardy. Made the back of my neck itch! We could not afford to give him room for the slightest suspicion that he might have been manipulated. Ashemimry (FO) was ready. He explained to the sheik that the weather had been moving to the west and would now prevent our going around it. NOTE: This was in keeping with normal movement of those storms and he would know that. We had also contacted the airline and they had advised to proceed to Taif or Jeddah. We asked him which he would prefer. He thought for a moment, half smiled, and opted for Jeddah. Giving him that choice was, I believed the clincher. Now I could breathe again. That part of the crisis was apparently over.

Now we had to turn towards the track for Jeddah and try to locate our position. We were still about two hours away and darkness was fast approaching. About an hour later, we could see lights of a town that we hoped was Taif. If so, we were off track about twenty miles south. I corrected to pass Taif to the north as I could verify the town for sure if White Mountain appeared soon. White Mountain was a mountain of marble and could be seen for miles, even at night. A great check point! NOTE: This mountain was owned by Bin Laden and was being mined for marble to be used in construction for holy buildings in Mecca. Yes, he was the father of the now, infamous terrorist, Osama Bin Laden.

Soon we could make out the ghostly outlines of the mountain and, by looking to the west; we could make out the faint glow of lights from Jeddah. We were almost "home." We landed with great relief after four hours and five minutes of tension and eager to off load our very dangerous cargo. Thank you very much, Mohammed N. Ashemimry. I wish you much success.

NOTE: When I returned to our apartment building two days later, Ashemimry was waiting for me. He thanked me for our trip and presented me with a very nice leather suitcase and a pen "for my son." I really did not want to accept, but realized I must or risk offending him. The suitcase is still with me and remains a treasured reminder of that dangerous happening and of the intelligent, resourceful young man who got us through it.

MARTI THE SHOPPER

From the first day in the souk, Marti was hooked. There were just too many "goodies" to be found in the shops and byways of that sprawling exotic market place. The sights, sounds and aromas were intoxicating. She no sooner got home from an adventure in the souk and she was looking forward to the next foray. All the women were advised not to visit the souk alone. Preferably always with a male as their companion, even a child. In the beginning, I would be available in between trips and of course David would also be along. He and I would take turns getting a haircut while she shopped, but soon I resumed cutting my own hair and David would be in school. She would then persuade one of her lady friends to go with her in a taxi. Sometimes Polly Vincent would be free from her duties in the Personnel office, and would go with Marti. Bob Majors' wife, Murphy, accompanied Marti on many occasions, but she soon began discouraging her as she tended to be a bit belligerent with the shop keepers. The male owners did not accept that behavior from women. Neither did the male Saudi shoppers. Once Marti tried taking our houseboy, Talbot, with her to the souk. She had him go find a taxi then pick her up. She surmised since he was Yemen, he could interpret for her while bargaining and he would suffice as "companion." She soon found out he was of little or no help. He did not speak the same dialect as the merchants and could not converse well with her either. Additionally, he did not help much with the taxi drivers as they apparently did not understand him.

The booklet furnished by the ladies of the airline covered many areas of dress and deportment for the female members of the employees. This was really a very valuable guide providing great information for newly arrived family members. Recommended dress for women was to cover exposed parts as much as possible, to include ankle length dresses or skirts with blouses with sleeves to cover their arms. Wearing a scarf to cover their hair was also recommended. Marti chose her own method of complying with the dress code and started a whole new fashion. I accompanied her to one of the well know tailors in the souk and watched as she explained she wanted him to make her a thobe. The ankle length, long sleeve, high neck garment the men wore. He was a bit surprised and made sure by questioning that was what she really meant. Soon he shrugged and got his tape measure. He took her measurements and told her to return in a few days. He would have it ready. It fit perfectly. Soon she had more of different colors and fabrics tailored. They were the perfect garment for the women and no objections were ever raised. She still has and wears some of those same "dresses." Shoes presented a further problem. I had mentioned earlier, streets in the souk were not paved. They were simply that part of the desert in that area left over after shops were built on either side. The space between shops left and right determined the width of that corridor, walk way or street. Very few of any of the "streets" were straight. None were ever built with automobiles in mind. Some would accommodate donkey carts but, with time, even they were becoming a big nuisance as more and more people arrived. The widest was Gaabel Street, the main entry off King Abdul Aziz Street. That's the one with the orange juice stand. I would guess it to be fifty or sixty feet wide. The very fine desert dust stirred up by constant foot traffic was quite a problem for the merchants, and they employed a method of keeping dust off the merchandise that created another hazard. From time to time, they would "lay the dust" by throwing buckets of water in front of their area. Now watch out for the mud! Marti solved part of the shoe problem by wearing only sandals, which were relatively inexpensive and allowed her to shake the dust out. Her favorites were those with thick soles.

She ventured further and further in to the souk, finding interesting areas filled with all kinds of "goodies," including hand crafted silver JEWELRY of many different styles. All of it was old, second or multiple "hand" and CHEAP. The very best kind! She had just found her calling and the collection had begun. She could spend hours just finding and acquiring a ring, a bracelet, or a necklace. Of course, acquiring one item might take several days of bargaining to satisfy her she had finally reached the very best price possible. She did not take this pursuit of antique jewelry lightly. Each piece had to meet all the requirements self imposed on acquiring it for her collection. She was not buying for a museum or for value or craftsmanship, but rather it must please her as a piece. Many of the pieces were made by Jewish craftsmen of a century ago and they were truly great, but a large number were sometimes crudely crafted and not of quality silver. Never mind the quality; those pieces are prized as well. One of the items in the collection is especially prized. It is a quite heavy, intricate silver belt given to her by the Crown Prince of Beihan, El Sherif Salih Hussain El Hubaily. He was a frequent visitor to our home and seemed to consider himself a particular friend. We liked and respected him.

One day she found a small antique hand made dark wooden chest, with hammered brass corners and nail studs in place to form designs. The chest was about eighteen inches long, fourteen inches deep, and twelve inches high. It sits in our living room and holds all her precious one by one collected pieces of antique silver jewelry. She can tell you where and when she acquired each ring, bracelet, toe ring, necklace, whatever and likely how much paid for each. Later she acquired her very own, "basket boy" by default. She had "hired" him once and thereafter, if he was not immediately available, one of the other boys would hunt him down and soon she would be graced with his smiling face and a friendly, "Allo, Madame."

The basket boys were of various ages and sizes, appearing to be approximately five to perhaps twenty years of age. They were all Yemenis, wore a type of cloth turban, a worn shirt, the traditional checkered or striped knee length skirt all of which showed signs of many hand washings. Their foot gear was some type of sandal or plastic "shower slipper" with straps (go a heads). Others were simply barefoot. Our boy appeared to be about ten or eleven years old and perhaps a bit small although sturdy. All carried a "basket," usually on their head held in place with one hand. Hence the sobriquet "basket boy." They would stick to you like glue and once he figured out what you were looking for, would steer you to the merchant with the best goods or bargain. They would also happily bargain for you, if allowed, and let you know when they realized you were about to pay too much for an item. One was a lucky person to find a good loyal "boy" to help them shop. Marti had a hard time trying to resist the need to "mother" him. She worried about his dirty worn clothing and was always making plans to buy him a new white shirt or whatever. Each time I was able to talk her out of it by explaining he would, without a doubt, sell any new garment she bought. Just give him a little extra baksheesh if she needed to help.

Her shopping was not confined to jewelry. We made many visits to the vegetable souks, buying items such as corn, watermelons, grapes, oranges and many other fruits and vegetables. Delicious watermelons and grapes were grown in this arid country. Watermelons came from several places, including the very dry desert area north of Riyadh, thanks to large areas of sub surface water. Excellent grapes were grown in the plateau area around Taif about a hundred kilometers west of Jeddah. Large amounts of vegetables were grown in the mountainous areas south of Jeddah. Terrace farming was really big there.

When we met Dick and Ruth Wood, a friendship began that still lives. Unfortunately Dick is gone some years now, but Ruth and Marti's friendship survives, even though we live in Prairie Village and she lives in Sun City, AZ. Both of the women were and are devout bridge players and compatible in thought and beliefs. They played bridge together in Jeddah for years and many times back in the states as their paths crossed through the years. Ruth happily joined Marti in the pursuit of bargains in the souk. They even walked from our apartment to the souk, a distance of approximately three kilometers over uneven terrain. Sidewalks were almost non-existent, and the traffic alongside their route was fast and dangerous. They maintained they needed the exercise and it was no more dangerous than riding in those taxis. Point taken.

On one of our trips back to the states to visit our parents and recoup, Marti found out my dad had some bells. Dad was long retired and enjoyed going to farm auctions where he found and bought a variety of antiques. Some were broken down wagons and buggies from long ago, antique violins needing repair, chairs, and organs, whatever. He would bring them home, repair, repaint, and sell them. He sold many wagons and buggies to Benjamin Stables in south Kansas City. This time he showed her some old cowbells, church bells, school bells and harness bells he had collected over time. This planted a seed in her mind; she might shop for, buy, and send to Dad some donkey bells. The city was filled with "donkey carts" hauling all sorts of materials. The preponderance of these were hauling water in a local made container crafted by welding two fifty five gallon metal barrels together end to end. This container was placed on a two wheeled cart pulled by a single donkey and driven by the operator, who was almost always a Yemen. (Saudi men did not do menial labor.) They carried water from the many wells to residents and merchants alike. Almost, if not all, donkeys had bells around their necks and some carts had bells on the shafts.

Shortly after we returned to Jeddah, Marti wanted to go to the souk to start her search for donkey bells. Naturally I had to go with her but my heart was not in it. Soon after we arrived, she spotted a donkey with just the kind of bells she wanted. She stopped the driver and started her dialog and pantomime in an attempt to convey her wish to buy the bells. I stood just far enough away to distance myself from the dealing, but close enough to establish protection. The Yemen and Marti did not speak each other's language and apparently was having very little success with understanding. Finally a Saudi who had been observing for some time decided it was time to offer help as a deal was about to be consummated. He explained to my wife, the Yemen thought she was buying his donkey, not the bells, and had agreed to sell. He would not sell the bells for that price. For some reason, I had a very strong urge to laugh, but was fortunate to suppress it. The nearby merchants and shoppers enjoyed the show. Later, Marti said she was really tempted to buy the donkey and keep it on the grounds of our apartment building. There was a wall completely around the building and the area inside was very large. However, the gate keeper and others in the apartment would not close the gates. She maintained the kids would have a great time with the animal and it would be well fed and cared for. She was always expressing her views about the poor treatment of those donkeys. Perhaps the thoughts of donkey doo scattered about the grounds and other unpleasant habits of the beast entered her mind and tipped the scales to no. In any event, her decision saved me from a rebuttal.

She did not give up on her pursuit of donkey bells. On another day we went through the "covered" souk, crossed the street and proceeded up the winding narrow path into the "old souk." The way was lined with shops of all kinds on both sides; however, as in the "newer souk," items of like nature were located in the same general area. Our destination was deeper in as she was in pursuit of bells and we had been

Capt. Porter with Barracuda
Caught in Red Sea

"The Shepard", near Abha, SA, 1975

The Shepherd

Marti in Bedouin Wedding Dress

told there might be some in an area we had not yet visited. Soon we were in the area designated as the "junk" souk, and many of the small shops were full of all kinds of cast off items of dubious origin and value. These shops consisted of "cubby" holes in what appeared to be a corrugated steel building of a single story, each with its own "roll up" front to close it off at night and during prayer times. Some of those long sheds had regular opening doors for each "shop" and they were used as "display" areas when open. Most also had large numbers of "spill out" of their wares.

Investigating each of these shops for prized pieces took a bit of time. One such place was to yield surprise and embarrassment. Marti started her spiel of limited Arabic, mingled with pantomime, verbal sounds of "Hee haw," "Tinkle, tinkle" etc. The shopkeeper answered with; "Yes Madame, I have donkey bells," in cultured English. She was rendered almost speechless and very embarrassed. Recovery was a bit slow, but she was finally able to consummate a deal and got her donkey bells. Later she got another set, now owning both old and new ones. These she proudly presented to Dad on one of our trips back home. One more donkey anecdote before we move on. One pleasant evening, while shopping in the crowded souk, weaving through a stream of people, Marti had an almost heart stopping shock. Unknown to her, a donkey cart had approached quietly from behind. Their soft hooves don't make a sound on that compacted desert and he did not have bells. The donkey reached out and nuzzled her from the rear. She instinctively put her hand back expecting to grab a hand. Feeling the unexpected, and strange object about did her in! Her reaction and fright scared the donkey and he blurted out an odd sound, and jumped, alerting all around.

In her investigative forays throughout the "junk" souks, she found, bargained for, and bought a large number of antique, exotic locks and keys. Some of those were entirely of wood. The collection included a pair of iron cuffs held together with a fourteen inch heavy chain. The merchant maintained it was a tether chain for camels. We were rather dubious as it appeared to be a leg restraint for a different kind of "stock." Anyway she brought all of them home and has two displays on boards to show off her trophies.

Another object of her frequent searches was for the perfect "Gahwah" pot. Gahwah is Arabic for "coffee." These pots were all hand made of brass, approximately the same shape and of several sizes. They ranged from approximately one cup to thirty or forty. They were shaped very much like our pitchers. All had a handle, an elongated spout, and a pinched waist, but differed from pitchers as they had a fancy hinged top with a spire. One could buy new ones almost anyplace, but Marti's goal was an old one stained by many camp fires. They made coffee by boiling the grounds over a fire and poured it by straining it through camel's hair inserted in the spout or using a "suitable substitute." One day she found what she was looking for. It was obviously very old, showing advanced patina, and was burned by many campfires almost to the top of the pinched waist. The total height was about twenty inches and the spout was beautifully curved. The merchant was very reluctant to sell it to her and was having a hard time trying to explain why not. He kept telling her the pot was "Moosh quaise," meaning "No good." Finally he went to the back of his shop, filled the pot with water and showed her the pot had a leak. She replied, "Malaish," in Arabic, meaning it is all right, or "never mind." She got the pot. He was perplexed.

Several days later, she came home to find Talbot, our houseboy, busily cleaning off all that accumulated smoke and patina from the Gahwah pot. She about went ballistic! Scared hell out of him! He had no idea what she was screaming about and tried without success to explain the pot was dirty and he was making it like new. Forget about it, he was lost from the start. He was very near to being without employment. Fortunately she regained some semblance of sanity, allowing her to back off before that happened. He was never quite the same about doing something on his own.

That same pot is still with us and ensconced securely on our antique Kuwaiti chest in its place under a hanging prayer rug located on a wall in our family room. Of course it is minus half of its smoke damage and patina that once adorned its shapely side. We have many other "treasures" Marti found in the souks and adroitly bargained for displayed and stored in our home. One of those other treasures is a brass Turkish style Gahwah pot. The come in different sizes depending on the need. Hers is about three feet tall overall with a controlled "pour valve" near the bottom. This type pot is made with a metal tube in the middle where a charcoal fire is set to make the coffee and hold the heat. A brass tea pot is then set in place on top. The whole thing is rather ornate and has fancy handles on each side. She still remembers where and when each was purchased and most of the time, how much she paid. I would expect nothing less from such a devout shopper.

Just a bit further into the junk souk was a large open area that had tables piled high with all types of old junk. More junk was stacked nearby or just piled on the ground. It was here Marti found her most prized antique. The prize was a castoff hand carved wooden door with a lattice like intricately carved upper portion. The openings in the lattice part were essentially square with saw tooth inner side. When those old houses were constructed, there was no air conditioning and they did not use screens. To provide cross ventilation and at the same time provide cover to prevent viewing the women inside, all windows and doors used this "lattice" work. Not all the work was identical, of course. The carpenter doing the work used his own style. The female members of the family could see out, but looking in was difficult. There was no finish remaining, having been bleached by the sun for many years leaving the door a light shade of gray. Marti knew at once she had to have that door, never mind hinges were long gone, the door knob was missing and there was a sizeable hole in the lower solid portion. Bargaining began immediately and soon the door became hers. Had she used her usual patience and tactics, no doubt the price would have been substantially less. The merchant sensed immediately she really wanted that door and refused to budge. Stu

Schlemmer, a young TWA employee from the States, was with us that day and helped me load the door on top of our Volkswagen. Stu was working in the TWA personnel office and would become one of our most treasured friends and companion on many of our in country and out sorties. He was also destined to become my unofficial "wine taster" when I started making my own wine. We are still very good friends some thirty plus years later.

That door, along with a large collection of artifacts, was shipped home to the States when we returned to this country in December of 1975. Not long after moving into our home in Prairie Village, Kansas, Marti convinced a friend, whom we had known in Saudi Arabia, to make her a cocktail table using the top latticed portion of the door. He did a great job of mounting and finishing the lattice work on legs that matched the present appearance of the top. A glass cover over that completed her table for which she is justifiably proud.

No doubt Marti is remembered fondly by the collective merchants of Jeddah, Cairo, Beirut, Taif, Abha, Karachi, even Asmara. The challenge and perseverance she exhibited was quite likely appreciated by all. Possibly some of the stories have become local lore. Well, maybe not, it's just a thought.

MORE FLYING

We departed Jeddah for Riyadh 0135Z with Convair SAR-4 for what was designated a Sana Charter. One crew would remain in Riyadh while the other would take the aircraft to Sana, Yemen. This was normal procedure, as the length of the flight required more than one crew. Further, the purpose of the trip was basically, to provide transport between the two capital cities, Riyadh of Saudi Arabia and Sana, Yemen.

Captain Cossairt flew the Riyadh to Sana to Riyadh portion and I would wait for his return and proceed back to Jeddah. This arrangement required me to wait six to seven hours for his return. With that time on my hands, I elected to go visit my friend, Lt. Colonel Ramstad, at MAAG unit located in the El Shark Hotel. We visited, played some table tennis and talked. Raider offered me some bottles of Beefeater gin to take back with me. I hesitated, then thought, since I had not been out of the country, I could return to Jeddah and go through the domestic side of Customs without a bag check. I happily accepted his offer with many thanks for, as I have mentioned before, liquor is hard to come by, and expensive if bought on the black market. When I returned to Operations to get ready for Cossairt's return from Sana, I took some items out of my black leather flight bag to make room for the booze. This is the bag all pilots carry with them into the cockpit for all flights. It contains flight and navigation books and maps required for flying in all required areas that might be visited. Also flashlights, pens, pencils and many other items each individual might consider essential.

The flight from Sana came in on time and all was soon ready for takeoff and return to Jeddah. The flight was without incident and landing was completed just after sundown on a beautiful spring evening. I retrieved my bag and proceeded to domestic customs without a care. As I started to enter the doorway to customs, a guard stopped me and said, "La, La, Sana, go there, pointing to out of country Customs doorway. I started to argue, but realized they would immediately become suspicious and check my bag for sure. Nothing to do now, but brazen it out. When one goes through Customs, the agent opens and checks each bag and marks it with chalk to indicate it is ok. Sometimes they may only open one or two bags, and mark them all. Occasionally, they will just mark all your bags without opening any. No doubt their intuition comes into play based on their long experience sizing up people. My black bag was a lot heavier than normal with the three bottles of gin, even though I had removed some items. Additionally, I worried about one "clinking" against the others, even though I had wrapped them to guard against that possibility. My goal, try to handle the bag normally.

I was the last of the crew members to approach Customs as I had made that small detour. With a friendly smile, I greeted the Customs agent in Arabic, set both bags on the counter and boldly opened my black bag partially, having turned it a bit sideways to prevent a quick glance in it. He immediately waved me to close it, saying, "Quaise" (good), as his chalk marked it. My goal now was not to show relief or all would be lost. As I reached for the zipper on my overnight bag, he again waved me off and marked it. Thanking him in Arabic and wishing him a good evening, I picked up my bags and departed. The back of my neck was at full "tingle" all the way to the exit.

Possibly I did not breathe until well out the door and on the way to my car. While walking I was thanking "Allah" for encouraging me to prepare my bags for "worst case" even though I felt confident I would simply breeze through domestic Customs. Never forget "Murphy's Law"!

Yes, I did know what I did was wrong and my conscience bothered me some. Later, I told Captain Jake Nahar (the King's pilot) about it and that it preyed on my mind. Jake said, "Don't worry about it, I will seek forgiveness." He spoke several sentences in Arabic over me concluding with "Allah Akbar." Then he told me I was forgiven. Jake had quite a sense of humor. So did I.

GO HOME?

In late April, 1966, we began discussions on how to continue David's education in the manner best for him. David would graduate June fifth from the local, "Parents Collective School." He had done really well in his year of school here and was happy with the arrangement; however, he would be in high school next fall and that was not available here. Most, if not all, of the families were sending their kids to schools in other countries such as England, Italy, Switzerland, Germany, Lebanon, even to the U.S. Some were successful; others became very troublesome for the young people away from home and proper supervision. Bob Majors had sent his teen age son, Billy to Notre Dame in Rome the previous year and seemingly was doing ok. Marti and I decided to go there and take a look. It so happened we arrived in Rome on a Saturday and proceeded out to Notre Dame to pay Master Billy a visit. We called ahead and with considerable difficulty located an official for information and permission to visit. The information he provided was very sketchy, hesitant and not encouraging. Proceeding to Notre Dame by taxi, we found the campus virtually empty with very few pedestrians. Consequently, we experienced considerable difficulty locating the priest we had talked to earlier. When we did meet, he informed us Billy was apparently not on campus. It appeared he and some of his buddies were in Rome for the weekend. Turning a fourteen or fifteen year old kid loose in a large city was not our idea of proper supervision. We thanked the priest for his time and departed much the wiser and ninety percent on the way to a decision on what to do about school. Also we had previously found that drug laws in some of these countries were rather lax and kids were taking advantage of it. Not good. Of course for that matter, kids were able to get drugs in Jeddah with very little difficulty, even though the penalties there could be very harsh. Later we learned one of David's friends in school had been caught with drugs and sent to prison. Prison in Saudi Arabia is not a good place to be. They do not feed prisoners, for one thing. Their relatives are required to take care of that little item. Things go downhill from there. He was there for many years, we understood.

We discussed our plans with David, informing him we would return to the states in late June to give us time to locate and set him up for school. The timing from this end was just right as by then I would have been in this country for eighteen months, qualifying me for a considerable income tax credit.

We sold all the items we had bought in the States and were not available in Jeddah for a profit, plus anything else remaining folks wanted. We packed the remainder, except for those items Marti thought we might need to get started in an apartment and shipped them off. I don't remember how many bags and boxes we took back with us, but Marti says we had 27 pieces of luggage. She had a good many "goodies" to bring along. Some were for her décor, some as gifts to friends and family. David was the keeper of the bags and he kept track of them all. Not an easy task to check and count each piece as they were moved around. We elected to go home the opposite direction to complete the round the world trip we started. Our route would be: Jeddah to Karachi Pakistan, to Bombay India, to Bangkok, Thailand, to Hong Kong, to Tokyo, Japan to Honolulu, Hawaii to Los Angeles and then to San Diego.

HOMEWARD BOUND

We flew on a Saudia aircraft from Jeddah to Karachi, waited two hours to connect with Lufthansa Airlines, and continued on to Bombay, India. We had to stay overnight in Bombay, but did not attempt any sightseeing as we had seen enough previously. Driving through the streets at night from the hotel was depressing enough. Many of the streets were wall to wall with people sleeping on the ground on each side of the pavement. Once we reached the airport, there would be about three hours of waiting for our transportation. For this portion of our flight, we would be on an Alitalia plane. Alitalia is the national airline of Italy. We enjoyed great service en route and had an excellent flight.

After landing at the airport near Bangkok, we cleared Immigration and Customs with minimum fuss, in spite of the many bags and boxes to account for and transport to our hotel. That might have cost us! Luckily, the Manohra Hotel had their transportation vehicle handy and would whisk us to their beautiful new location. Staying there for a few days was well worth the time. We took a tour up one of the muddy subsidiaries of the very wide muddy Chad Phraya River that ran through the city of Bangkok. The long motor boat we were in had an outboard motor with a long shaft protruding almost horizontally to the surface of the river. The propeller was barely covered by water. This allowed the operator to travel through very shallow water and through water lilies growing in some areas upstream.

Many domiciles and shops were built on the river banks with parts of them extending out into the shallows on stakes. These included tourist stops along with food and the usual souvenirs of many kinds. The natives bathed, washed clothing, urinated, defecated and played in those polluted streams. We were told they also used that water to cook with and to drink.

About a mile up river from the last tourist shop, we encountered a wall to wall outdoor market consisting of many boats laden with each merchant's fruits, vegetables and many other items native to that area. I knew what some of those items looked like, but could not identify them, nor wished to in some cases. Everything was very colorful and all the people were friendly and courteous. Constant bartering filled the air with shouted bids and demands. Our boat operator deftly worked his way through the boat clogged "market" area. From there, we endured the long bumpy ride back across the waves created by the quite heavy boat traffic. We "dodged" many boats, large and small on the way.

That evening after dinner in the hotel, we attended a show featuring the Thai Dancers. There were men and girls in their native costumes performing separately in exotic, intricate dance routines. All had their faces painted in exaggerated fashion showing off the girl's beautiful doll-like appearance. The girls wore a lower garment that could be described as a "pantaloon." They also wore a jewel encrusted "helmet" that culminated in a spire for the top. The men's faces appeared more "Gargoyle" like, perhaps depicting fictional characters in their ancient history. In another all male show, the men were in the clothing of their ancestors and depicted events of the past. The dancing of the girls was very gracefully accentuated by coordinated movements of their beautiful little hands and super long artificial gold nails. These nails were fitted on over their own. Altogether a very interesting and beautiful show.

The next day, we visited many pagodas and shrines. Perhaps I could remember which ones, if they had been possible for me to pronounce. We also saw one seated solid gold Buddha. Inside another shelter we stood beside the fifty-five foot "Reclining Buddha." He was completely covered in gold leaf.

That evening, our dinner in the hotel was followed by a depiction of a Thai wedding complete with traditional costumes and rituals. David was invited to come forward, sign the guest book and congratulate the bride and groom. The event was quite solemn, colorful and interesting. How traditional and accurate I do not know; however, the staff vowed it was indeed a "real" wedding.

The next day was a bit more restful with only a little sight seeing, some shopping for Marti and goofing off (investigating) for David. After an early quick meal, we proceeded to the IUMPINEE STADIUM to see some "kick boxing" or THAI boxing as they tagged it. The boxers are matched in weight brackets, and the card showed five matches plus three "main events." They do wear boxing gloves; however, the gloves appear to be about half the size or smaller than ours. The feet are bare except for taping of the ankle for about six inches continuing with a wrap of the instep. They box in the accepted manner while attempting to get in position for a strong kick to the opponent's body, apparently preferring mid thigh. After a few kicks of this nature, the thigh of the "kicked" begins to redden and weaken. In the first match, the loser was kicked in the same spot on his mid thigh so often, he could no longer stand. It is the kick that usually decides the winner.

We had good seats and were grateful we had not accepted the offered position nearer the ring. A bit of blood and sweat occasionally splattered those at ringside. Marti surprised me for going in the first place and more so by staying as long as we did.

HONG KONG

June the 15th, 1966. We departed Bangkok on Alitalia Airlines heading to the fabled shopper's paradise of Hong Kong. We were authorized two hundred pounds of free baggage by Saudi Arabian Airlines, and that usually was honored by most other carriers, even any overage one might be dragging along. Alitalia was not inclined to be so generous and were insisting on charging all luggage over sixty-six pounds as overage and levied a heavy penalty. After a few heated discussions, the manager agreed to charge extra only on that weight over two hundred pounds. I agreed and paid; knowing when to back off.

The approach to Kai-tak Airport at Hong Kong is not for the faint hearted. The very rugged hills surrounding Hong Kong require a very steep approach to the runway down between apartment buildings on each side. We looked out our right side windows and were eye level with laundry hanging on the balconies of one such apartment building. The runway itself is built on landfill that extends out into the bay and is not as long as it should be for those big jets. The pilot must aim for a spot as close to the approach end as possible and stick it close.

We had hotel reservations at the Hong Kong Hilton and were advised to look for the hotel limousine service after arrival. After we arrived at the vehicle and the driver had loaded our baggage, we learned we had landed in Kowloon and would have to take the Star ferry across the bay to Hong Kong side to find the Hilton. So we did. Most of the shopping areas were on the Kowloon side, so we rode the ferry back and forth every day. Indeed, Hong Kong lived up to its reputation as a shopper's paradise. Shop after shop, street after street, beckoned with all kinds of desirable goodies at unheard of prices, especially for folks like us. We had just come from a stay in a country not known for shopping of this kind to this paradise for the afflicted.

Your imagination will have to suffice for enumerating the many items we collectively ended up with. However I do think it might be interesting to learn, we three each had a pair of shoes handcrafted by Mr. Lee Kee, Boot and Shoe Maker LTD of Kowloon. Completely done and delivered in two days! Prices: Men's German calfskin for $9.00, Kangaroo for $10.00. Ladies shoes were comparable in price. I still have a folder Mr. Kee gave me with samples of nine different leathers to choose from, each shown in six choices of color.

We set aside one day to explore the narrow winding streets of Hong Kong side, climbing the many steps to the different levels, experiencing the colorful sights and sounds of that bustling very native area. That trek was very much worth the time and effort we had to put in.

Sunday the nineteenth of June, 1966 on David's fourteenth birthday, we would depart Hong Kong for Tokyo, Japan. Marti had the hotel send a cake up to our room to celebrate. Unfortunately, they were a bit late and we had only time to partake of a single piece of it before hurriedly picking up our gear and rushing out the door. Back across the bay on the ferry and to the airport. Here I was to have another encounter with a different Alitalia manager over excess baggage charges. The case for me to be granted relief from the excess charges is quite weak. Much thought had gone into this subject since my previous encounter over excess baggage charges. Now better prepared, I used verbal smoke and mirrors to muddy the waters sufficiently to allow the Alitalia representative to save face as he approved the allowance.

TOKYO

Soon we were winging our way north to Japan and after an uneventful flight, duly arrived at Tokyo International Airport on the nineteenth of June. Taxi service from the airport to downtown was one hundred dollars. A bit steep for our purse. However, an airport limousine service rate was quite reasonable and would transport all our baggage as well. Again we would stay in a Hilton Hotel, which was in our favor in more than just favorable rates. Inadvertently, I should think, we were assigned to a Japanese style room. This would not suit our lifestyle at all and I called the front desk. We were given another more suitable room. The Hilton was just across the street from the Sanno Hotel, a U. S. Military run Hotel for transit personnel of the armed forces. The Sanno had a small Post Exchange and a cafeteria serving food American style. Of course we were welcome to use that facility and did so. Tokyo would not prove to be economical and we would curb our activities accordingly.

The next day, Marti wanted to visit the highly advertised world class shopping area of Tokyo located on the Ginza. This location was said to rival New York's Broadway area for great stores and volume. That may be true; however, I can't vouch for that, but I can testify to the huge throngs of people we encountered. The taxi drivers certainly were competitive and worse, they drove faster and took more chances than Marti cared for. There were street cars in Tokyo, and the taxis used their tracks, dodging only to avoid head-on crashes with the oncoming street cars. Brakes were used sparingly, usually only to avoid impact, not for stopping. The traffic noise was disconcerting with horns blaring, tires squealing, and street cars ringing their bells. It was fortunate the taxi driver could not understand the invective hurled at him by Marti in between her screams to "Slow down," you $%&# idiot!" When we departed the taxi, David had to help her free her hands from the grip she had on the assist strap.

Shopping was a bust. The throngs of people constantly in motion on the streets and in the stores were just overwhelming. Marti cannot tolerate heights, including those scary views one gets from traversing those open areas on escalators. All the stores were loaded with those open air people movers and Marti's resolve was fading fast. Marti agreed on one more taxi ride having recognized the necessity. After we entered the taxi, Marti proceeded to tell the driver how she expected him to drive on the way to the hotel. He nodded his head enthusiastically to everything she was saying as he blasted off with squealing tires and blaring horn. We spent the rest of the day relaxing at the Sanno Hotel.

Tokyo's Gray Line Tours took us for a "Meet Japan Tour" the following day. We were allowed in and through a "typical" Japanese home. Interesting, but not for us. The National Gymnasium complex was huge, modern and overwhelming. Marti really enjoyed touring one of the Tasaki Pearl Company Farms. They did not offer enough of a bargain, so she passed on pearls. We also drove past the wall and one of the entrances of the Emperor's Palace. That complex takes up an awful lot of space right in the center of Tokyo.

HONOLULU STOP

The morning of June 24, 1966 would find us winging our way to Los Angeles via a stop at Honolulu. Japan Airlines was the carrier and there was no hassle over excess baggage. Not only that, they had upgraded us to First Class and we received full attention all the way. The flight was great with arrival at Honolulu on time. Here we would go through Immigrations and Customs, for the U.S. Customs targeted us immediately with all those bags and parcels. They took my declarations and started through all bags. They intended to charge me tax on all our possessions, maintaining we were Foreign Nationals having arrived in the U. S. after being a resident of Saudi Arabia for over eighteen months. Needless to say, this came as a bit of a surprise and started me thinking back over what I had been told at our embassy in Jeddah. Recalling a paper the embassy had given me on that subject, I started going through my briefcase searching for it. While searching, I began explaining the circumstances as outlined to me and how their interpretation did not apply in this case. They seemed to think I had actually become a resident of Saudi Arabia, but I explained I had been on temporary duty from TWA for a specific purpose and was returning after my job was accomplished. Knowing that in a confrontation with Customs I would lose, I adopted the sincerity approach. At this point, I located the document the U.S. Embassy in Jeddah had furnished me. The Customs supervisor looked it over and pointed out it did not specifically cover my situation. His interpretation was a little loose and after reading it over, I sensed he might be wavering. Now for my sincere approach; agreeing with his feelings, but at the same time building on my temporary duty status. After more conversations and explanations, he waved at his inspectors to clear things out and wished us a pleasant trip on to the mainland. He had accepted my plea.

NOTE: My wife still relates the above story in a manner that does not agree fully with my account. The answer is simple. She maintains I was lying so much in the discussion; she had to leave as she feared she might make a correction and foul up the situation. That remark was not intended as an accusation, but rather her quaint way of recognizing when I deviate from what she thought I would say. She did the right thing but for the wrong reason. The U.S. Embassy had briefed me on several possible situations for our route. Marti was not and I did not attempt informing her. What she overheard me say probably sounded as though I might be lying. Actually I was starting to lay the ground work for a plausible story that might influence the inspector. Little lies might inadvertently creep into a story of this nature, but are not necessary. Perhaps even a bit of obfuscation might occur. There are degrees of truth and that is what promotes serious discussions. One must find a middle ground where both parties are satisfied with a truth they can accept. See? I did not lie! Very much.

Our flight on to Los Angeles was great and we slept most of the way. Arrival in Los Angeles was the usual hassle but the drill was accomplished with little difficulty and we proceeded on to San Diego on Western Airlines.

TWA STATESIDE

Settling in with Marti's mom in San Diego was not an easy operation and never fully completed, but there was a feeling of semi completion at least. Her parents had always welcomed us with open arms and did all they could to make us feel at home. All of us were worn out after that long grueling flight, having to care for and shuffle all those many pieces of luggage during each stop. We were never sure if our baggage was being off loaded from one carrier to the other during these changes occurring at layovers. Going through Customs with so many pieces was quite a chore and more wear and tear on our nerves. David, as usual, was of immense help and lightened the load considerably. It took us about two days to allow our bodies to get back in tune with this part of the world.

We stayed in San Diego to visit with Marti's mom and other family, enjoying the great weather and stateside surroundings. I retrieved our two cars, a Pontiac Grand Prix and the Sunbeam Alpine (Roadster) from storage and put them back in proper operating condition. We planned on towing the Sunbeam with the Pontiac on the way back to Kansas City and load most of baggage in the cars. Marti opted to return via air as she did not relish the long ride over the desert and beyond. David would go with her and be her guide and helper. They left after me, and arrived in Independence the day before I made it.

Soon we started a search for a place to live, preferably near where David could attend a school. We settled on The Danish Village Apartments, just off Metcalf Avenue on Seventy Ninth Street in Overland Park, Kansas. David would go to School at Broadmoor Junior High, just one block south of our apartment.

That settled, I proceeded to the TWA Flight Operations Training Center located at 13th and Baltimore in downtown Kansas City. Here I met with a Mr. Glen Hersh, the Flight Operations Ground Training Manager. Mr. Hersh gave me a rundown on the training program and took me around for introductions. He was a very competent and interesting gentleman. He assigned me to an instructor for orientation and for me to expect joining a ground school class for the Convair 880. Additionally, this same instructor would be helping me with the Convair 880 Performance Manuals with a view to expanding it into a complete teaching program. Mr. Hersh also introduced me to Mr. Don Crowley, the Director of Ground Training. He, too, was a friendly, personable gentleman and made me feel very welcome.

I was about to become a full fledged member of the eight to five brigade. Very soon, I realized what a sophisticated training program this airline had developed. Later I would learn TWA had far and away the very best program of any other airline. Also, TWA was very safety oriented and maintained a comprehensive program for pilots and flight attendants. An outstanding safety record attested to that fact. When I completed the Convair class, I was assigned to and completed the Flight Safety Class. Very interesting, and thorough. All of the class participated in a practice evacuation of a mock up of an aircraft cabin with smoke, noise and simulated fire. Additionally, all were indoctrinated in the use of several different aircraft doors, both in normal mode and emergency. Not only that, we used the doors in an emergency mode, deploying the escape chutes and sliding rapidly down them. The 747 slides were especially fun (fast) to use, as they were quite long due to the size of the aircraft. The flight attendants were advised not to wear nylons as they would burn off in a heartbeat (and burn them) due to the friction. I remember one safety instructor advising the flight attendants the slides on the 747 were long and steep. Therefore, they would be very fast and they would go down them "lickety split." The girls thought that was funny. The Safety people took things even further by simulating a ditching (landing on water), launching of life rafts and evacuating the passengers. They used a local pool for these events and later the pool located at Breech Academy in Overland Park, Kansas.

Of course, during this "break-in" period, I was meeting many people in the course of getting situated and daily activities. Pat Pierson, Glen Hersh's secretary, was perhaps first followed by Anita Smith, Don Crowley's secretary. Both were very efficient and would be very important in smoothing the path for me and everybody. Anita was particularly personable with a wide friendly smile for all. I wonder if Anita still has her pet squirrel? Naah, that was long ago. Bunky Moorehead was probably first of the supervisors or nearly so, followed by Mark Antes, John Buckmaster, Bob Larson, Bob Hague and Lou Tournoy. Lou was in Safety and would remain a lifetime friend.He was an efficient supervisor and an expert in flying safety matters. Bill Stansberry was teaching Power Plants at that time and worked with me for a while. Bill was a light airplane pilot instructor and glider enthusiast. Much later, he volunteered to give my son David his first airplane ride. He named the day and I took David out to a small airport located at State Line and 135th Street. From that initiation ride, David went on to acquire his private pilot's license.

They kept me quite busy for the next several weeks and time really passed quickly. In the meantime, Marti and I used our weekends searching for a suitable house to move into. Our requirements were a bit restrictive as the house would have to be in the right neighborhood (close to school), all on one floor, suit our needs, and the price had to be right. During the winter, we found the right house and it had been empty for a while. It was owned by General Electric and been the home of one of their employees, whom they had transferred to another city. Now they would like to sell it and get it off their books.

We made the right offer and bought it. The house was located at 6417 West 100th Street Terrace, Overland Park, KS. The house was white, had four bedrooms, all on one floor, a full basement and a nice neighborhood. David would transfer to Nallwood Junior High School and would later go to Shawnee Mission South High School. My daily commute would be a little longer, but don't forget, I had a Sunbeam Alpine Sports car! Meaning, of course, there was some fun involved in wending my way down through the traffic. We soon moved in, got our household goods out of storage, and Marti would be a busy person for quite a spell getting our new abode in order.

Instructing was challenging work and so was the learning process. Before going back to Saudi Arabia in 1971, I had completed classes again on the Douglas DC-9, and Boeing 707. Initial class on the DC-9 was in Saudi Arabia and the

707 was accomplished in the Air Force before my retirement. Later I would complete the course for the Lockheed 1011.

Within the week, I met Ben Nicks, who was the Manager of Publications and Stores, which was located in the basement. His supervisor of stores was Marty Shaw who was a very efficient, friendly person always with a smile and desire to help. I liked them both. Later I would learn Ben had been a World War Two B-29 pilot and that we had been "neighbors" in combat. He was on the island of Tinian and I was on the adjacent island of Saipan flying B-24's. The two islands were separated by about a mile of ocean. I still see Ben almost every month at our retiree luncheon. Ben is one of the truly nice guys.

While still in Convair 880 ground school class, I would get to take a trip as an ACM (additional crew member) on a Convair 880. The flight was from Kansas City to New York to Boston and return. All went according to schedule and up to the final approach to Boston. The weather at Boston was great, wind right down the runway, and approach was uneventful. I was seated right behind the captain and had an excellent view. Just before flare for landing, a great flock of starlings rose up in a cloud right in our path. Nothing could be done at that point except land and hope for the best. On the roll out while slowing down, the flight engineer and captain were monitoring engine temperatures. The engineer called out, "Temperature rising on two and four." The captain ordered both shut down. Shortly after turn off and proceeding to the gate, number one engine temperature started up and it too was shut down. We were parked short of the usual gate, and the passengers were bused in. We got off the aircraft and were talking to the ground crew to get them started on checking for damage. The flight engineer walked over to number one engine and stuck his head in to look for visible damage. We have all heard of projectile vomit at some point and had even seen examples of it. However, what now transpired was no doubt of world class vintage! Bill turned his head just quick enough to project his vomit quite a distance. The mashed up odor from all those turbine masticated birds coming from that hot engine was stupefying! A slight breeze wafted a bit of that my way and I almost joined Bill in evacuating my lunch.

The ground crew used high pressure water hoses to run water through the engines to clean them out. What a mess! Later they would run the engines up to check for proper operation. After a through checkout, the aircraft was cleared for flight and we returned to Kansas City without incident. The lesson? Watch out for birds! They can make you ill!

The assignment to The Flight Training Center was a great change for me and an even greater challenge. There would be many hours of study and creativity involved in every hour of every day. I was to meet a large number of involved and efficient people in the years ahead. All of the pilots, flight engineers and flight attendants, except those assigned to the New York Domicile, would pass through Kansas City at one time or another during their career.

Once a month, we could and did take a flight to places of choice, such as New York, Boston, Chicago, Los Angeles, Las Vegas, San Francisco, etc. Later we would spend a week at a time providing recurrent training for pilots and flight attendants at some of those same domiciles.

Concurrent with my studies in Convair 880 classes, I had been working on a lesson plan for a class in Performance on the same aircraft. Using performance information from the Manufacturer's Technical Manuals, I extracted the pertinent data, and then entered it into a format that could be taught using slides and graphs. Knowing how to use this performance data quickly and easily was essential for the pilots. Each takeoff had to be evaluated for length of takeoff roll, stopping distance, and takeoff speeds for that aircraft weight, that runway, that temperature day, wind velocity and aircraft weight. Soon after finishing the ground school portion of training in the Convair, the Performance plan was completed.

The routine was good and the environment was great. The number of really nice hard working professional people I met while employed by TWA is phenomenal. Supervision was accomplished, professional and efficient. One does not always or often find supervisors that are both competent and easy to accept in every way. My compliments have been extended to many of them quite often.

About two years after I arrived in the Training Department, Mr. Crowley was replaced by Warren Berg as the Director of Training. Warren turned out to be the type of manager I would like to be. A very nice guy and very capable. He still has lunch once a month with the rest of us "Old timers." About this same time another Air Force dropout came to work in the department. Jim Williams was a pilot in the Air Force and kept his commission in the active reserves until retirement several years from then. Jim went right into the training program for the Boeing 707, doing a stellar job. Later he would move into Safety and become the manager of that unit. Jim is a very likeable and conscientious person. Great work ethic and an excellent supervisor. He, too, is a member of our retired lunch group.

About this time, I became aware Jack Rhyner, Lt. Colonel USAF, Retired, a trusted friend from my Air Force days at McGuire AFB in New Jersey, was looking for a new job. After getting his approval, I approached Glen Hersh about an interview for Jack as an Instructor. The interview was readily granted, completed, and in due time, Jack arrived and was put to work. He later retired from TWA much later than I and now lives in Atlanta, Georgia with his wife, Marge. Another of my old friends from Air Force days, Ben Evans, Lt Colonel USAF and retired, came to mind and I called him. He was in banking in Austin, Texas and after a brief rundown to him about this type of job, he too asked for an interview. Duly granted, interviewed and hired, he was soon reunited with us. Ben left TWA after a few years and took his homesick wife back to Austin. Both have since passed on. Hope you had a good flight, Ben.

The Art Department had some very talented artists who would prove to be good friends and valuable coworkers. John Woody was the supervisor and a dedicated employee along with his expertise. Dick Marshall was an excellent artist and friend. We played many rounds of golf together through the years. He also was responsible for the art work on the much appreciated gift given to me on retirement from TWA. Dick drew a twenty by thirty inch caricature of me with a remarkable likeness and several events depicting my preferences for leisure activities. When it was presented to me at the retirement ceremony, the drawing contained one hundred and eighteen signatures of TWA well wishers. I was suitably impressed and almost at a loss for words to express my appreciation. Thank you, Dick. That gift was framed and has been displayed on the wall in my "computer" room for years. Rose Dickeson, another in the Arts Department, was an excellent artist and an interesting person. She was a divorced mother of one and very talented in many ways. Rose was quite interested in flying and flew light airplanes every chance she got. Many years after we had both retired, I learned she was in Arizona and contacted her via e-mail. She then owned her own airplane and kept herself busy at many things. We still correspond.

Another very interesting person then working in the Training Center was Rodion Rathbone, the son of Basil Rathbone, a quite famous movie actor from the thirties and forties and later. Rodion had been a navigator on TWA aircraft for years, and when that position was eliminated by the advent of jets with their computerized navigation, transferred to the Training Center. When younger, Rodion had acted in many movies as an extra but soon tired of that. He was not on good terms with his father and opted to get away from him and that artificial life style. Rodion felt abandoned by his father while growing up. He was raised by his mother in England and attended British schools which, according to him, were too bloody strict. Rodion was very bright and I enjoyed talking to him and trading repartee. His sense of humor was very much in line with mine. He too went to Saudi Arabia about the time Fosters did. His wife joined him there and provided another very interesting person for the many social events. She too had been a movie actress and was very beautiful in her youth and an animated conversationalist.

Bob Foster came to work for TWA during this time and he and his wife, Maribeth, would become great friends of ours. In 1971, Bob and his family would go to Jeddah, Saudi Arabia to work in the TWA Training center. Their two children, Roberta and Mark, went with them. We did not know it at that time, but within a few months, we would join them. David was now in Kansas State University in Manhattan, Kansas. We had accomplished our goal by coming back to the States in 1966 of putting him through a good high school, preparing him for further education. Now he was mature enough to live on his own through college and we could return to Saudi. We had enjoyed our previous stay there and the pay was much more than stateside, and included Income Tax relief while there.

BACK TO SAUDI ARABIA

Captain John Rhodes, a senior TWA captain, was also the general manager of Flight Operations Training. His office was in the TWA Training Building at Thirteenth and Baltimore where the rest of the Training Department was located. I had been on friendly conversational terms with him for many months. In the late summer of nineteen seventy one, I was headed for the JFK Flight Operations Training Center in New York City. While waiting for the TWA flight to New York, Captain Rhodes appeared and, after the usual greetings, divulged he too was headed for New York on the same flight. We sat together on the aircraft and talked all the way there. During the conversation, I told him my wife and I would soon be going back to Jeddah. He offered the thought there was a pretty good supervisory position open at that time, and would I be interested? Captain Rhodes explained the job opening was for the position of general manager of Flight Operations for Saudi Arabian Airlines. I knew from past experience what responsibilities went with that position and, after some thought, replied; "Yes, I would be interested." Captain Rhodes then replied, "I will offer your name for consideration and attach a letter of recommendation." He was headed for Corporate Headquarters for a meeting and would take care of that while there.

Three days later, I was at the JFK Airport for return to Kansas City and coincidently, Captain Rhodes was also. Again we had an enjoyable visit on the way home. He advised he had submitted my name for the job opening in Saudi Arabia and my chances looked very good.

Three weeks later, John called me up to his office and told me with regrets the position had been filled at the direction of the airline's CEO, T. W. Tillinghast. He had appointed his son-in-law, Hank Noon to fill the position.

We would soon begin preparations for departure to fill the original position for which I had applied. We sold our house, but delayed the closing of the deal temporarily. I prepared for departure, while Marti would remain behind to complete all the details of the move. In addition, she would wait until I could arrange housing for us. We also sold the Mercury Cougar we had been driving, but stipulated later delivery as Marti would need a vehicle after I left. The couple who bought the car wanted it right away and offered Marti a Volkswagen to drive until she should depart for Jeddah. She agreed and drove that until she departed weeks later.

In the fall of 1971, I arrived in Jeddah to be greeted just outside Customs by Bob Foster, Dike Artley, and Rodion Rathbone. A much different greeting than when I first arrived in 1965. They escorted me to the Al Haramain Hotel where I would take up residence once again. I would live here until proper housing could be assigned for us. In less than a month, we would be given an apartment in the Ashour apartments located north on Medina Road about a mile and a half from Jeddah Souk. The apartments were just across the street from the well known Blue Mosque. One could and did identify location by referring to it. The complex consisted of two apartment buildings, each five stories in height, surrounded by a ten foot wall. Our apartment was on the second floor and was quite spacious. There were three apartments on each floor. One was inhabited by a young pilot and his recently married bride. A maintenance person with his wife was in the other. We would rarely see either couple, as our schedules was quite different. Marti wanted a drawing with dimensions of the rooms and layout including positions and sizes of windows. The drawing was soon on its way. She could then plan on curtains and other necessities for decoration.

Marti was ready to travel by Christmas and David was on holiday break, so he could travel with her. She welcomed his company and considerable help for another rigorous trip by air.

Automobiles were easier to purchase now and I had already bought a new Toyota Corolla four door sedan with air conditioning. The Fosters, Artleys, and Rodion were on hand along with me to greet Marti when she arrived, so we were not wanting for transportation from the airport to our abode. Nor did we have to worry about fixing or procuring food for several days. Our friends made sure we were not wanting. Additionally, we were invited to eat with the military in the MAAG house anytime. David enjoyed the trips out to the creek with me to scuba dive in the Red Sea, but soon had to return to the states to continue with his studies at K-State. We would miss him very much.

My schedule had already resumed with Flight Operations Training and I was now in a ground School class for the Boeing B737 Jet, along with associated training. Previously I had been through schools for all the other Saudia equipment and only had to review the systems and performance of each. Soon I had returned to routine daily schedules. Socially, we were soon caught up in the social scene with not only old friends from our previous stay, but were meeting new ones as well.

Bunny and Ed Kaufman were in our apartment building two floors up and across the hall. He was a long time TWA employee and was currently the treasurer for Saudi Airlines. They would become lifelong friends along with their two children, Gaye and Brian. Ruth and Dick Woods were also in our building one flight up and would become our very good friends. Ruth and Marti were bridge friends and walking friends. They both enjoyed the many bridge groups in the various companies and embassies located throughout Jeddah. The two "girls," Marti and Ruth, would often walk from our apartment building to the souk, a distance of about one and half miles, and return after their shopping. They were no doubt frowned upon by the Saudi men for that act, but they both wore long brightly patterned long sleeve "galibeas" made for them by the tailors in the souk. That fact would serve to soften the Saudi's view of western women somewhat as it would serve as an illusion they were "conforming."

Thinking back about the girls sharing many experiences reminded me of the day Stu Schlemmer and I offered to take them to see the king's palace. Back in the nineteen fifties, King Abdul Azziz Saud ordered a palace be built in Jeddah to be used for entertaining foreign dignitaries. All the embassies were located in Jeddah for the most part because of religious issues. Foreigners were simply not welcome in the capital city of Riyadh. Contracts were let and the building began along with the accompanying "baksheesh," a very necessary part of any endeavor. The entire compound was encompassed by a ten foot wall about four miles in circumference. Many buildings were built along with the huge sumptuous palace all connected by winding paved streets. Palm trees along with many tropical plants, even banana trees, were generously planted throughout and alongside the streets. Lamp posts adorned all the streets and the scattered small gardens. The palace was huge and floored with beautiful marble from abroad and the local sources. The main entrance was spectacular, tall, ornate and beautiful. When the staff was assembled and began preparations for the arrival of the king, they discovered there was no kitchen. The space for it was there but there were no contents, just bare ground. Baksheesh siphoned off a bit too much this time. Realizing that if this became known by the king, all would suffer greatly, they concocted a bizarre plan to outsource food service for the upcoming visit by the king and the invited dignitaries. When it was time for the first meal, they prepared all the food in kitchens located about a mile away at the airport facility. The prepared food was then loaded in many vehicles and rushed to the palace for serving. All went well and heads did not roll this time. The king never found out. When we visited, we drove right on through the huge open gates and investigated the grounds by driving around for a while. Occasionally we would see a native here and there within the complex, but no one approached. Soon we arrived at the main entrance to the palace, parked, and walked up the very wide marble steps to the main door. There is an accompanying photo of Marti and Ruth ascending that spectacular stairway. Stu and I entered the open door and explored the spacious beautiful interior, but the ladies declined for fear of encountering a native caretaker.

About two years later, the palace was reopened at great expense to entertain a head of state from Africa. When all electrical power was restored, the city of Jeddah experienced a power failure. They solved this for the extent of the visit by shutting down all power to sections of the city on a revolving basis. We never knew when we might lose lights and air conditioning. All were relieved when the visit was concluded and our power came back to an almost reliable condition.

Chuck and Betty Frey were in Building Two. Chuck had been an instructor in ground school in Kansas City and had recently come to Saudi Arabia to teach in the Flight Operations Training Center located near the airport.

Ken and Joann Kennedy were in that same building and would be great friends in our social group for the next four years. Kennedy was the assistant to the director general of the airline.

Many entertaining social gatherings took place in the various apartments over the years. Included in those events were our neighbors, Dick and Lida Mason, who resided on the floor above and opposite from our apartment. Both of them were ardent bridge players and fit right in with the mixed groups. Dick and Lida bought our 1974 Chevrolet sedan when we departed Jeddah in December of 1975. He paid cash for it three months before we left and took possession when we left. Nice of him to do that. However, it did worry me every time I drove the car in that dangerous Jeddah traffic for fear the car might suffer some dents and scrapes, if not worse. Picture New York traffic, only with drivers who had been camel or sheepherders just off the desert or over from Africa who had never driven a car or seen one. They knew about the gas pedal and the horn but had little respect for the brakes. They depended heavily on the horn and Allah. Rules? Who could read? We would see the Masons much later in the Overland Park area when they too, returned from Saudi Arabia.

We renewed our friendship with Joe and Polly Vincent and observed their kids, Randy and Scot a bit more "grown up." "Smokey," their grey cat, was still around and friendly as before. We would have many more enjoyable social gatherings with them as we had before. We considered them as "best friends" and still do, even though we are again separated. They in Florida and we in Prairie Village. Through them we met Stu Schlemmer, a very nice young man working in Personnel. Stu was about twenty years our junior and single but fit right in with our life style. He had an apartment in our building on the fourth floor.

Soon Stu would be joining us going to our evening meals at the MAAG House and many times to the movies the military showed on the roof of their building. Often there would also be civilian Saudi employees there as well. The Saudis did not allow movies in the city but chose to ignore the fact of one at a U.S. military installation. Those movies were of much value to all of us that had permission to attend. The embassy also had a movie in their main building and we attended that one when there was a different picture being shown. Stu was very good company and fit right in, even though there was a considerable age differential. We shared most beliefs and could discuss many subjects equally. He was also an avid photographer and I shared that hobby with him. He accompanied us through the souk many times while he and I surreptitiously took pictures of the people and places in the souk. We would keep watch for each other as a cover. We learned to spot the ones to watch out for and managed to stay clear of trouble.

There were shacks were in many empty lots scattered throughout Jeddah and were home to many foreign workers from various countries. For the most part, they appeared to be from Pakistan or India, but could have been from almost anywhere. The little girl pictured at the end of the book was Pakistani and was always neat and appeared clean. She had a bubbly personality and was eager to speak to us as we passed by. She would hold out her little hand and giggly ask for baksheesh. We rarely offered any, but the big smile always stayed with her. We often remarked how impossible it seemed that a clean, neat little girl could live in such apparent squalor. I can't help but wonder whatever became of her.

Later when I began experimenting with making wine, Stu would come down to our apartment and help me evaluate a batch when it was deemed ready to bottle. We would note the color, "nose" and taste for future reference. After bottling, I allowed about three months of "aging" before calling Stu for another taste test. We found that some wines had not changed in that time, some had changed for the worse and some had definitely improved. Apparently depended on the type of grape used or in one case cherry. After about six months all had much improved in "nose" and taste. The cherry became very smooth and seemed stronger in alcoholic content. One had to be careful in the amount they drank.

Before I started to make wine, I had read a lot about wine making. However, none of the books or booklets addressed making wine from bottled juice. Making wine from local grapes was indeed possible as there were some excellent vineyards up on the plateau east of Mecca. That was ruled out, as we did not have the facility to process the grapes and get rid of the waste without possibility of calling attention to the endeavor. On a trip back to the states, I visited several distributors of wine making paraphernalia and pamphlets. None of them were of much help; however, I did buy yeast from one of them along with fermenting supplies. One of the individuals did give me a crucial tip that would prove to be of great importance. He cautioned me to not try using any bottled juices that were pasteurized, as they would not ferment. That just about ruled out any American product and some European as well. After we returned to Jeddah, I canvassed the local stores for juices. There were some excellent raw juices imported from Germany, France and Switzerland. I purchased some of each and gave them a "taste" test before deciding on which to start with. Later I would learn they all would make good wine, but with a distinctive taste of their own.

My wine was never for sale but we were invited to everyone's dinners as they soon learned I would bring wine for dinner. That is one way to become popular. Before we left, some of those three and four year old wines had become very tasty indeed and some had deteriorated so much I decanted them to the sewer.

When it became known we would soon be leaving Jeddah for good, we received many urgent pleas for the remainder of my wine supply. Several grateful people received a case or two of my remaining stock. That should insure we would be remembered, at least for a while.

BAGHDAD

My trips into Baghdad were infrequent for which I was thankful. The airport was well controlled and easy to locate near the confluence of the mighty Tigris and Euphrates rivers. Although the entire terrain was flat and without distinctive features to aid in orientation, the rivers compensated. The difficulties began on the ground. An aura of mistrust and suspicion prevailed amongst all our contacts with operations, maintenance and Customs. When we were driven to the hotel, the driver was evasive about why we were not going to the Continental, where we expected to go, but rather we were destined for the Baghdad Hotel. The Baghdad was rather second class at that time. As you might gather if you could inspect the towel with the name of that hotel on it. Somehow that towel found its way into my bag and Marti found it on unpacking. Very strange. When we would check in, the clerk on duty would invariably remind us not to venture out into the city in the evening. It would be much better for us to have dinner here in the hotel than to possibly encounter disgruntled persons in other places. Rather vague in their warnings but we decided to heed the "suggestions."

When we went through departure proceedings, an aura of suspicion walked with us especially transiting Customs.

I would very much have liked to inspect the city's market area (souk) and the people in their daily activities, but were always denied one way or another. The overall atmosphere here was much worse than in Damascus.

MEDINA EMERGENCY

We had some shuttle flights to make from Jeddah to Medina, taking Hajji's to and from Medina for that part of their pilgrimage. Medina is the second most holy site for Muslims. Mohammad fled here from Mecca after being attacked for his teachings. Medina is also his burial place. We had completed two round trips and were now on the third. This time at night as the sun had set about thirty minutes ago. Not too much of a problem, although their beacon was not working, but I knew the lights of the city would show up against that very dark terrain. It was a moonless night and I knew I would have to be careful as the city was surrounded by mountain peaks and dark old lava flows. The lava partially surrounded the airport and had built up into a narrow plateau ending just before the end of the runway. The lava was so dark and dull, it just soaked up light making it very difficult to judge height, especially at night.

The idea was to make your approach for landing just a bit higher than normal, adding a few feet for the wife plus a wee bit more for my son. Then be prepared for a quick power off to facilitate landing while glancing quickly from the altimeter to outside and back. And don't hold your breath. The landing was a piece of cake. All went well with the offloading of passengers and reloading for the return flight to Jeddah where we would quit for that day. We taxied out to the active runway, lined up and applied power for takeoff. The takeoff was normal and when airspeed and climb out was achieved, I called for gear up and landing lights off. Within seconds, the cockpit was filled with fog which smelled like hydraulic fluid. I was by this time flying strictly instruments as it was pitch black outside and there was no discernible horizon. Just as soon as I identified the smell of that fog, I had called for gear down to stop the hydraulic pumps and eliminate that very explosive fog. All it would take was a spark from a radio or some other electrical switch to blow us out of the sky. When we had gained sufficient altitude, I started a turn to initiate a return pattern to the airport. Instrument flying was made much more difficult by the fog and the fact the mist was not kind to my eyes. I cautioned the copilot not to use the radio to inform the tower of our difficulty as it might spark. We would simply have to continue an approach and landing, while praying they would not turn the runway lights off before we got back on the ground. We were supposed to be the last flight for the night and we knew they would be in a hurry to shut down and go home. Without runway lights, we would be in big trouble for sure as it would be almost impossible to judge our height above the ground even with our landing lights. Under these conditions, I much preferred not to use them anyway due to the possibility of causing an explosion when they were switched on. So far the only good news was the fog was dissipating and runway lights were still lighted. I may have called on Allah a wee bit, and I know for a fact Farouk did. I could hear him. When finally after turning on to final approach, the fog in the cockpit had dissipated enough I dared turn on the landing lights. It would become a catastrophe should they turn the runway lights off as I neared the ground without landing lights. When over the end of the runway, I eased off the power and set her down at a relatively high speed as close to end as I could because the landing was without flaps. Not knowing where the leak might be, I could not chance pressurizing the hydraulic system. Turned out to be a fortunate precaution as a pinhole leak was located right at the flap solenoid valve in the cockpit. That pinhole leak under great pressure caused the explosive prone vapor that occurred in the cockpit. We used all of the runway and, seconds after turning onto the taxiway, all airport lights went off. We had no contact with the tower and no greeters. We were strictly on our own.

After engine shutdown, we deplaned the passengers and Farouk explained to them the situation. I allowed them access to their baggage and they carted it off to the terminal building. After securing the aircraft, we retrieved our gear and followed the passengers. Some of the passengers left their baggage and walked into town. The rest of us made the best of it by attempting rest on the floor or wherever. Terrible night!

The next day, Jeddah sent an aircraft up with a maintenance crew to fix our sick bird, leaving maintenance behind to do the work and returned to Jeddah with us on board. Another fun night in Saudi Arabia.

One might ask, "Is flying really all that safe, then?" The answers are many. One answer might be as follows. Yes, providing the pilot knows his equipment thoroughly, has instant recall, has the nerve to do what will save the situation and is imbued with a large measure of luck. Or one might also believe in divine intervention. Certainly in this case we had a load of devout Muslims on board who were no doubt fervently exhorting Allah to deliver them back safely on the ground. Perhaps it is some of both. Then, of course, there is the situation where a mechanical failure occurs so catastrophic, man cannot cope or a weather condition so severe the aircraft cannot withstand the forces involved. This is a no. NOTE: Later I would learn there were many devout Muslims who believed dying while on the Holy Pilgrimage would be welcomed as a glorious ending to their lives. This caused me to rethink just how many positive prayers were going on in the cabin for a safe landing. ???

LANGUAGE

Marti and I had rudimentary skill with the Arabic language, but I was still attempting to learn. Going to class was not an option for either of us. Memorizing Arabic words phonetically was my chosen method. Then when the occasion arose where I would be in the company of an Arab for any period of time, I would practice putting those sounds together in a sentence. A bit awkward, but was working rather well. On many occasions, my attempts fell flat or were sometimes hilarious. Once when I was on a flight through Dharan to Bahrein back to Dharan for refueling, two of our crews met in the lobby of the beautiful new terminal building. One of the Saudis suggested we enjoy some ice cream in a new facility adjacent to the lobby. The ice cream availability was news to me and I was ready to try it. Ten crew members, eight of whom were Arab, got ice cream and we sat at one of the tables to enjoy. During the conversation, I thought to improve my Arabic. After asking if "tough" was the correct pronunciation for ice and "hales" was correct for cream and receiving corroboration, I proceeded to put them together. Then, I said," This must be "Tough Hales." Silence followed my remark, followed shortly by a giggle from one of the female flight attendants, then general good natured laughter from the Arabs. Joining the merriment, I asked, "Then what is the proper pronunciation?" They all chorused, "Ice cream." We simultaneously burst into merry laughter. That gaffe has stuck with me for a very long time. That was something I should have guessed. Anything foreign that was introduced to them stayed with the name they came with. There was no Arabic equivalent. Airplane was airplane, car was car, McDonalds, was McDonalds, ice cream, was ice cream, etc.

TENNIS AND GOLF

This time I had remembered to bring golf clubs and a couple of the latest tennis rackets with me.

We would play many rounds of golf on the grounds of the U. S. Embassy before our return to the states. Surely I mentioned earlier about the fairways being sand and the greens raised platforms of a mixture of sand, tiny sea shells and some kind of binder, probably an oil product. Anyway, the sand had a pretty high content of salt and would really eat away on the metal of the clubs. Still, when we departed four years later, I sold the set for what I paid for them. After returning home, I again played a lot of golf and found my shots out of any sand trap were as good as most professional's. That didn't last, however, as I did not have sense enough to shoot for the traps, where I could make a decent shot to the pin.

My tennis equipment included a Model 2000 Wilson racket and Model 3000. The 2000 was "loose" or "soft" strung whereas the 3000 was "tight" or "faster."

Anyway I liked to start with the 3000 first and later switch to the 2000. The ball would come off the racket slower but with a lot of spin on the ball. Not sure if that was legal or approved, but it was fun. I would switch back if the guys objected, and sometimes even when they didn't, if they caught onto the spin too easily.

Four of us pretty much had a set day and time each week to play and many times in between. The weather was pretty hot, running just above 100 degrees Fahrenheit most days. We drank lots of water. My playing partners were Ed Kaufman, treasurer, Fred Biesceker, vice president of finance, and Larry Stapleton, vice president of marketing. We played on courts located on the embassy grounds and occasionally one or more players would join giving a bit of respite to us one at a time. Fred had been vice president of finance for Braniff Airways before retirement from that airline. He was a real nice gentleman and we would have many social engagements where he and his wife, Fern, were involved. Some were at their home and of course they were invited to our affairs. Fred and Fern had a banana tree inside their villa wall. Some enterprising entrepreneur had imported several of those trees from Africa, and they had been planted in a good many of the recently constructed villa enclosures. The bananas were short and fat, with a rather thin skin. The good news was they were very tasty and slightly sweet. The Biescekers invited a large number of guests for a banana split party using their bananas and home made ice cream. The party was a great success! We were invited to their home for a party in early December. Marti had accepted and, as the date grew close, started to worry if David would make his flight on TWA in time to join us for the coming Christmas. TWA was on strike at that time and there was doubt their schedule could be kept. The night of the party had crept up on Marti and she had forgotten our commitment. Shortly after the time for us to be there, Ed Kaufman showed up at our door. He was there to inquire if we intended to attend our own party? Turns out the Biesekers were giving the party in honor of our wedding anniversary on the thirteenth of December. We quickly got dressed and proceeded red-faced to the party waiting for the guests of honor. We were forgiven.

Larry was a very outgoing person with a great personality and was a long time employee of TWA. Just a great guy to be around. And of course Ed, too, was a long time employee of TWA with whom we would enjoy the company of him and his wife, Bunny, for many years. Those were the good times.

Picture taking was forbidden, as I no doubt mentioned before, but I persevered and spent many a day looking for good shots and then much more time waiting for the exact moment. I took a photo of a Bedouin woman wearing her wedding dress in the normal course of her duties. She was aware of my presence and, at one point, threatened me with her staff and approached my car. I left and circled around and waited for her to come around the corner of a wall. After the wedding, the dress became an everyday garment as it was too expensive to be idle. It would be worn and washed until worn completely out. Her duties were many and varied and in this case, she was tending a herd of goats. She herded them through the outlying streets, stopping at every garbage pile in turn. The goats would then get busy performing their duties as a special part of the scavenging team. The rest of the team consisted of humans, dogs and cats, in whatever order they had agreed on. When the Hajji's were in town, I would spend many hours waiting for a shot of a good subject and timing to avoid detection. Yes, once in a while someone would notice and before they could act, I would depart quickly.

BEIRUT

Beirut, Lebanon was a very important city in and for the Mid-East. The city was known as the "Paris" of the Mid-East and aptly described. The city was mixed Muslim and Christian. Beirut was famous in World War Two for the proliferation of spies from several nations. Many of those spies stayed in the Hotel Normandy, where we would make our headquarters on almost every trip to or through Beirut. The Normandy was on the corner of Rue de Phoenicia and the Rue de Sour and overlooked the extensive beautiful Port area.

My first trip into Beirut was in October of 1965 where my introduction to that historic hotel and city would begin. The lobby of the Normandy was beautiful and very well kept. A wide wooden circular staircase caught one's eye while approaching the check-in counter. All the attendants I could see were dressed to greet new arrivals. All had on white shirts with bow ties. After checking in to the hotel and getting settled in my room, I proceeded to the ground floor and across the spacious lobby to the small bar along the wall.

The bar was very efficiently operated by a Lebanese named Anwar Lameh. Anwar was not only the bartender, but the man to see if you had a problem or needed a tailor, jewelry, license plate, or whatever. He would pick up his phone, call someone and soon have your answer or the product would be on the way. We learned to trust him. When Marti wanted to look at diamond rings, Anwar told us who to see and where to go. We walked to the jeweler, picked out a diamond and the mounting she wanted, and he crafted the setting for her. The final deal was better than we expected. She later in the states had the ring appraised for more than twice the cost.

Many of my flights were into and out of Beirut, so I had many opportunities staying at the Normandy. My first breakfast there was quite a surprise. Entering the dining room was my first surprise as it was quite large, with many tables covered with white linen and formally set with silver. Even the salt and pepper shakers were silver along with a rose in a small vase. The waiter was promptly at my side dressed in black tails with white shirt and black bow tie. The suits were shiny with age and many cleanings through the years, but were neat and pressed. The shirts also showed their many launderings and ironings and they too were neat. The breakfast was delicious and enjoyed, but the coffee was not to my taste. Rarely did I have a decent cup of coffee in any European or Mideast country. Well, actually, never.

One could buy almost anything in Beirut. Prescription drugs could be bought without a doctor's prescription and was on a regular basis. Many pilots flew into Beirut with a list of frozen meats to be bought and transported back to friends in Jeddah. Ham and other pork products were available here and forbidden in Saudi Arabia. Passengers on these flights participated in this mini-smuggling as well. One lady we know quite well returned from Beirut with several pounds of bacon wrapped around her waist hidden under her girdle. The heat generated by her body, exacerbated by the heat in Jeddah on arrival, caused the bacon to exude juices which not only ran down her body but caused an itchy rash. The rash would serve to remind her for many days that crime does not pay.

On another visit to Beirut, Marti and I stayed in the beautiful Hotel Phoenicia which was newer than the Normandy and much busier. The bar was very large, well decorated, and the whole back bar was clear heavy duty glass which allowed a view directly into the swimming pool. There was a constantly moving "stage show" as those at the bar drank, talked and ogled the swimmers. Some of the swim-mers had no idea they could be seen through the glass and some strange sights could be observed at times. There were some very embarrassed swimmers on occasion.

Another time we stayed in the Le Vendome Hotel, a small boutique style building with all French décor. Each room was beautifully decorated with French provincial furniture. The rooms were a bit on the small side and that was the only drawback. This hotel was near the St Georges, Phoenicia and Normandy, all close enough to walk.

It was a sad time to witness the demise of Beirut through the machinations of Syria and a radical bunch of Muslims. Marti and Bunny Kaufman would be witness to some of the shooting from the twentieth floor of the Holiday Inn some-time later after their return from Cypress.

CYPRESS

I was in many cities throughout the world, some I vis-ited many times, and some I visited many times, and some Marti and David were with me. To name a few, one would have to include: London, Frankfurt, Berlin, Madrid, Paris, Barcelona, Lisbon, Cordoba, Seville, Milan, Rome, Venice, Geneva, Heidelberg, Naples, Tunis, Athens, and Nicosia.

Just before we decided to go to Cypress, I had read an article in the Stars and Stripes written by Hugh Mulligan, Associated Press which is quoted in part as follows: "On the island of Love Muslim minarets sprout from gothic cathe-drals, Irish and British soldiers play football together, Arab and Israeli diplomats shop in the same supermarkets, while United Nations troops from six nations keep the Greeks and Turks from committing intramural genocide."

Cyprus is non-aligned, as the olive branch on its flag pro-claims. It comes by its soubriquet, 'The Island of Love," from the mythology of Aphrodite, the goddess of love, who was born of the foam where the Mediterranean washes the rocks at Paphos on the southwest coast. Marc Antony gave the legend life by giving the island to Cleopatra as a love of-fering.

As soon as I wrote Nicosia, an incident involving Marti, my wife, came to mind. We visited that city on the island of Cyprus in 1973 along with our friends, Bunny and Ed Kaufmann, and Stu Schlemmer. We flew into Nicosia from Beirut, thence to the local Hilton Hotel. We made arrange-ments for a limousine to pick us up the next morning for a guided tour of the island. We started off to the west from the Hilton and followed the main (perhaps only)—- to a small village that had a castle ruin nearby. Quite interesting tour really, although our guide proved to be deficient in English. But we were able to get the gist of his explanations somehow. He at least could converse with the local populace and opened up some interesting doors for us. It seemed the grape harvest was underway and there was some celebratory wine-tasting going on. We joined the fun.

One small village after another as we progressed around the island, heading south and then swinging back to the east. We traveled part way around a "mountain" (1951 meters) to get to Paphos where we did a little wine tasting, etc. Then on to Limasol where we shopped, took pictures and tasted some wine. We saw many areas of grapes growing mostly on the sides of hills, it seemed. Also, numerous huge trucks loaded with newly harvested grapes. The juices drained from the backs of the trucks and were staining the highway purple for miles, especially on an upgrade. This made the roads quite slick in some places, and there were numerous signs along side the highway warning motorists of that fact. We stopped at a couple of the fields where harvesting was in progress. The people doing the work were very friendly and offered grapes for our approval. The grapes were excellent.

On towards Larnaca. We saw a sign directing us to a big castle named Kolossi. It looked massive, all right, as we ap-proached on the entry road. Naturally it was located on higher ground, adding to its formidable appearance. It was built in a huge square with apparently just one entryway. It could only be reached by ascending a flight of open stairs and across an open platform that could be raised to deny entry. At ground level, there was an opening affording entry into what was described as a "dungeon." A large filigree iron double gate to this area was ajar and visitors could go in and look around if so inclined. We opted (all except Marti, as she is afraid of heights) to head for the staircase leading to the upper level(s). It is only fair to point out that the rest of us had been imbibing (wine tasters) but Marti did not drink. Maybe she had a total of one glass. Anyway, while we went on up to the top of this big "fort," she stayed below. Soon she decided to take a look in the dungeon. There was a step down into it and she misjudged the height as she stepped in. When her foot did reach the next step down, her ankle turned due to centuries of worn-cupped area in the stone. She lost her balance and launched herself towards the interior of the dungeon. Marti grabbed onto the gate as she went and it swung into the darkened interior right up against the wall. It was pretty gloomy in there, and she could not tell how far it might be to the floor, so she just hung on desperately. Some British tourists saw her predicament and came to offer assistance. One politely asked if they might help. She shouted in a semi-panicked voice, "Get me down from here." One answered, "Quite right." She wasn't more than about ten inches from the floor, so they had little difficulty. She soon realized her ankle was giving her a little pain as the good Samaritans assisted her out of the dungeon. When we finally came down from our interesting tour of the upper levels of the castle, we got a bit of surprise when Marti related her mishap. She was walking fairly well at this time, but I gave her some assistance as we headed for our vehicle.

Back in the vehicle, we headed for Larnaca where we would have lunch and perhaps a bit more wine. By the time we got there, Marti's ankle was beginning to swell and was becoming quite painful. We found she could not put any pressure on it at all. Stu and I assisted her in and out of the restaurant, one on the left side, the other the right. She put her arms around our shoulders and we carried most of her weight. While we ate, the restaurant people fixed a bag of ice for her to pack around the ankle to help reduce the swelling. Soon we continued our travels and in due time arrived back at the Hilton Hotel. We attempted to get a wheel chair to get her from the car into the lobby and on up to our room. One could not be located, so Stu and I half walked and half carried her in and through the lobby. Marti and Bunny started giggling and that rippled on to us. Ed led the way grinning and shooing people out of the way. We made quite an entry as we carried/dragged Marti across the lobby with our breath giving away the secret of our indulgence (in wine), giggling as we went. Everybody there watched our progress with awe or whatever. At best they should have realized we really enjoyed the quality of their wine as evidenced by our demeanor. At worst, well, maybe the thought of "crazy Americans" might have occurred to them. (See photos)

The next morning we were to depart for Beirut. I called the manager of the hotel to ask for a wheelchair. After a search, one was located in a closet someplace. The hotel people came to our room and wheeled Marti down to and across the lobby with some fanfare. Right on out to our waiting vehicle which then transported us to the airport. We asked Mid-East airlines people for a wheel chair, and that request soon caused a jurisdictional dispute between the airline and the Greek airport representatives. The dispute centered on the issue of who was responsible to provide the wheel chair. There was an awful lot of arm waving and foreign language shouting going on for a while. Finally, a wheel chair showed up from somewhere and whisked Marti off to the waiting jet. She was quickly ensconced in a convenient forward seat. The door was immediately closed, as she was the last passenger to board.

Beirut arrival was the usual hustle and bustle with shouts, curses (Arabic style), and much movement with very little apparent direction. Eventually the chaos lessened and we got transport to the Normandy Hotel to await a flight back to Jeddah. I took Marti to the American Hospital where she was attended. They would not treat her until I paid Lebanese cash for the x-ray. Since I did not have any, having just arrived back from Cyprus, I had to go find a money changer to convert my riyals. It was Sunday and would have a hard time finding one. Finally got back with the cash and the X-ray revealed no break. She was bandaged and issued a pair of crutches, which proved to be quite unwieldy.

Back in the Normandy. We had rented just the one room as our wait for a flight was uncertain and we needed a place to "park." All our baggage was piled in the middle of the room. Marti and Bunny were seated on a couch, the rest of us were seated around the luggage. We had bought some Cyprus wine and brought it with us. We knew we could not take it back to Saudi Arabia. So Stu, Ed, Bunny and I were drinking what we could, so we need not leave it behind. For some reason, Marti decided to get up from the couch. She hung on to the crutches to help lever herself up. When finally standing, she put the crutches in place under her arms, put her hands on the handles and tried to lean forward. The crutches were a little long and that action caused her to be raised up at the shoulders and launched forward straight onto the pile of baggage. Bags, crutches, and Marti tumbled all over the room. We quickly determined she wasn't hurt and almost simultaneously burst into uncontrolled laughter. She joined in the merriment as well. The sight of sober Marti standing up and being launched onto that baggage was more than our restraint could handle.

Flights out of Beirut were more than full and all of us could not get on the flight. The men could get on as we had to return to work, but Marti and Bunny would have to stay overnight for the next flight. They were able to get a room on the twentieth floor in the Hilton Hotel, just a block up the hill from the Phoenicia Hotel. Bunny went shopping for clothes and some time later returned with a shop keeper rolling a rack of clothes into the room for her to try on. Marti was a bit surprised and upset with that procedure and reluctant to relax. Anyway, Bunny kept some of the dresses and the shopkeeper left, much to Marti's relief. Bunny ended up taking all the dresses back the next day. That evening, the girls were out on the balcony when they heard some popping noises coming from the street twenty floors down. When Marti realized it was gunfire, she told Bunny to come back inside, they might get shot. Bunny declared it was all right, she wanted to watch as the bullets couldn't reach up that far. Marti kept urging her to come back inside as she knew better. Fortunately, the girls were able to get on a flight back to Jeddah the next day. The memory of those events has stayed with us throughout all the years.

DAVID

While David was in college he frequently made use of the free passes afforded to family members and returned to Jeddah for R & R. We looked forward to his visits and enjoyed his company, including his diving forays in the Red Sea. I would go along with him but did not dive. Not having attended any classes in underwater exploration and a lack of desire and equipment, I stuck to snorkeling above, while he dived below to mingle with the fish. From my vantage point, I could watch him swim amongst the fish and coral banks far below, as the water was very clear. Sometimes he would get so low investigating the drop-offs, it became a bit difficult to follow him. Many times I saw schools of barracuda checking him out for edibility. And shadow forms of sharks doing the same. Those views gave me some very anxious moments at times as I performed my duties as a semi-safety net. There were so many varieties of aquatic life in those waters that could sting, bite, or eat you, I chose discretion and stuck to snorkeling. Even then I was not completely spared those dangers. While walking to the shore through the shallows, I stepped on something that surprised me and stung my foot with such severity, my voice shattered the tranquility with great volume, causing nearby sea birds to take flight in droves. True, the underwater life was truly beautiful and fascinating, but not worth the risk for me. David seemed to thrive on the risk and rewards.

Just getting to Jeddah carrying his sixty pound air bottle was a feat in itself. He had to carry it along with his other baggage between planes on every change of equipment or carrier, plus to and from hotels on layovers. During Christmas break, many students would return to Jeddah from the states and many European cities to enjoy the holidays with their parents. On one such trip, a large number of kids converged on London on their way and were greeted with full loads on all carriers. They had to scramble to find hotel accommodations, and many ended up crowding into one or two rooms for each of the nights of waiting for space available. Of course David was encumbered with his heavy unwieldy air tank all the time. After some delay, David took a chance to at least get closer to Jeddah and boarded a flight to Cairo with no assurances of space on to Jeddah. Luckily the delay in Cairo wasn't too long and he made it "home" along with baggage and air tank.

The derelict ships in the harbor fascinated David from first sight. There were quite a few abandoned hulks pulled up into the shallows and stranded, apparently without anyone guarding them. One day he could not stand it any longer and decided to investigate. He took a small inflatable raft, loaded his fins and snorkel along with other gear, and headed out to one of the wrecks. He was able to get on board ok and found that on this ship, at least, there was a guard or an attendant of some kind. He was a friendly type and showed David around the ship, where he observed the steering mechanism was intact along with most of the instrumentation. The ship was indeed inoperable and would no doubt remain so possibly forever. He left the ship and returned more enthused than before to go to another ship as soon as possible. Marti and I did not learn of his adventures until a bit later. To continue with his pursuits of the mysteries of these abandoned ships, I must interject some background to set up his last and largest foray out to one of the larger ships.

Don and Eileen Lohrengel, good friends of ours from our stint in TWA Flight Operations Training Center in Kansas City, had arrived for duty in Jeddah not too long ago. David began been telling Don about the ships in the harbor. Don was in his late thirties and much more mature than, but just as adventurous, as David. However, David had the knowledge and expertise. Don was duly impressed and, without too much encouragement from David, agreed to go with him out to one of the ships. There were many hazards associated with this activity and one of those was the presence of many sharks foraging for their natural food amongst eaters of the garbage discharged by all the ships in the harbor. They made plans and soon were on their way. They got on board and were able to investigate to their content without interference. They climbed down from the deck on the ship's ladder and were soon on their long trek through the shallows towing the inflatable raft loaded with their gear and whatever. When they neared the shore, some people could be seen along with a couple of vehicles apparently waiting for them. Apprehensions set in as they got nearer when it began to dawn on them those people were police. Don and David were taken into custody and interrogating began. What were they doing out on the ship? Did they remove any items? Who gave them permission? What were their names? Who did they work for? Saudi Arabian Airlines was notified and the word got to the personnel people. Stu Schlemmer called in the "fixer" to go see what he could do. The "fixer" was a "retired general" from Sudan who may have departed the country a step or two ahead of the new regime in Sudan. In any event, he was hired to perform unnamed duties which might arise in the normal course of events. He was bright, quick minded, personable and had a good command of languages. I think an overall short description of him might easily be "con man." In short he applied his skills of obfuscation, persuasion, and geniality to soon gain custody of Don and David. They were escorted back to Saudi Air personnel office where they were then released. There were no more trips out to the ships in the harbor.

Later, David and I both had an adventure with the police of a much different nature.

IN CUSTODY

David went with me one day, as I had some scheduling information to check up on. We drove towards the airport in my 1972 Toyota proceeding with caution and complete concentration on avoidance of the hazards all around. Luckily, traffic wasn't really all that bad. When we approached the entrance to the "Old TWA compound," where TWA flight operations is located, I signaled for a left hand turn and stopped waiting for an oncoming car to pass. As I heard the terrible sound of rubber screaming on the pavement, I glanced in the rear view mirror in time to see a taxi cab approaching rapidly in my lane with his brakes set and sliding out of control. I released the brakes, slammed the gear shift into what I hoped was first gear and floored the throttle. Unfortunately, I had hit third gear and, although we did move forward, it was not enough to avoid the taxi. First and third gear are both forward on this gearbox and even had I hit first gear, it would not have avoided the impact as time had run out. He slammed us in the rear and accelerated our car ahead some more. That forward movement was enough to minimize the damage to my car and limited the amount of repair necessary. Steering right to the curb to get out of the way of other traffic, I stopped, got out of my car, and ran for the driver's side of the taxi. The driver of the oncoming car I had waited to pass before turning had also stopped and was running to beat me to the taxi. He got there quicker reached inside, removed the keys from the ignition and put up his hand, shouting: "Hold it, hold it! Police," in English. I knew from his uniform, he had to be police and no doubt an officer as the uniform was very neat and fit him. He proceeded to inform me he had seen the whole thing, knew who was responsible and to take it easy. Turned out he was a major in the Jeddah Police Department and was just on the way to work. He explained Saudi law required all parties involved in any accident must be taken to the police station where responsibilities would be established. He asked if my car was drivable and if so, did I know where Station 99 was?

After checking I answered yes to both questions even though the trunk lid was open and would not latch. We tied it down with rope. He then directed me to proceed to the station, check in with the officer on duty and wait for developments. When David and I checked in with the officer on duty, we quickly found it was not going to be quite that simple. The duty officer spoke very limited English, but did get us into the correct waiting area even though we were very dubious. We were seated along a wall in hard backed, hard seated chairs just four feet from the duty sergeant's raised "office." He was seated on a platform in a hard backed swivel chair, with a raised counter in front of him, which contained about ten identical phones. While we waited, we observed him answer a phone when one rang, answer, "Nam! Nam!," hang that one up, grab a different phone and again, "Nam! Nam!" repeating until he got the right phone. Sometimes it took as many as four phone pickups to get the right one. (Nam is Arabic for Yes and typically the way they answered a phone.) It was very funny the first time and became more so each time as we both knew the other was making every effort to keep from busting out laughing. We did not dare to look at each other. Fortunately about this time there was a diversion when the cab driver arrived with some of his male relatives and was seated to our right in line. Now back to the duty sergeant comedy for a while as we waited. Later, the major arrived, coming directly to us explaining about the relatives and about what would now occur. He then commenced a conversation with the relatives in Arabic and after a bit, returned to us. He said the relatives understood the cab driver was at fault and promised to pay for all damages if I would, "forgive" him. My first question was, "What happens if I don't forgive him?" He answered, "We will keep him in jail until the debt is settled." Next question, "How do I know they will actually pay the damages if I forgive him?" He answered, "Have the repairs made, bring the bill to us and the relatives will pay promptly." I forgave him amongst much rejoicing from the cab driver and relatives with many "shukrans" (thank you) from all. David and I were duly "released" and drove home to Marti with another adventure to relate.

CAIRO

We traveled to Cairo, Egypt twice, once in December of 1965 with David and again in 1974 when Stu Schlemmer joined us.

David was thirteen years old in 1965 and attending the ninth grade in the American School in Jeddah. We were able to arrange a mutually acceptable schedule to begin a mini vacation to Cairo. Our departure from Jeddah in a Saudi jet was accompanied with the usual semi controlled noise and confusion, but never the less successful.

Arrival in Cairo was accompanied by more humanity seemingly milling about accompanied by many voices shouting in multiple languages, none of which seemed to make much sense to us. Nevertheless, we shuffled through the lines with the rest until confronted by a uniformed person at a counter who asked to see our passports. He proceeded to ask seemingly obnoxious questions which were at times very difficult to answer as the meaning was unclear. We were instructed to fill out a form for each to list the amount of money and travel vouchers we carried into the country. Also list any jewelry being worn. As an incentive to list everything properly, I suppose, we were informed we would also be required to submit a list on departure. The lists must match.

All was well so far, now for the turmoil at the cab stand with our baggage. Preparations had already been done for this anticipated ordeal while still on the airplane. I had reviewed the city map to locate the hotel in relation to the airport and the approximate route to have a ready answer as to the probable streets involved. Also having asked recent travelers to Cairo for going rates from the airport to The Sheppard's Hotel or other places in the city would help. The first cabbie gave in a bit easier than I anticipated and we were on our way to the world famous Sheppard's Hotel on the Nile River.

We found the Sheppard's Hotel to be very nice, but not "sumptuous." Our room was quite nice and had an acceptable view of the Nile. When we departed a few days later, one of the employees apparently misplaced one of their coat hangers in my luggage. It was a very nice wooden hanger with the name of the hotel printed boldly on the top portion. I still have it. We settled in, looked around a bit, while David investigated the entire hotel and the hotel grounds. He would come back loaded with information on many, if not all, aspects of the surround, some of his intel would even prove to be of convenient usage.

Our plans for the morning were a leisurely breakfast and then go to the National Museum located in Cairo. We understood it opened to the public at 10:00 a.m. and was scheduled to close at 4 p.m. Upon our arrival, we found the posted times to be correct, but the museum was not open and no information was posted as to when it might open. Luckily, almost directly across the wide street, there was a large souvenir shop which of course attracted Marti's eye immediately. The large sign over the doorway read, DING DONG BAZAAR. Crossing the street, we found a large sign out front, which proclaimed:

"ALL KINDS OF EGYPTIAN & ORIENTAL GIFTS. LARGE COLLECTIONS OF OLD AND MODERN JEWELLERY, PRECIOUS STONES, HIGH CLASS BROCADES AND OLD EMBROIDERIES, WORKS OF ART IN GOLD, SILVER, BRASS, SILK, LEATHER, INLAID WORK, TAPESTRY, RUGS, CARPETS, EGYPTIAN PERFUMES, AND WOODEN CAMEL SADDLES, ETC, ETC."

No way to keep Marti out of there. Right after we entered, we were greeted by a slender Arab man in his forties, with a thin mustache and an exuberant personality. He wore casual western clothes and glasses. He introduced himself as "Ding Dong" and proclaimed he was the owner and would gladly show us around the store. Later we found out he was Bassili Tawadros and was indeed the owner of this and two other similar stores in Cairo. Marti would have much preferred to graze peacefully throughout the numerous "goodies," but he was not to be denied. Later, as the time approached noon, he guided us up to a second level which housed more interesting collections and two or three tables with chairs. He sat us at a table and proclaimed he would order lunch for us. Our protests of not hungry, etc., fell on deaf ears as he was determined to prove his hospitality. He did not realize it, but we were already fed up, that is, convinced of his good intentions. We coped without pleasure and all of us ordered bottled beverage for our drink. We did not wish to abuse his obvious attempt to please in all ways, but I am not sure we really succeeded.

There is no doubt in my mind, Marti bought some really nice items from him, but I cannot recall a single one. If I did ask her, she would search back through her memory and tick off each item, telling exactly what she paid for it after her bargaining. But I won't ask.

The next morning after a leisurely breakfast, we loafed for a bit and then prepared to visit the Pyramids. Oddly, we thought, it was quite cool in Cairo even with the sun shining as it was. We were not prepared for this, but dressed as warmly as possible before venturing out to the area of the Pyramids in the desert beyond the city limits. We went by taxi, as that was the most immediately available means of transportation and most mobile. As we left the city limits and entered the desert proper, we saw some beautiful Arabian horses being ridden at a rather vigorous pace. Sand was literally flying from their hooves as they ran. Quite a sight. Soon the Pyramids appeared ahead and to our left. They appeared small at first but grew larger as we approached and soon we were looking up at the largest one. Just short of the Pyramid was an Arab with several camels, fully accoutered for dress and saddled for riding. The Arab set about offering rides to each of us and predictably, David offered to get on one first. That was quite a sight! The animal was squatted down on all four legs tucked under his huge chest and abdomen and David was helped a bit to get up in the saddle. Then, at command of the Arab, the beast unfolded by raising his hindquarters first, causing the rider to pitch forward quickly and then, just before he falls off the front, the animal raises his front end to pitch him back into the saddle, hopefully. David handled that pretty well, I thought, and was soon walking the camel around to get the feel of riding one. I was next and no doubt did not handle the whole procedure as gracefully as my son, but got on board just the same. The crown jewel of all this was we finally persuaded Marti to get aboard a camel. We were able to get her up on the saddle all right, but things got real dicey when the camel started up with his hind end. She was hanging on to the pommel with a death grip and let out a piercing scream that startled the camel so much he got up in front much sooner than he intended, thereby keeping Marti from departing the saddle and flipping over his head.

From this point on, all she wanted was to get back on the ground. She had a short ride, which she declared was the last one. We left right away and proceeded to the entry of the Pyramid. We were greeted by a rather smallish young Arab in western type clothing who offered to show us around in and out side the largest Pyramid in the group. Close up, one could see the sides of the Pyramid were not smooth but were built by placing very large rectangular stones end to end, then the same size and shape stones on top of that layer, but recessed almost the width of the first row. We got a very good spiel about the history of the Pyramids and how they might have been built and when. He then informed us he held the honor of the record time to climb to the top and return to ground and would we like to see how fast he could do it? Now we could appreciate the difficulty of climbing that imposing edifice, not only because of the height, but each stone or level, required springing up to the next which was about three feet. Without further preamble, he was on his way. I can't describe his technique of level to level, but he was fast. He was at the top in five minutes, and seemingly falling on his way back down. He made that in less than two minutes, not even out of breath. We had no reason to not believe his claim of a record and certainly admired his agility.

He then took us into the Pyramid and along a very narrow lighted passageway and the up a narrow set of stairs hewn from the solid rock. Marti was not happy in this environment and made noises about not going any further. We discouraged that tendency by pushing on. At the top of the stairs, which was about half way to the top, was a small chamber, then a larger chamber which was described as the resting place of the crypt that had contained the remains of the Pharaoh. It was almost as though the end did not justify the means. We had the feeling of disappointment and entertained the question in our minds of, "Is this all there is?"

The Sphinx was a bit further out in the desert and was in the process of rehabilitation, so we left it for the future. The following day we took a taxi to the entrance to the souk and strolled through each street, then over and back through another. The streets were crowded and noisy as usual, with pedestrians, donkey carts and motor scooters filling the width both ways. Sometimes it was difficult working one's way over to one of the shops when Marti spied something interesting. Some of the narrow streets were covered, but most were not. The interesting sights and sounds seemed endless, raucous and at times brilliant. Marti found one store with so many goodies it was almost impossible to pull her away. They had one display with loads of jewelry and she had to examine all piece by piece. I took many photos, one of which was of a weaver busy working on some kind of fabric. He appeared to be a man in his forties seated on the floor with his lower legs stretched in front of him. They were out of sight within the confines of the wooden framework of the weaving apparatus. We watched for a bit, but he never looked up. We enjoyed the trip and vowed to come back another time. That vow was not fulfilled until February of 1974, and this time Stu Schlemmer accompanied us instead of David, as he was in Kansas State University at that time.

We stayed in the same hotel and actually did some of the same things, but I think more of the souk bit than last time. There was to be a show of some kind at another hotel that supposedly included an actual Arab wedding ceremony. We made reservations and ended up with an excellent view of all the happenings including the highlight of the whole thing as far as Marti was concerned. Directly within our view was a huge winding staircase down from the second floor. Prior to the appearance of the bride and groom, an ensemble of musicians was heard from the top of the wide staircase which got our attention as they started a descent. In their midst was a belly dancer energetically showing her wares and expertise. Marti said she had to be around fifty years old, and no doubt weighed in the neighborhood of one hundred eighty pounds. She was fat, her makeup was intense, and so was she. Never mind the age and the fat, she was really good! She made that fat ripple and moved every part of her body at the same time. Down those stairs she and the musicians came with her gyrating from one side of that wide staircase to the other. The musicians were just as intense, loud and exuberant as she. They continued with their act for some time after achieving the ground floor level. The sweat just rolled off their faces and bodies, while she flung droplets everywhere as she pivoted. Marti was really impressed and declared she was the best belly dancer she had seen. When the bride and groom appeared and made their way down the staircase, it was an anticlimax. No pun intended. We departed Cairo fulfilled.

ABHA

Prior to 1972, Saudi Arabia did not allow tourists, not even those of us who worked and lived in the country. For whatever reason, they decided to test the waters in that area and authorized some tour groups to be set up for certain towns in the country. As soon as we found out, we investigated the how and when. There was to be a tour to the southern mountainous region of the country very soon and we were fortunate to be included. Stu Schlemmer also signed up and we managed to stick together for the adventure. This area of Saudi Arabia was designated The Asir Province or District, controlled by one of the sons of King Saud. In this case, he was Prince Khalid Al Faisal, Governor of Asir. He was a fairly young man who had been educated in Western schools and whom we later found could speak excellent English.

A small group of Saudi employees, including us, were flown in a Convair 340 twin engine passenger aircraft from Jeddah to Khamis Mushayt, elevation 6500 hundred feet, thence to Abha which had a field elevation of about 7000 feet. From the airport at Abha, we were taken to the Hotel Aseer in a small 16 passenger bus. The hotel was two stories and had perhaps twenty rooms. The rooms were average in size and were fitted with modern conveniences, but not to Western standards. For example, there were no door locks. When I complained about this, the answer became obvious; there were no doors. They had solved that problem, at least to their satisfaction by hanging a cloth drape over the doorway. We were not pleased. Stu Schlemmer had a room of his own on the second floor and noted there was no door, receiving the same answer as we had. During the night, Stu's bed was so bad; he took his blankets and lay on the floor. Shortly after finally falling asleep, he was rudely awakened by a terrible clanging coming from directly below his room. He had the additional misfortune of a room directly above the kitchen and the noise was coming from the breakfast activity below. Naturally the hotel was of new construction and had no resemblance to the other buildings. The buildings in the rest of the town (village) were of mud brick construction and of indeterminate age. We knew they were old as the streets were many times a foot or foot and a half above the entry door sill of the shops or dwellings. We were told this was because the streets through time had built up due to the wind carrying dirt and depositing it on top of the old. The town of Abha was small and a bit primitive from our standpoint. Somewhat similar to small towns in the United States in the 1880's. The people were all Muslim, of course, and very sensitive to outsiders, so we were duly cautioned to respect their sense of decorum. We were the first westerners in the town and would have to be very discreet. An American educated Saudi in his native dress would be our tour guide and would supervise the tour. He was friendly, personable and had a fairly good grasp of our English.

After settling in our rooms and freshening a bit, we got back on the bus for a tour of the souk and surrounding area. This was "market day" for Abha as it was the fourth of five surrounding villages which had an established day for its turn at marketing goods. Tomorrow it would be the village of Khamis Mushayt's day. Sometime in the past, they had named their village with the prefix Khamis to indicate their market day. Khamis is the Arabic word for the number five. The architecture in this part of Saudi Arabia was all of mud brick held together with interlocking wooden poles and straw. Some of these buildings were six and seven stories in height and most were slightly tapered towards the upper region. Many of the tops are decorated with modified crenation on the perimeter and whitewashed. Some whitewash the frames of windows or whitewash a wide band around the edifice. The whitewash added some pizzazz to the appearance. Many of the rural buildings were of very solid construction with very small high narrow windows resembling Middle Ages castles with their arrow slots in the walls. Additionally, we saw many tall mostly round buildings with some narrow slot-like windows higher up. We were told these were built in strategic positions in the country side as watch towers in troubled times.

All of this area was mountainous. We were at about seven thousand feet, and there were peaks all around up to two or three thousand feet. Most, if not all, the peaks were terraced for farming and the greenery against dark rocky areas was beautiful. We would get to see some of this type farming close up. They grew a bountiful diversified crop which we would later encounter in the market place.

Our next tour destination was to be the "hunting" lodge that had been built for King Abdul Azziz Saud many years ago. Lore has it that the king was actually there one time after it was built and it had been empty since. Our drive was through a rather scenic area of light green grazing fields for sheep, rolling hills and small mud brick buildings with mostly flat roofs. Occasionally we saw people in the fields tending flocks of sheep. Due to the terrain, we did not see the lodge until we were almost there. The building was quite long, three stories in height and of more modern construction than anything else in this part of the country. When we first arrived, there were only one or two persons visible in or near the lodge. We were escorted to and in the lodge and were free to walk almost anyplace. There was no furniture, none of the doors were locked, many being left open all the time it appeared. After going through the lodge to the west side, we could see the lodge was perched on a precipice allowing one to look to the south and see many miles into Yemen with myriad peaks and valleys in sight. Looking to the west allowed you to see far down a fog enshrouded valley almost to the Red Sea. To the north were more peaks dotted with terraces colored with greenery of the crops. By the time we had walked the many rooms of the lodge and came out to the northwest end, we were surprised to see many more local people had gathered. Likely we were the catalyst and the local populace wanted to see what the infidels looked like. There were several small boys looking us over and came quite near, responding with smiles and chatter when we tried talking to them. Nearby and approaching was a local in an aging formerly white thobe, with well worn sandals, and a faded Kufiyyah ("skull cap"). His right arm appeared to be shrunken and almost immobile as he held it up across his chest at all times. He was of slender build with a thin gaunt face showing his prominent nose and cheekbones. He was playing some sort of tune using only his left arm on a flute like instrument which was a tube about sixteen inches long with appropriate holes along the length. The kids urged him on and he walked amongst us without acknowledging us in any way. We gathered he was there in the hope of receiving "baksheesh" from the infidels without having to notice them. Discreetly I took several shots of him without protest from anyone. Yes, I slipped him a bit of baksheesh. (See photos)

It was pretty cool up in the breezy mountains but we were not dressed for it, so the tour of the Lodge was cut short. Back in the bus for a short tour of the countryside and soon I saw a local tending a flock of sheep in one of the meadows. After prevailing on the tour guide to stop, I went over to the small slender Arab tending the flock. His beard was short, trimmed from his sideburns across his chin, and almost white. His mustache was neatly trimmed and salt and pepper in color. Judging from his smooth skin, I would guess him to be in his early forties. He was seated, wearing the traditional Arab clothing with the addition of a very large sombrero-like head piece hanging on a strap around his neck. The hat was woven straw or local plant and had a very wide brim, and I think it was used solely as an umbrella to protect from the sun. His demeanor was relaxed and friendly, so I tried to converse with him in my very limited Arabic and hand signals. He was willing and helpful and understood my request for a photo. He posed in his seated position and responded when I got him to stand for another shot. When I looked in the viewfinder to frame the shot, I was startled to see him with his "sakeen" (traditional long curved knife) raised in the stabbing position. I clicked the camera and jumped backwards with a racing heart. He was vastly amused. Slowly recovering, I laughed too and got another shot or two before waving goodbye to that shepherd with the big sense of humor.

We continued on through the countryside, finally coming to a stop near a sprawling castle-like long, low building that appeared to be built entirely of rocks and some kind of mortar. We were to learn the entire building consisted of one room after another built on to the original part as the family grew through the years. We were allowed inside and walked into one room after another, sometimes climbing or descending a flight of very narrow rock stairs to gain further access. We were able to ascertain at least three levels in the complex. Some rooms had colorful rugs on the floors with pillows arranged along the walls. Along the wall of one of the larger walls was a huge "fireplace" with a grate in the center and large heavy iron pots hanging or setting on the sides. The room was the kitchen and the fireplace was their "oven." We were surprised to note the ladies of this rambling house did not wear veils or cover their faces in our presence. Some did have a face covering dangling from one ear, but just didn't bother to hook it up. Seems that was a fairly common thing in the countryside. We were shown another "walk in" oven on the outside of one of the abodes. Going in the narrow low entry required stooping, but inside was a large area and a very large oven. The lady of the house demonstrated how the oven was fueled and used to bake bread, cook other foods, heat liquids, etc. Their fuel was anything they could find that would burn. We had already noted from arrival the number of people with vary large bundles of twigs, small limbs and or dried grasses of some sort being carried by men and women on their backs. There might have been other sources for fuel, but we did not see many large groves of trees anyplace. We headed back to the town of Abha and our hotel to prepare for dinner. Our meal at the hotel was not noteworthy and I shall not attempt to describe the food or service. That also applies to the breakfast at the hotel the next morning. In all fairness, I must remark the box lunch we were afforded the following day was not bad. The next day was also to bring with it an experience that none of the group has ever forgotten, I am sure.

The night was memorable in that we got very little restful sleep and the breakfast was again unmentionable. The tour got off to a slow start as they wanted to wait until the market place filled and began to hum. We went for a short tour around and through the town, seeing some interesting sights but the ladies were anxious to shop in the souk. Soon we entered the busy souk area and started on our rounds. Many

Arab women were busy hawking wares and more doing their usual shopping. Most, perhaps all, wore some sort of face covering, but not like those one sees in Jeddah or Riyadh. We were careful not to stare or bump the locals, giving way when necessary. In our group, Stu, two of the other men, and I had cameras and were using them from time to time as unobtrusively as possible. But apparently not careful enough. There was a sudden surge of sound and movement at our end of the souk and we found ourselves surrounded by armed scruffy looking soldier-police. They were very threatening with the weapons and shouts for us to stop. About this time, a jeep drove rapidly up, stopped and an apparent person in charge drove up, dismounted and quieted the rabble. He did not speak much English and we spoke inadequate Arabic, so it took a little doing to sort things out. He was insisting we all be loaded in vehicles and transported to jail. I spoke up and made it known that was not going to happen. The women could not be treated that way and we would not allow it. He was demanding my camera when another official arrived and was brought up to speed by his counterpart and me. Stu was standing by me and holding staunchly as well. After a bit more discussion, I proposed to go with them to jail or wherever and sort this out while the others remained here in the souk for our return. My camera remained in my possession. The peon soldiers would "guard" the remaining group until our return. Stu had already volunteered to go with me and the officers, and I immediately accepted his offer, thinking two would be better than one in this case. We got in one of the jeeps and roared off, making a detour to pick up another person who turned out to be an English speaking dentist they decided might be helpful.

We still did not know where we were headed, but decided it was a good thing to have this dentist along just in case things turned sour. Soon we pulled up in front of a walled area and were told to get out and follow them. We walked about thirty feet to a huge intricate double gate that was beginning to open. We could then see a large entourage of neatly dressed Arabs following a regal personage who caused our captors to turn servile in demeanor and rightly so. This was Prince Khalid Al Faisal, Governor of the Asir Province. He was a son of King Faisal. He had been informed of our "arrest" in the souk and had directed we be brought to him, rather than to jail. It turned out there was no need for the English speaking dentist, whose English was not that good anyway, because the Prince spoke excellent polished English. He greeted us with respect and we responded in like manner. He queried our captors in rapid Arabic, and then turned to me. He informed us we had been accused of taking photos of the local people in the souk. He asked directly if we had done so. I said, "No we had not, but if we had it had been inadvertent." I continued, saying, "During our many travels in the world, I had always taken pictures of my wife in many places to help identify where we had been. I did take a picture or two of her in the souk." I knew I could not reasonably deny having taken a picture, as I had been seen and I was carrying the camera with the evidence. The above was the best I could come up with on the spur of the moment. I have no idea what the Prince told our captors, but I think he seized on my story and used it to appease the officials. He turned to us and invited us in for lunch. Declining as gracefully as I knew how, it was necessary to explain I must return to the others as soon as possible to relieve their anxiety. Fortunately he accepted, but did extend the invitation to all. We were quickly escorted back to the souk and reunited with a very anxious group. Later I learned my wife did not appreciate her guard pointing his rifle at her and pushed it away. Then caused him some difficulty by insisting she was going to shop while waiting and he could just watch. She was pretty lucky. Those very low paid peons are not known for judgment or patience.

When we departed the next day, the Prince was there at the airport to see us off and apologized for our inconvenience. We were welcome to come back and next time let him know and we could accept his offer for lunch. Very gracious act on his part. I was very impressed.

IRAN-AFGHANISTAN 1975

Not wishing to make this a travel log, I will leave out a lot about our travels to the surrounding countries during our last four years in Saudi Arabia. Beirut was our most favorite place to visit and we did as often as possible. The last big trip we scheduled was in May of 1975, and that would be our first and last big adventure in these countries. We scheduled a visit to Shiraz, Iran, thence to Isfahan, Iran and lastly to Kabul, Afghanistan. Stu agreed to accompany us and one day we were on the way. Arrival in Shiraz was to give us a challenge immediately as all the hotel rooms were full for some reason I have forgotten. After some scrambling, we located rooms in the Count Hotel. A brief tour of the rooms we were assigned caused an immediate reversal and exit from that "flea bag." Further scrambling got us rooms in the Cyrus Intercontinental Hotel. This was much more to our standards for a suitable abode. We did an awful lot of walking the next day, seeing some very beautiful sights including a centuries old building with beautiful grounds. The well tended gardens extended front and back. Later we approached a huge mosque and were informed we could enter if we liked. All women had to have a head covering of some sort and, if one was needed, it would be furnished for the visit. The huge interior was well worth the visit.

A taxi ride out beyond the city limits brought us to the ruins of the Persepolis, which dates from the reign of Xerxes. Very interesting to stroll through the large area of the recovered portions. Magnificent pillars rose high above our heads and we strolled through what was uncovered of that vast antiquity. We walked the parts still remaining of The Staircase of The Apadana. The Palace of Darius the Great was next, followed by the Palace of Xerxes. We also viewed the ruins of the very large building that once harbored the King's harem. He must have really had his work cut out for him. We stayed in Shiraz only a couple of days and then onto Isfahan, Iran via Iran Air. Here we were much luckier on choice of accommodations. We registered at the fabulous

MARTI WAITING FOR HEAD SCARF TO ENTER MOSQUE, IRAN, 1975

Our driver & car top of Noon Cannon Mountain, Kabul, Afghanistan, 1975

Shah Abbas Hotel. The outside perimeter was egg shell coloring and consisted of Arabic columns topped with arches. The art work in the public rooms of the hotel and all of the hand painted tile work on and in the mosques and palaces was absolutely fabulous. We enjoyed our brief stay in this fantastic hotel. We were treated very well on the streets of Isfahan and within in the many shops Marti needed to check out. I have a large number of slides showing Marti shopping in the souk and elsewhere. Time does allow me to do justice to all the beautiful old palaces and mosques we saw and admired. Too soon, we were at the airport waiting on our flight to Tehran, followed by a wait for our flight on the Ariana-Afghan Airline to Kabul, Afghanistan. For those who might harbor a longing for caviar, they had kilos of the stuff for sale in the duty free shop; one pound of Beluga would be about eight dollars. We did not purchase any, I can't stand the stuff!

Our flight to Kabul, Afghanistan was called and we were directed out to an Afghan Air Boeing 727 for our long flight above the rugged country to our destination.

We arrived at Kabul on a clear cool spring day and one could see for miles. The snow covered mountains in the near distance were beautiful. Kabul is the capital of Afghanistan and is located in a fertile valley at an altitude of six thousand feet. The city is dominated by two high hills, the Asmai and the Sherdawasa, separated by a narrow gap through which flows the Kabul River. We negotiated Customs and Immigration easily and had little difficulty choosing a taxi for our ride to the Hotel Inter-Continental, Kabul. This hotel was the very best in Kabul, but not the luxurious type one finds in other countries. We had a fairly long ride from the airport, going through most of the city to the outskirts on the opposite side.

Our choices for sightseeing were twofold: Go by bus to the various attractions, or rent a driver with a vehicle of his own to show us the various sights and towns.

We chose the personal driver, one who spoke pretty good English and whom we were assured knew the area well. He wore western style clothing at all times and was clean and neat. The option was a good choice.

With him along, we chose to walk the streets of the bazaars where almost everything one can imagine is sold in small shops or simply out of carts pulled by a donkey or a person. One can even purchase poppy pods from itinerant vendors. Are they potent in that form? I don't know, but one young lad we saw seated with a basket of pods for sale was eating one with a very faraway unfocused silly look on his face. The streets through the bazaar were unpaved and not as wide as one would expect. But they were almost always busy to the point of being crowded most of the time with ninety five percent men strolling the market area. Most of the men wore a turban of one sort or another on their heads, mostly rather loosely wound. They also wore well worn "pan-taloons" of a sort with a layered look of several garments above. Such as sweaters, vests and a long shirt like loose garment that was notched on either side. That shirt reminded me a bit of men's "nightshirts" I had seen pictures of that were described as worn by men in the 1880's or early 1900's. Half of those wearing that sort of outfit had clothing that was patched, patched, and patched many times. A very large percentage of these men also favored western style suit coats as their top garment. Never-the-less they appeared neat and proud. We did not encounter beggars anywhere. Some women would be seen occasionally entering the better shops almost always wearing the Chador (or "Chadorey," an almost complete covering from the head down of thin material). The few women we encountered without head covering were either westerners or Bedouin. There were many shops with a stock of all locally made guns of some type. Fancy adornments were the theme on pistols and long oddly shaped rifles. The urge to pick one out for purchase and ship home was very strong, but in the end better judgment won. Marti loved every minute we wandered through the streets of the exotic goodies, but we ran out of time for that.

Her next experience gave her something to remember for many years. The Animal Market was on the road from Kabul

KABUL AFGHANISTAN BUSTLING SOUK STREET

KABUL, AFGHANISTAN ONE OF MANY SHOPS WITH HAND MADE GUNS, 1975

KABUL. AFGHANISTAN, MARTI IN MIRROR

to the Kabul Gorge and a visit to see the animals was indeed an experience. The animals on display for sale or barter were many and varied. The merchants spruced up their donkeys, camels, goats, and sheep, whatever, with carving of their fur or hides in fancy whorls or variations of designs. Some would even use henna, especially on the donkeys to enhance their "beauty" with the red color. One of the merchants got Marti's attention with a huge camel on a tether he was holding and urged her to take the rope and hold the camel while a picture was taken. With great reluctance and temerity, she gingerly took the end of the rope in her hand and the camel took a step or two towards her. She was already frightened of the monster beast and stepped back some more and of course he followed. The merchant saw her plight and released her from the rope just in time to prevent her bolting the area. The camel meant no harm; he was just very sensitive to the slightest pull on that rope on his tender nose. Luckily I have a photo of that!

Earlier, I mentioned the two hills that overlook the city and the Kabul River. One of those hills, the Sherdawasa, is famous in two ways. One, there is a cannon on the top that was once a part of the fortifications of the city. Two, the cannon is now known as the "Noon Cannon" as it is fired daily to announce the time as twelve o'clock noon. Our driver recommended we travel to the top as the view from up there was fabulous and we might be in time to see them fire the cannon. We loaded into the vehicle and he circled around the base of the hill to access the road to the top. Soon we started up the hill, rounding the hill in a spiral as we went. The trail was not much wider than the car and there was no railing on the down side. Marti is afraid of heights and within minutes, she realized there was nothing but sky visible on the left side where she sat and immediately started speaking loudly with a tinge of terror in her voice, "I don't want to do this, go back, turn around, no no no." The driver explained we cannot turn around and cannot back down, we must continue. We moved Marti over to the hill side of the car so she could no longer see the empty space, but that did

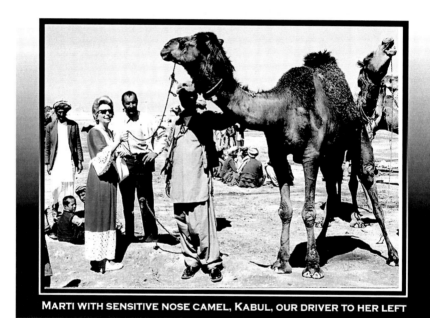

MARTI WITH SENSITIVE NOSE CAMEL, KABUL, OUR DRIVER TO HER LEFT

"Noon" cannon, Kabul, Afghan 1975, overlooks the city.

vehicle with roses on bridle and neck, Nerr Ghazeni, Afghanistan

not help. Admittedly, that road was scary and I was not feeling all that secure either. She continued to rant about going back all the rest of the way to the top. There she announced she was not going to go back down, no matter what. We did see the almost antique wheeled cannon held in place with some carelessly placed stones. Soon we found the soldiers attending the cannon. Both in their dirty, wrinkled uniforms were sound asleep, one under the cannon, the other in the shade of a big rock. Hard for me to believe those two clowns would know when it was noon, let alone fire that cannon safely. The view from our vantage point was indeed fabulous and Stu and I took several pictures of the surrounding area and of the cannon. Marti did return down the hill with us, protesting all the way and terminating with, "Never again." Can't say I fault her for that view; the trip down was even worse than going up. Without comment, I felt the same way she did and, if there had been a way out, would not have gone back down the same way we went up. Later I asked our driver, what did one do if they met a car coming down as you were driving up? He just shrugged his shoulders and had no answer. That made me feel no better.

Walking the streets of the newer part of the city was equally interesting as the old part, just so much different. There were broad paved streets with many shops lining the sidewalks tempting Marti along the way. Street vendors with their small carts abounded selling clothing, socks, pots and pans, along with many other goods. Two young lads attached themselves to Marti trying to sell her a "butterfly" knife; a type of switchblade made by hand out of brass and steel. She bargained with them as we walked down the street. They kidded her, laughing and joking in their language with some mixed in English as they giggled and quoted their price. Finally they let her have the knife at her last offer and went their way, still laughing and giggling.

We saw the hotel where the Western hippies stayed who were there to purchase and use the readily available hashish and other drugs. The kids were notorious for their lack of appetite with little interest in food due to drugs and money.

Potter at Istalaf

Marti on path, Istalaf, Afghanistan

One of the interesting disturbing signs we saw was a chalk board message near the doorway which read; "Peanut butter sandwiches, ten cents."

Another day we prevailed upon the driver to take us to the town of Ghazni, about two hours south of Kabul. This town was once the capitol of the Ghaznnavid Empire, which stretched from Persia to India. The tomb of Sultan Mahaud, the most famous ruler of the empire, is located there. The streets were wide but unpaved. Our car and possibly two others were the only ones in town that day. The rest of the vehicles were all horse drawn, some with two wheels and others with four. Many of the teams were festooned around their heads and necks with roses. We did not linger, but did take the time to visit and view the nearby famous Minarets of Ghazni, renowned as one of the finest examples Islamic architecture in existence

Our driver suggested we go to the town of Istalif, about an hour north of Kabul. The town is known for its brightly colored pottery produced by its craftsmen. The drive there afforded an excellent view of the snow covered mountains and some Bedouin encampments along the way. By the time we arrived near Istalif, we had climbed to a much higher elevation and were likely around seventy five hundred feet. We had driven through trees on either side of the road alongside a beautiful lake. The driver had to park below the village and have us walk up as the streets were not suitable for automobile traffic. The pathway was narrow in places, widening out here and there.

The open areas were mostly rock covered and winding through and between the houses and old buildings on the way up the hill to the potter's home and place of business. We were greeted by several children right at the beginning of our climb and they stayed with us all the way, chattering merrily as we slowly made our way up that rather rough climb. When we entered the shop, the owner-potter was working on a pot of some kind at his wheel. He greeted us from his seated position and continued shaping and moving the foot pedal that turned the wheel. All around the shop there were many colors and shapes of his completed work. Before he finished the project he was on, Marti had already spotted the jewelry he had on display. We enjoyed seeing the work being done and admired his work, but not to the extent of purchasing any. We would not have room to bring back all the unusual and beautiful things we saw. However, Marti still has some of the jewelry he had made. The children had left us as soon as we reached the potter's door, but picked us up as we left to provide their cheerful company back down through the village. Our return took us through an open area where two stalwart youths were busy "fleshing" out a large prime all white goat skin on a frame. They were removing all vestiges of flesh in preparation for curing the hide.

On the way back to Kabul, we met and passed two groups of Bedouins moving from one area to someplace else. There were many donkeys, several camels, a good many carts and a rather large number of people, all carrying loads of the necessities of life. One camel was saddled with what appeared to be a folded up tent. Some of the people were carrying large bundles of sticks, for future cooking fires I presume. Everybody carried something, plus a few with items on their heads as well. What an unusual, colorful, dedicated sight that was, we waved and most cheerfully waved back or smiled.

We saw and did a lot more than written here, but I promised there would be no travelogue. We did go on a drive to view the Kabul Gorge and were thrilled to be in such a historical locale for a brief time.

We enjoyed our visit immensely and wanted very much to continue exploring that vast country very much, but time had run out. Without a doubt, these were the friendliest people we had encountered throughout the Mideast. No exceptions. There were some Russian soldiers in the city, and any encounter between them and the Afghanis revealed some latent animosity towards them. Occasionally, one of the men would remark after passing a Russian, "We don't want them in our country." With great reluctance, we scheduled our return to Jeddah, and departed this trod upon, unconquered country. With that terrain and their indomitable spirit, it is no wonder to me so many from the past have failed in their attacks.

The Afghanis enjoyed a game played on horseback, both as a spectator and as participants. The arena or stadium was rather large in area to accommodate the teams of riders and horses. The bleachers were on sides and ends, but not tiered very high. The teams consisted of about eight riders on each side and wore colors for identification. The game was played using a stuffed calf or goat skin, which one team member would grab and protected by his team mates would attempt to transport said heavy skin to the goal line. The other team attempted to retrieve the object and or prevent the other team from reaching their goal. The game was fast, furious and filled with mayhem. Most anything was fair, it seemed. They were all great riders and the steeds quick and agile.

BIN LADEN

Back to our hum drum life in Jeddah. Sherif still came by for visits periodically, which of course we enjoyed. Saleh, our Yemen caretaker or guard who resided on the first floor, regularly had visitors almost daily. Some of who were very important personages and a bit of a surprise. Sherif visited him on many occasions, and more than one of the Bin Laden family could be observed in and out once in a while. Mohammed Bin Laden was an entrepreneur who had gained the blessing of the king and was building an empire by contracting all manner of projects throughout the Kingdom. He was already making huge sums of money and would continue to grow. He had his own airplane and pilot who, for some unknown reason, was attached to the airline. Each of the pilots in turn had been hired by the airline and assigned to him to be used as he saw fit. The job was considered to be prestigious and financially beneficial to the individual, but very confining. The pilot had to be on call twenty four hours a day and would "burn out" from time to time. He was required to land on all sorts of runways and, on many occasions, to pick out a likely spot on the desert near where

Mohammed wanted to go and set down. Mohammed Bin Laden had many sons and amongst them was a lad of about seven who would grow to be one of the most controversial and notorious of them all. His name was Osama. I never met him, but I did meet the father and several of his other sons who were then grown. One day as I returned from Flight Operations, there was a beautiful cream color 1958 Packard convertible parked right in front of the entrance to our building. The top was down and the two tone (blue and cream color) leather seats were beautiful and appeared right out of the showroom. The rest of the car was also spotless. Now this was in 1973 and I knew there had been no Packards built since 1958 and this car appeared new. Actually, the odometer only showed two hundred plus miles. Immediately I went in to see Saleh to ask where the owner of that car was. The owner was seated in Saleh's room and rose to greet me. He was one of the Bin Laden boys and was happy to give me the history of that convertible. His family had owned the Packard Dealership in Saudi Arabia in 1958 when they stopped making those cars. His dad had simply stored the remaining Packards under sheds in a fenced in area near the old souk. When I expressed strong interest in seeing them, he took up the challenge with exuberance. He said, "Come with me, we'll take a ride." We quickly jumped in and he was off, speeding out the walled area with little regard to other traffic. Already I was beginning to regret my hasty impulse. When we entered nearby Medina road headed towards town, he did slow down a bit and drove with the traffic. When he exited the traffic circle located just outside where the ancient walls of Jeddah once stood, he entered a narrow street I had not previously used. From that point the narrow walled, mostly dirt (sand) streets were not familiar. These streets were narrow and not straight, but rather jogged one direction or another. The very worst part was he did not slow for the blind corners at cross streets, but used the car's horn repeatedly. This was not good for my sense of safety and well being! Perhaps at this point I was a bit apprehensive or terrified might be the better term. Not soon enough, we came to a corner where he turned a corner amidst a cloud of dust and came to a stop in front of a walled in area and blew his horn. Within seconds, a gate opened and we drove in, coming to a stop in front of several covered parking stalls. Under the roofing could be seen several automobiles in two rows, facing each other. Bin Laden told me they were all Packards from the year of 1958 and all were parked here new, when the dealership closed. They were of various body styles, four door sedans, two doors, convertibles, and colors. Most had never been driven since parked new, but some had a few miles on them, having been driven by family members from time to time. These cars were not for sale, he informed me when I had asked. They were available for any of the extended family if they chose. Naturally I wanted his convertible, but there would be no chance of that. Needless to point out, I survived the ride back to the Ashour Apartments and thanked him very much for his generosity in showing me the Packards. Many years later we learned his brother, Osama, had emerged in world history as an Islamic fanatical hate monger and avowed enemy of the United States and western world. Then my mind wandered back to those days and I pondered the differences between him, his brothers, and his famous father. The label of "bad seed" comes to mind.

There is so much more that could be told, but what I have covered his should be enough to convince most folks things are just different here in the Mid-Est. Some of the stories untold are just as interesting as those above, but must of necessity remain with the past.

LEAVING SAUDI ARABIA

We think our time has come and plans were soon in the works to sell off our worldly goods and begin the long trip home. This time, no long way around for us. We shall go direct to London, stay overnight then on to New York and then Kansas City. Our "estate sale" went very well, and my remaining cellar of home made wine was gone to various buyers or friends very quickly. Golf clubs, tennis rackets, everything was sold in very short order.

Our friends gave us a very nice going away party, complete with very nice gifts and well wishes. Crown Prince of Beihan, Sharif, gave us a book written about his family, titled, "QATABAN AND SHEBA" by Kendall Phillips in 1955. He wrote in the flyleaf the following: "To my dearest friends and closest family to me personally. My friends, Porter and his wife Marti I put these words for memory and History. Signed: El Sharif Salih Hussain El Hubaily, 13-11-75." (Those numbers reflect the Arabic date.) We received many other fine gifts, including a gold pair of cufflinks with the crossed swords and palm tree motif of Saudi Arabia. They were crafted from twenty three karat gold and are quite soft and fragile. One must wear them with care. Their sincere well wishes were invaluable.

Our plans were soon firm and we departed Jeddah on a Saudi Arabian Airlines Lockheed L1011 aircraft for Paris-London in December of 1975. We stayed in the Heathrow Airport Hotel for the night. After a good meal and pleasant evening, we retired for what we hoped would be a restful night in preparation for the tiresome flight home. That was not to be, at least for me. About 2 a.m., I was awakened by a terrible pain in my right side, which grew in intensity and seemed to migrate around to my spine. My first thought was to call for help, and then realized where we were. I could not bring my self to surrender to the not so tender care of Great Britain's socialized medical facilities. Vowing to not give in and not waking Marti, I suffered in silence until thankfully the pain subsided enough for me to fall into a troubled sleep. About two hours later, the pain returned with a vengeance and I rose up in agony. Again, I held out hoping to somehow make it on that airplane to the United States in the a.m. Luck was with me and I made it through the night and the travail of the rest of the flight and on to Kansas City. There is no way I could have justified my decision not to go to the hospital in England to Marti, so I kept my own counsel. After repeated attacks in the following months, I checked into the

KU Medical Center in Kansas City, Kansas for diagnosis. After a full day of testing by four different doctors with no diagnosis, I left frustrated. After a week, I went to Richards Gebaur Air Force Base to see the flight surgeon, seeking a second opinion. Instead, I was ushered in to for an interview with a Master Sergeant who was the Air Force equivalent of nurse physician. After a brief interrogation and cursory examination, he suggested I probably had gall bladder blockage. After two attempts to prove the diagnosis, it became apparent; my gall bladder was almost completely blocked with debris. Within a month, I had surgery at St. Luke's Hospital and my gall bladder was removed.

In the meantime, we had safely returned, with me reporting back to Flight Operations Training Center at Thirteenth and Baltimore in downtown Kansas City. My primary duties during this period were reviewing the systems and characteristics of the Convair 880 four engine passenger jet aircraft. Additionally using the Manufacturer's Performance Manual, I would set up and rewrite a lesson plan for flight engineer and pilot's classes.

We had moved in to an apartment soon after returning to Kansas City and Marti was busy with realtors looking for a house. She stipulated we wanted a ranch, all on one floor, three or four bedroom with a level lot and an adequate two car garage with entry facing the street. The realtors were not very smart as some were attempting to show split levels, side or rear entry garages and unleveled lots. Marti changed realtors more than once. She had looked at about two hundred homes, most of which she would not enter for obvious reasons. We had turned to Jay's Realtors and were lucky to have a female representative who was on the ball. Shortly after she took over, we got a call from her about a house that would come on the market in a couple of days and we should take a look. We went with her to see it as she explained the couple was in the middle of a divorce and wanted to sell. The house was as advertised, with all on one floor, a big two car garage, level lot and a really cool large family room. We made an offer shortly after leaving the premises and were accepted that night. We moved into 4908 West 83rd Street, Prairie Village, Kansas in June of 1976. Finally through the next few years I would go through classes in all of Trans World aircraft, including the DC-9, 707, 727, L1011 and the 747. In addition, I would be scheduled for trips to various cities in the system and provide pilot and flight attendant training while there. Luckily, I would get to stay a week at a time in places like Los Angeles, San Francisco, Seattle, and Chicago, and sometimes reluctantly in New York. It did not take many trips there for me to feel unwanted or a target. One had to watch every turn a cabby would make on a ride to your destination to keep charges in line. One had to remember and offer a certain amount to take you to your destination. If accepted, relax; if not, get out of the cab. On one of my early trips to Los Angeles, I took and left a golf bag with clubs and other necessary equipment in storage in one of the hangers. Then, of course, I played golf in my spare time while there. Sometimes while en route to San Francisco through Los Angeles, I would run over to the hanger and pick the clubs up and proceed. I loved golf.

When I returned to the Flight Operations Center from Saudi Arabia, I was reunited with most of the same people that were there when I departed four years ago. There were also some new faces who became good friends, too.

The years rolled by with mostly routine regularity, with some very exciting moments added here and there. Therefore, I won't elaborate on that phase as almost all of the most interesting events occurred in the Mid-East. My basic plan was to retire from TWA when I reached age sixty. All airline pilots had to quit flying passengers after reaching age sixty although they could qualify as flight engineers and continue to fly in that position. Some did just that, although I suspect their ego suffered considerably. Many of my older friends had stayed on past sixty in a non-flying position and had developed a medical problem or died without satisfying their dreams of pursuing a completely indulgent life style. The option of teaching in Flight Operations Training Center was open to me and I was urged to do so by management, but I had other plans. I loved golf, hunting, fishing, etc., and chose to retire while still physically able to enjoy them. Marti was in complete agreement, so I requested retirement to be effective shortly after my sixtieth birthday. My boss asked to stay on for a bit longer and I agreed to a sixty day extension.

The retirement event for me was really great and was very much appreciated. Among other very nice gifts, including a watch was a thirty by forty inch artistic full color caricature of me depicting some of the hobbies I was known to pursue. Additionally, it was signed by one hundred and nine of my friends and coworkers. The artist was Dick Marshall, an employee in the Arts Department of TWA. I had it framed and it still hangs in my view as I type this. Many thanks to Dick and all of my friends at TWA for the memorable send off.

Some comments have been made that I wrote almost exclusively of the internal flights in Saudi Arabia. I realize the comments are well founded and so are the reasons. Those flights are by far the most interesting of all because they required eyeball, computing, judgment and some luck to find the way across the desert country. There were no radio aids or radar aids of any kind. The whole old way of flying took me back to my roots and I really enjoyed it. Out of the country flights were mostly routine and of little interest to be chronicled herein. By this time, I could have been flying Lockheed's L1011 and even Boeing's 747 to all of the international destinations. I chose not to. Later, I would find out it was best for me. I volunteered for all of those internal flights, just for the exploration of the desert country and interest in the people. Many times I have made the boast I could go back there and fly most, if not all the internal routes by memory. I could recall every marble mountain, every unusual outcropping, every jabal (mountain), dry wadi, or any other landmarks I had made use of for positioning. I have read about the "trackless" desert many times and have found that most of the desert areas are crisscrossed with camel caravan trails and watering holes. One just has to learn by observing and I did a lot of that. Many of those camel trails have been augmented by the more recent truck and automobile traffic.

Trans World Airlines was truly a great airline in its time. Unfortunately, first, Howard Hughes robbed the coffers, and then Mr. Tillinghast took the reins and further weakened the financial position of the airline. Carl Icon, the robber baron, bought a controlling interest in the airline after TWA had fought its way back to profitability. He then proceeded to methodically divert airline assets for his own enrichment. By the time TWA management got rid of him, they were deeply in debt. Years later, astute handling of the remaining assets allowed the airline to resume its position in the hierarchy of the airline industry. Then catastrophe struck again, when a person or persons unknown shot down Flight 800 over Long Island. This act was the beginning of the end for the once proud airline.

Leonard V. Porter, Jr
Captain, Trans World Airlines

ABOUT CAPTAIN PORTER

Leonard V. Porter, Jr. was born 30 May 1921 on a farm near Smithton, Pettis County, Missouri. His parents were Leonard V. and Frona M. Porter (Crabtree). He was the fourth of five children, two girls, three boys, all deceased except himself.

He moved with his parents to Kansas City in 1923. They first stayed at 532 South Hardesty, moving to 409 South Quincy (1924), then to 438 South Denver (1925 to 1928), 418 South Hardesty, (1928 to 1932) and to 533 South Hardesty (1932 to1957). Leonard Jr. graduated mid-year 1939 (actual class of 1938) from Northeast High School, Kansas City, Missouri. He had previously attended Thatcher Grade School and Northeast Junior High.

While attending high school, he worked at his father's ice house selling ice and driving a pickup truck, delivering to local residents on a regular route. He also worked for Demmings A.I.D. Drug Store at Independence and Hardesty (one hundred yards from home). He started as a delivery boy, "graduated" to "soda jerk," and later assumed full duties as a clerk. This helped channel him in a positive direction as he worked for and with people who influenced him very much. In later years, Mr. Demming's son, Bob would become a good friend. He too, had worked at one of his dad's drug stores as a "soda jerk."

After graduation, Leonard worked in Kansas City area for a while, and then went to California. He stayed with friends looking for work. Working on a dairy farm was not for him. Then he got a job at the only restaurant at Van Nuys Airport and a place to stay. This was in the San Fernando Valley, just north of L.A. The owner of a large aircraft hanger on the airport also owned the control tower. He offered a trade of a room in the tower AND instruction rides in a Luscombe single engine airplane for him to provide security for the un-manned tower. The owner also had in that big hanger several exotic one of a kind aircraft. Very intriguing. Fun times! He also met and dated a few aspiring actresses through introductions from his good friend, Bill Campbell. He and Bill had gone to grade school together. Bill had moved to California with his parents in the early thirties. Many movie stars used that small, close to Hollywood, airport and were frequent visitors to the restaurant.

He returned to Kansas City in 1940 and soon gained employment with Chrysler Motors Parts Corporation located in the Fairfax area of Kansas City, Kansas. In April of 1941, he met a girl he had casually known in high school. She was Martha L. Kilcrease. Little did either of them know or even suspect how important she was to become to him. They began dating in rather a slow fashion, not really going steady but slowly gaining momentum. On 13 December of 1941 they were married in Olathe, Kansas. Martha said her parents could not afford a big wedding and mine certainly could not, so with her concurrence, they took a long drive to Olathe on a Saturday night. They spent the night in the former Bellerive Hotel in Kansas City, Missouri. Both parents knew of the plan.

Martha was working for a photo studio at the time and continued to do so. They moved in with her parents at 3604 Central, Kansas City, Missouri. (The house is no longer there.) Also, the Ice house and residence at 533 South Hardesty is no longer there. The land is now part of a parking lot for Walgreen's Drugstore. Chrysler downsized their work force and through union rules, Leonard was "laid" off. He took a metals working course that qualified him to apply for employment with North American Aviation. That company was building B-25 bombers for the war effort. The aviation plant was located in the Fairfax area, and was the same site as now used by General Motors for its huge complex. He worked there until recalled by Chrysler.

Leonard enlisted in the Army Air Corps in 1942 and was accepted as an Aviation Cadet. After receiving his wings and commissioned as a 2nd Lt., he trained in B-24 Liberator Bombers and went to combat against the Japanese in the South Pacific with his crew of ten good men. He was awarded the Distinguished Flying Cross for a difficult dangerous mission against Iwo Jima and seven air medals for other accomplishments including the sinking of a Japanese vessel. He had several other awards during his military career for a total of fourteen. He was able to complete his education in the military.

Leonard retired from the Air Force after twenty two years in the rank of Lt. Colonel. Soon after retirement, he was accepted by Trans World Airlines as a captain.

After sixteen years with TWA and reaching the age of sixty, Leonard chose to retire and enjoy the simpler life of golf, hunting and fishing in addition to carrying out the details of the "wish list" of his adoring wife, Martha (my words, not hers).

THE GOLDEN YEARS

From the time of our retirement, we did have some golden years; we traveled some more, visiting friends in Los Angeles, Phoenix, New Hampshire, etc. More than once in many cases. We visited relatives in San Diego and looked it over as a possible retirement destination as we had other places. San Diego area had been building ever since we departed in 1966. We judged it to no longer fit our needs and went on to the Phoenix area where Ruth and Dick Woods had retired. Again we determined this area had become a different place, building going on everywhere and it was too hot. Finally, we decided the Kansas City area was more hospitable and would more likely accommodate our life style.

I loved to hunt, fish and play golf and the Midwest area had plenty of all three. Luckily I met an avid fisherman, hunter and sometime golf companion in the person of John O'Leary. He had retired from Hallmark as the Vice President of Marketing and had a wide range of friends in the hunting and fishing community. Oddly the day I met him, he was a member of the same golf foursome as I. He was friends with John Leavy who lived at Lake Quivira and he had invited Stan Pruitt whom I already knew. Stan in turn, invited me. That was a double lucky day for me as not only did I meet John, I shot my first hole-in-one on the tenth hole. That was in 1983 and I was sixty two years old. Since then I have made three more holes-in-one. While a member of the Public Links Senior Golf Association, I enjoyed and maintained a seven handicap for several years, winning many tournaments. These tournaments also included TWA's annual golf tournaments, held in many great golf courses. They included Scottsdale, Tucson and Phoenix, Arizona, Vail,. Colorado, Tarpon Springs, Florida, North Carolina and the Blue Monster eighteen in Florida. My trophies include a win in each of them.

John and I hunted birds every year in the fall, walking miles every day sometimes for several days at a time. Our quarry included quail, pheasants, prairie chickens, Hungarian partridge, three kinds of grouse and turkey. We met some wonderful people who allowed us to hunt their land. We fished many places as well.

Bob Demming was introduced to me and I had the privilege of hunting with him for years. Charles Fillmore joined my circle of hunting and fishing cronies. Charlie was also more of a golfer and we have played many holes through the years. Charlie is my sponsor at Unity Village, near Lee's Summit, Missouri. That allowed me to become a member of the Golf Association at Unity Country Club.

Through conversations, I learned Bob Demming and I worked for his father, each in one of his dad's drug stores as soda jerks. This was during our high school years in 1937 and 1938. He has invited me to hunt at his duck lodge near Urich, Missouri for many years. Mary, his wife has been a great hostess for all of us hunters. He also invited me to fish with him every year. Thank you, Bob and Mary. Many thanks to all.

We took a vacation, traveling to Hong Kong again via many airlines as usual. Marti needed to revisit as she had not fully satisfied her shopping instincts the first time there. This time we ended up on TWA for our return and were routed through Guam. We fully expected to be "bumped" by space available passengers waiting there and were so advised. However, while I was processing through Immigration, Marti was bypassing procedure and had us scheduled to continue with that flight on to Honolulu. Marti had learned a lot through the years, and I was pleasantly surprised. Although admittedly, I was drawn to staying there for a visit to the area I had camped in during WWII.

LEONARD V. PORTER
CAPTAIN RETIRED

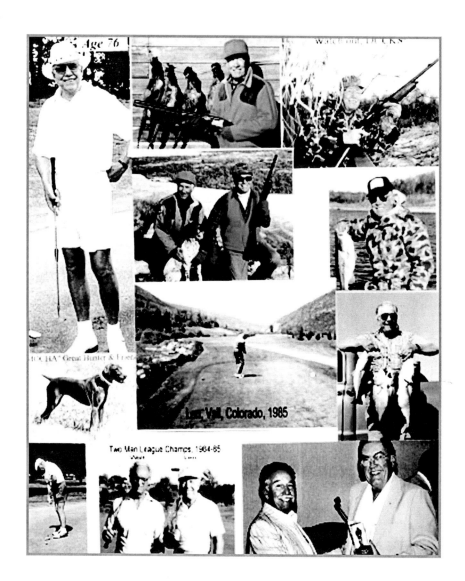